OUR
BELOVED
CRICKET

To Ian

Dave Walker gave it the okay I hope you enjoy it!

OUR BELOVED CRICKET

FROM VILLAGE GREENS TO LORD'S

There's a good Essex story on page 109

BRIAN SCOVELL

Best wishes

Brian

20/9/2013

FONTHILL

FONTHILL MEDIA
www.fonthillmedia.com

Copyright © Brian Scovell 2013

A CIP catalogue record for this book is available from the British Library

Typeset in 10.5pt on 13pt Sabon Lt Std
Typesetting by Fonthill Media
Printed in the UK

ISBN 978-1-78155-215-5

CONTENTS

Dedication

To the Stonemans and the Owen-Brownes who played such a big part in my joyous career as a social cricketer. Hugh Stoneman, who played for Cornwall's Minor County side and several wandering clubs, was a delightful private detective who specialised in speeding up society divorces. He was my first captain of the Woodpeckers CC, founded in 1936. Educated at Blundell's School, he was a true Corinthian who espoused the Olympic spirit. His son, also Hugh and an Old Blundellian, had similar qualities but he hit the ball much further than his father.

The Owen-Brownes came into my life in the early 1960s. Colin and Kim, who went to Portsmouth Grammar School, were identical twins who both could throw a cricket ball more than a hundred yards. They were quick bowlers and gave the ball a clout with the bat. Colin, who rose to become managing director of the *Evening Standard*, was cruelly cut down by amyloids, a fatal disease which he caught in Pakistan at the age of 38. His son Patrick succeeded me as skipper of the Woodies in 2004 and his elder son Alastair still plays as a talented all-rounder. Kim has three talented cricketing sons – Rupert who is the most talented, Jamie, a big hitter who works in the Far East and Toby, who scores glorious centuries amidst occasional ducks.

To the Woods, father and son. Alan, a former deputy head of a comprehensive school, comes from the far West, like the Stonemen, and recently retired in his mid-fifties. He scored more runs than any Woodie, took key wickets and fielded brilliantly, and he is a good man. Robbie, his elder son, is a batsman-wicketkeeper.

To the Phetheans – Nigel, the granddad who was still playing recently, and his family, including two grandsons, Olly and Alfie, who played with him. There have been hundreds and hundreds of Woodies from all over the world and I salute them all.

Finally, to Gavin, my son who broke records as a schoolboy at St Dunstan's School and represented Kent at junior level. He needs 15 more hundreds for his 100 centuries, but is probably too busy now being a TV director of cricket around the world. He personifies the family tradition of the Woodies.

To those many former Test players I have written about in his book, I thank them for brightening up our matches and apologise if any of them take offence. I don't think they will. I hope not.

BRIAN SCOVELL

August, 2012

Starting Out With
the Head Bangers

Walking through the fallen leaves on a beautiful autumn's day at Kelsey Park, Beckenham, my son Gavin, the international cricket TV director, suddenly asked me, "Have you thought about having a seat dedicated to you at your favourite cricket ground?" I said I haven't given a thought to it. "You should," he said, "you've had a Freedom Pass now for a few years. Time is running out. What about Tilford?"

My wandering club The Woodpeckers have played at Tilford since 1969, making it our oldest fixture: it is one of my favourite grounds among the 500-odd I have played on around the world. It has two squares and is on a slope leading down to a river where on a good day, hordes of people take their children to paddle in and chase newts and other forms of life. The slope from the highest point down to the huge oak tree at the bottom is around 30 feet, three times than at Lord's. The top-side square is drier and if there is rain around they use that one. Normally they use the other square and the boundary on the river side is no more than 35 yards. That's one of the reasons why I love batting there: the snick through the slips usually ensures a four without having to run. The opposite boundary is far in the distance, around 130 yards. It's unique, the only cricket ground of its type in the world.

We look on our matches at Tilford, the ground which was used to film A. G. Macdonell's hilarious book *England, Their England*, which features a chapter about a village green cricket match and was broadcast by the BBC in 1975, not as first team club cricket with everyone shouting and sledging and trying to win almost at all costs, but a form of rustic cricket to be enjoyed. Both sides will include elderly gentleman, others in their mid-twenties with a vast thirst for good quality beer, and young whippersnappers, often as young as nine. Shezhar Mohammad, grandson of Hanif Mohammad, made his debut for the Woodies at Ockham in Surrey in 2001 at that age, and may well be a Test player within a few years.

Macdonell was a Scot and when the book was published in 1933 he depicted the visiting side as posh people from the big city, usually members of a men's only club, taking on the village side which included artisans, farm workers and gardeners with the squire and one or two professional people making the number up. The result didn't really matter: it was about having a grand, boozy time on a day out to the country. Now of course class distinction is fading away, although our team has plenty of ex-public schoolboys who work in the City and train on hooch (the word meaning alcoholic drink and used in the 1920s and '30s).

One of the most copied cricketing pictures of an England village cricket ground features Tilford's Barley Mow pub, built in 1765, which is right next to the road alongside the ground. When the BBC shot the film, they had the road painted green to make the ground bigger on TV. There was a wonderful series of shots of a fierce-looking "Terror Thommo" type fast bowler appearing above the brow of the hill with a shaking batsman awaiting his fate. Close to a quaint, medieval little bridge across the River Wey, the pub was owned for many years by one of England's greatest eighteenth-century cricketers, "Silver" Billy Beldham. He was the W. G. Grace of his time and the pub is virtually unchanged from his day. The pictures filling several rooms capture the essence of village green cricket and the tales from past days are still repeated. The Woodies have been involved in several hilarious incidents, which are all true and verified, and much more entertaining than those A. G. Macdonell wrote about in his book.

WG is known to have played at the Green at Tilford where the game was first played around 1750. Tilford CC started their club in 1885 and many famous personalities have played there, including Tony Hancock and Sid James who put on 75 in a charity game. Courage the brewers, British Airways, Rover cars and many book publishers have used Tilford's ground in their advertising and books. Lord Coe, the chairman of the Organising Committee of the London Olympics, owns a £2 million house near Tilford and he has played in a charity match on the Green, but at the age of 56, he is unlikely to be included in a match involved with the Woodies. We might show him up. Seb's recently married second wife, Carole Annett, retail editor of *House and Garden*, is daughter of the Warwickshire and England cricket captain Mike (M. J. K.) Smith. I've known Mike for more than half a century and he is a top man, also a very modest one.

The Woodies played in Tilford's 125th anniversary year and there was a massive turn out, most of them arriving well ahead of time, ready to have picnics with their families. I noticed there were signs warning people not to park on the road up from the river. Some years ago Gavin set a record for the ground by hitting ten cars in that road while making a big total. Most of the owners were soldiers from nearby Army barracks taking their children out for a day's paddling. They probably hadn't seen the dents until they arrived home.

In the absence of Gavin and the current captain Patrick Owen-Browne, his best friend known as POB, Australian Ross "Swampy" Marsh captained the side. Looking at the bare, parched pitch which appeared to be ready to break up, he decided to bat. Nevertheless, we made an above-par score of 254-9 with "Swampy" being bowled for 2, playing across the line.

Tilford had several youngsters and one of our recruits – 47-year-old Pakistan-born swing bowler "Snacks" Quarishi from the City – swept them aside with startling figures of 6-2-25-5. The Pakistan trio of spot-betting criminals were in the news at the time, and someone said to him, "Have you been taking lessons from Mohammad Asif, Mohammad Amir and Suliman Butt?"

He roared with laughter. "I haven't played for ages," he said. "I've got a bad back!"

Two brothers batted together and the 15 year old who scored 18, the top score, was given out lbw. His brother at the other end said angrily, "Wouldn't have hit, too high!" The boy walked off dejectedly and as the new batsman arrived, his brother said, "It was never out, watch your legs, get forward otherwise you've had it!" Naturally no umpire likes to hear that, but no further finger signs were needed. The others were all bowled. After the game ended, some of our players were standing outside the pavilion and the loquacious elder brother approached our umpire. This sort of thing happens at the end of Premiership matches when the manager storms up to the referee demanding an explanation. To our delight, we heard the young man apologising. "Sorry mate," he said. "I got carried away. What really upset me was that your bowlers were kept on so long that we didn't have a chance. They should have put on some rubbish bowling (he turned to the direction of The Count, our lob bowler Neil Runkel), and then we could have got 140 or so in the last 20. The bowlers that came on were even better than the first two." Maybe we were too hard on them because the home side were bowled out for 65 and the margin of victory, 191 runs, was a club record for the Woodies. We were intent on winning our eleventh win in a row, another record. And with an Aussie captain, no favours were on hand.

The drinking outside the pub, filling the road which at that time is usually deserted, went on until dusk. One of the wives of the Tilford team said, "Thanks for coming. It was wonderful to see so many happy people here today – children, parents, everyone, all enjoying themselves. Well done." Terry Cartwright, the former captain and now fixture secretary, said, "We look forward to seeing you next year and we'll be signing up one of those Pakistanis to give you the same treatment!"

The club uses one of village cricket's poshest pavilions. First built in 1894, designed by Sir Edwin Lutyens, the world famous architect, and named after him, it has been revamped at the cost of £500,000. It is used as a community centre on the top side of the ground. Tilford has been promoting the friendly Big Society for many years, long before David Cameron thought of the idea, and the village shop is run by residents who are volunteers.

We have always had Australians, and other Colonials, in our ranks. In one match our Western Australian swing bowler Simon "Sav" Hare was moaning on the Barley Mow boundary about the incessant rain and having to retrieve the ball after a succession of sixes went over the pub into a wooded area behind. Having been in a winning position, the Woodies were suddenly confronted with being beaten by a big hitting Australian from the home side. After the next six was thrown back by a spectator, I said to Simon, "Next time the ball comes back, hurl it into the river."

The river is 70 metres from the pub – too far for most amateur cricketers to reach from a throw. When the next six was struck Simon, who had a very good arm, picked up the ball and did what he was told and the ball disappeared into the far side of the river.

"Skipper! Did you see that?" shouted the portly home umpire.

"What?" I said.

"That man deliberately threw the ball into the river."

"Well, he comes from Western Australia and he's a bit of an odd chap," I said. "I'm afraid you'll have to produce another ball."

After a delay – when our reluctant fielders announced that the original ball wasn't to be seen – the umpires agreed to take a dry ball from the dressing room. With a relatively new ball, Simon bowled his fellow Australian with a big inswinger and the game drifted on into a draw, with everyone drenched.

In another game there, Mike "Spack" Pringle, a former Australian Rules player, dived and caught the ball close to the ground in front of the pub. He got up and held the ball aloft, roaring like a one of England's young fast bowlers when the stumps go flying. An elderly spectator sitting on the stone wall shouted, "You cheating bastard, your foot was over the line!"

Mike advanced towards him and the man's colleagues, some of whom appeared to be rather cowed by the sight of this burly, muscled part-time cricketer, and got up as though ready to take evasive action. But Mike suddenly broke into a smile and said, "Listen mate, the catch was completed before my foot crossed the line and when we get in the bar shortly I'll be glad to buy you a pint. And your mates."

"Oh, all right then," said the man. The captains agreed that the wicket should stand and when the match ended in a draw, the teams went straight to the pub rather than the pavilion. Mike was working in the City at the time and qualified for big bonuses. "Drinks all round!" he shouted to the barman and the spectators joined in the cheering.

In 2009, the Woodies were on the way to victory when a 57-year-old batsman from another village, a ringer, came in to bat: his front leg was hit in front of the stumps and there were tumultuous appeals for lbw. I was umpiring and had to admit that the finger was raised so quickly that everyone thought I was in the pay of the bowler.

"Too high," said the batsman.

"Oh no," I said, "it was on the roll. You have been given out. Please leave the wicket and make way for the next batsman."

The batsman started muttering and turned to Fred Pennell, our wicket keeper who lives in Tilford, and said, "You ought to withdraw the appeal."

Fred, a friendly teacher who shuns controversy, said, "Okay, I thought it was a bit high as well." The batsman started to take his guard again.

I interrupted and said, "You're out, Sir."

"But the keeper has withdrawn the appeal," he said.

I reproved him, saying, "The fielding captain hasn't withdrawn his and except for the keeper, all the fielders think you are out which is why they appealed in the first place."

A stalemate ensued. Patrick Owen-Browne had been shielding himself under the 800-year-old Tilford oak tree some ten yards inside the boundary at deep cover and had played little part in the drama. Realising that a row might erupt, he walked up the slope on to the square and announced, "All right, let him stay there. He doesn't look as though he will remain there for too long."

Play restarted and 95 minutes later, the ignored batsman came in alone, unclapped by players on both sides with an unbeaten 87 to his name, with the Woodies soundly beaten. Back in the visitors' changing room, Fred threw his gloves down in disgust, apologised profusely and went for a shower on his own. Later in the pub the batsman and his wife sat alone outside and no-one spoke to them. The Tilford captain explained, "He's not one of ours. He comes from a village up the road. Only came along to make the number up."

When I first played for the Woodies in 1966, I failed to ask the few founder members why they chose the name. Everyone knows that the woodpecker, one of the most beautiful and colourful of birds, uses its beak to bang into trees to send loving messages to others. But why are they able to carry on doing it without damaging themselves? Jason Palmer, the science and technology reporter of BBC News reported on 27 October 2011:

> Their heads move some 6 metres per second at each peck, enduring a deceleration more than 1,000 times the force of gravity. Researchers say that unequal upper and lower beak lengths and spongy, plate-like bone structure protect their brains. The findings could help design more effective head protection for humans. For years, scientists have looked at the anatomy of their skulls to find out how they pull off their powerful pecking without causing themselves harm. They have little 'sub-dural space' between their brains and their skulls so the brain does not have room to bump around as it does in humans.

Clearly the man, or men, who chose our name had experience of banging his heads into hard objects and launching a cricket team of all sorts, mainly from poor-quality players, and must have realised there were permanent hazards ahead, like arriving at a game with three players short or someone leaving the match ball at home. The high incidence of players being hit in the head without wearing a helmet was another factor. You needed hard-headed players who could take a blow without flinching. It is not a matter to boast about, but in my 40-odd years playing for the club I was probably hit in the head more than anyone else. I can recall six occasions. The first was on a rain affected pitch at Beddington CC, when an 18-year-old bowler struck me on my left-side jaw and I had to retire briefly for treatment. When I returned, a similar rising delivery shot up and I turned my head the other way and the ball hit my jaw on the other side. "I think it knocked it back into place," I said. I spent six weeks with a wired up jaw and it now still gives me a slight reminder when chewing sticky toffee cake.

In 1978 another 18-year-old tearaway aptly named Steve Deathridge was bowling at me on the beautiful ground of Withyham in East Sussex, and I edged a bouncer into my mouth, breaking six teeth. Audrey, my wife, drove me to hospital through heavy traffic and an Indian doctor said, "Sorry, it's a dental problem. Go to your dentist." Next day I did, and my dentist said, "You have a fractured jaw as well." It caused another six weeks of acute discomfort and I had to pay £500 for six crowns. We had three Australian ear, nose and throat specialists in our side: Ross Elliott, brother of the disgraced John Foster of Foster's lager and Carlton, the Aussie Rules club, Mike Jay and Rob Thomas, and none of them detected my broken jaw. Mike said, "You can't blame us. We didn't have a chance to examine the injury." Years later, Rob, a fine all-round sportsman, suffered a cardiac arrest while on a run. Mike said, "It was a Dustin Hoffman job. This man stepped forward and saved him from serious damage."

On a tour of Barbados, a squash player was bowling to me in the nets when I top-edged a full toss into my right eyebrow. The English doctor, John Manning, did such a great stitching job that I gave him a copy of John Snow's autobiography which I had with me. "He's my favourite cricketer," he said. A few years later I was facing a Wasim Akram-type left arm bowler on another stunning, in both senses of the word, ground at Knowle Park, and he let go a beamer. As I bent and pulled my head back, I felt a thud on the back of my head and it was like hearing church bells in full sound. One of our wives was a former nurse and despite my protestations that I was fine, she persuaded me to go to the nearby Sevenoaks Hospital.

The kind lady wrapped bandages around my head and on the way to the hospital, Audrey had to stop for directions. The couple we approached took one look at my bandaged, bloody head and walked quickly in the other direction. They thought I must have been one of those football hooligans. We finally reached the hospital and a doctor said, "It's only a small cut and some swelling but take it easy and don't go back to play." Back on the hill – the National Trust decided to stop staging any more matches soon after because of lack of water – I saw that seven wickets had fallen. "I've got to go out there," I said to Audrey. I padded up and when the next wicket fell, I walked out like a survivor from the Crimean War and was clapped in. Mr Akram put himself on again and his first ball was a bouncer which I managed to fend away with my left glove. "You've just put me in hospital and now you want to do it again!" I said. He didn't say anything funny, or apologetic, but at least he bowled properly afterwards.

During one of the five tours I have been on to South Africa, I was trying to sweep a legspinner at one of the country's most prestigious schools and the ball shot up from my toecap and hit me on the chin. Blood flowed and I had to retire to the pavilion. One of the wives, another nurse, said, "It's nothing really," and walked off. A boxer doesn't know what damage has been inflicted so I went to the dressing room looking for a mirror. There wasn't one. And there wasn't one in the main pavilion either. But I wetted a piece of newspaper and stuck over the area to stop the bleeding and went back to the middle after the next fall of wicket.

"I'm so sorry sir," said the legspinner. "I hope it hasn't caused any problems."

"Not at all," I said, "no stitches, only the *Sunday Sun*!"

Over the years I thought The Woodpeckers should be renamed – The Head Bangers CC. Woodpeckers are indestructible, especially in the head. I first joined them in 1966 when I was writing a weekly column for Gary Sobers who, in my view, was the finest all-round cricketer of all time. He was a Corinthian, a man of principle, but the only problem about him was that I had great difficulty in contacting him – well before mobile phones. During a rain break of a Test match, I was skimming through the ads of *The Times* and saw one saying the Woodpeckers wanted quality players to play social, wandering cricket around London. I took my 1954-vintage Remington Rand typewriter from a rather bulky wooden case and knocked out a cheeky letter claiming that I was another Sobers, opening both batting and bowling and being an outstanding close fielder.

Some days later I received a letter from the President, Tony Cadman, inviting me to a meeting at the Dorchester Hotel in Park Lane. I rang him and he seemed pleased when I said I would be available. When I arrived, I sat across from three very happy, bulbous middle aged men who were keen to sign me up immediately. "I'm only an ordinary third team cricketer," I said. "It was a bit of a joke."

"Don't worry," said Tony, "I like your style."

My first game took place at the old Westerham CC ground at The Squirryes, next to a seventeenth-century manor house close to the house where William Pitt the Younger, the Prime Minister (1783-1803 and 1804-06) lived occasionally. Now it is an Indian restaurant. As I turned to drive up the unmade road to the ground, I saw a white Bentley parked on my left and sitting it in was Tony Cadman. I stopped and said, "Broken down Tony?"

"Oh no," he said, "I don't want to take my vehicle up there, it would get mud on the wheels!" Not worried about getting mud on my Triumph Herald, I gave him a lift. In the one sided defeat, I scored a quick duck, bowled well below the standard of Gary Sobers and dropped a simple catch at first slip. Afterwards, John Boyd-Carpenter, the secretary, congratulated me and said, "I suppose you want to play against next week!"

From that time on, I was a regular, depending on my duties working for the *Daily Sketch*. The club had few outstanding cricketers and one of them was the former Ugandan international all rounder John Nagenda, who bowled fast and hit the ball very hard but was unreliable. The year before the top brass signed some younger players from a teacher training college. They included Matt Wall, our redoubtable retired left-handed opener, and a deputy head, Paul Davidson, our small ginger-haired medium-pace bowler who bowled line and length and took a club record of 451 wickets, and a teenager from Shepherd's Bush by the name of Mick Hogan. Yes, he was Irish. Mick was an embryonic Botham and I fixed up trials for him at Middlesex and Surrey but he failed to turn up. He was never coached but bowled at close to 80 mph with a high action, played some wonderful attacking shots and held some brilliant close catches. Within 18 months he had disappeared. He might have played cricket as a professional if he had any ambition.

Paul was the gutsiest sportsman I've ever met. He was a diabetic and though he loved cricket, he loved the girls more in his early years, often letting us down and apologising and saying, "Met a young lady. Sorry!" But we always forgave him. He was a brilliant school teacher in a very tough school. On one occasion a group of rowdy young boys were on the rampage and were advancing up the road to the main entrance with bricks in their hands, looking for trouble. The police had yet to arrive and the staff were terrified. But Paul came out the door and walked straight towards them and started calming them down, and eventually the young men dispersed. He was a top-class goalkeeper, despite being only five feet six inches. He was still playing football at the age of 58 until gangrene set into one of his legs and it had to be amputated. He was talking about a comeback when I saw him in the Gillingham Hospital, but a week later, he died of MRSA. It was a terrible loss to humanity.

In 1967 Tony Salisbury moved to a top job with Southern TV in Southampton and retired from cricket. Within days, Boyd-Carpenter died at the wheel of his car after a heart attack at the age of 60 – his pretty wife Stella who was 34 years younger was elsewhere – and I was asked to become captain. I said I would only do it if I was left to run the whole club and the others agreed. For the next 40 years I filled all the posts, and with help from good, sound men like Alan Wood, Patrick Owen-Browne and Gavin, it worked. We turned it into a family club, encouraging the members – who weren't asked to pay a subscription – to take their wives, partners and children to exotic parts of Surrey, Kent, Sussex and Hampshire and make it a day out in the country. Two survivors, Hugh Stoneman Senior, who played for Cornwall's Minor County side, and his son Hugh Stoneman Junior, known as "Bingo", set the pattern.

Senior was a delightful man who worked as a private detective exposing rich folks' adultery cases, among other things. He was a slow inswing left-arm bowler, good enough to take 9-33 against a team of West Indians representing Lewisham Hospital, the best analysis by a Woodie. When I consulted Senior about a possible change of bowling, he would always say, "Put 'Bingo' on – he'll bowl them out!" When I would ask Junior, he would say, "Dad, he's got the measure of them." Paradise for them was to bowl together all through the innings. I never let them do it though. "Bingo" was a successful artist and printer and sadly he died at the age of 58 not too long after his parents departed.

Another great character was the Fleet Street sports writer and author Bob Harris who had three 8-wicket hauls. Bob was a junior at Warwickshire and bowled off a 25-yard run and delivered every type of ball, including googlies but not the doosra, which hadn't been invented by then. Any suggestion that he should be taken off was greeted with an angry response. Once at Hertford Brewery, on a sizzling hot day, he ran up and suddenly collapsed holding his heart. Everyone gathered round, and we all thought he'd had a heart attack because he looked ghost-like.

"You'd better finish his over," I said to Paul.

Bob's eyes slowly opened and started to get up. "I'll be fit to continue, thank you," he said. And he bowled another 21 more overs.

Another character was John Campbell-Watson, whose young wife Virginia scored for several seasons. He injured a foot – he claimed a bone had fractured – and for several weeks he strapped a batting glove to his boot when he played. Probably the first and only time to see a cricketer putting a batting glove on to his foot.

In the post-Second World War years, we had an outbreak of Owen-Brownes. Twin brothers Colin and Kim played, and in the field they spent a lot of time trying to beat each other on long throws. Over throws piled up. Both threw the ball more than 100 yards. Sadly, Colin died at the age of 38 and his son Patrick is now captain. Alastair, his elder son, plays as well and three other OBs, Toby, now a regular, and his brothers Rupert and Jamie, whose father is Kim, have played occasionally. Alan Wood, another former deputy head, has scored more than 12,000 runs and he is our second leading scorer with 24 centuries. His son Robbie is a successful batsman-wicketkeeper and the family links continue with Nigel Phethean, our over-sixties bowler who still makes an odd appearance, playing in the same side with his 15-year-old grandson Ollie Gower. We even had lady players. Rebecca Watkinson, whose father David (another teacher) took 283 wickets for us without seeing them because he finished his bowling delivery looking into the ground (like Jimmy Anderson used to), played several times and was in the U19 side in Kent.

We could put out a Test team because these players all played for the Woodies, starting with Willie Rodriguez, the West Indies spin bowler in 1972. The others are Sarfraz Nawaz, Salahuddin, Aftab Gul, Billy Ibadulla, Alimuddin, Aamir Sohail (Pakistan), Danny Morrison (NZ), Geoff Lawson, Michael Slater (Australia), Ian Bishop (WI), T. K. Sekhar and B. S. Chandrasekhar (India). The ebullient Danny Morrison, now one of NZ's most popular cricket commentators, hit the winning run at Tadworth in 2004 coming in at 11. He once held a record for the number of Test ducks, but he insisted, "I won't bag a duck time!" and he was right. He struck the winning runs, a four through long on. In Tadworth's innings, he swung the ball both ways at medium pace but after eight tight overs for a return of 1-14, he tweaked a hamstring and took himself off. I can tell you – none of our leading Woodpecker bowlers would take himself off. Never!

2

Broadhalfpenny Down Wasn't the Birthplace of Cricket – True!

Long hours of research has established that nine true men of Woodies played at Broadhalfpenny Down on 10 June 1984, the so-called cradle of cricket between 1765-1796 when Hambledon CC, a humble village side in Hampshire, beat All England on numerous occasions and claimed they were the best side in the world. Most people think that cricket was first started in Hambledon, but that is a myth. It was propagated by John Nyren, the son of Richard Nyren, the founder of Hambledon CC who ran the Bat and Ball pub next to the ground. Nyren Junior wrote a book entitled *The Cricketers of My Times* – actually it was mainly ghost written by someone else – and it was the one of the first books to spread the word around the land about England's foremost cricketers.

In those early days there was a mix of country gentry and yeomen in the teams and betting was rampant: a forerunner of today's spot betting. Incidentally, the ICC reported that there were 56 cases of cricketers who were approached by illegal bookies in the 2009-10 season so it still continues. News Corporation's sleuth Mazher Mahmood, the Fake Sheikh, have only exposed three so far – the Pakistan trio of Salman Butt, Mohammed Aamir and Mohammad Asif. Mazher, born in Birmingham in 1963 from parents who migrated to England three years earlier from Pakistan, claimed that he brought more than 250 miscreants to book including Sven-Goran Eriksson, John Barnes, Ian Wright, John Fashanu, Joe Calzaghe, John Higgins, the Duchess of York, David Mellor and many more.

At their annual dinners, Hambledon Cricket Club had six toasts, and the number 5 was "The Immortal Memory of Madge". The club records indicated that Miss Madge was not a real person, but the female vagina. Or this is a Wikipedia invention? Like much cricketing lore, you never know.

In the early to middle 1600s, cricket was played spasmodically on village greens in the South Downs of Hampshire and Sussex and the Weald of Kent, and there is a record of one game played at Bourne, Kent, in 1637. No-one knows the place and date when the first match was held but it certainly wasn't at Broadhalfpenny Down. Alan Wood, our much respected opening batsman who scored 12,234 runs for us (a record), took 347 wickets with his offspin and caught 137 catches (second in the list behind wicket keeper Jim Baker who took 142), retired as deputy head at one of the most roughest comprehensive schools in London on Friday 22 July 2011, the day the Woodpeckers played at the ground against the Broadhalfpenny Downs Brigands CC.

When I congratulated him on his early retirement – escape from Colditz someone said – he reminded me about a match in 1984. Apparently the Jack Frost Xl, then mainly run by John Campbell-Watson who played for us for many years and is still revered, had problems in fielding a side so we took the fixture on. We batted first on a green pitch with little bounce and the opening stand put on 43 (Wood 32, Scovell B. 20) and the rest – Colin Blunstone, the singer, songwriter and guitarist, Qamar Ahmed, Gavin Harper, John Peters, Derek Wheeler, Campbell-Watson and the number 11, Gavin Scovell (4) managed to scrape up just 49 more runs, and with extras of 13, the total came to 118 from 53.3 overs. There were no sixes. A man named Scarborough had figures of 20.3-9-27-7.

Qamar, who recorded a first ball duck, came up to me at tea and said, "Use the old ball and I'll see them off." He knew his cricket and I agreed readily.

His first ball pitched well outside leg stump and John Peters, our keeper, jumped in front of second slip to catch the ball. Qamar smiled. "They won't make 60," he said.

Ginny Campbell-Watson, our supremely efficient scorer, shouted, "What's the bowler's name?"

"Qamar," someone shouted back.

"What about his surname?" shouted Ginny again.

The man smiled as he said, "Qamar Sutra".

Qamar reeled off six maiden overs, and with the other opening bowler named Phillips bowling five maidens as well, the Brigands failed to score a run in 35 minutes in 11 successive maidens while losing four wickets. Qamar played first-class cricket in his youth in Pakistan and once dismissed Hanif Mohammad. "I was close to being selected for the Pakistan team," he once said.

He continued to take wickets and ended with Lakeresque figures of 18.4-10-10-6, and he was four runs out about the team total – the Brigands were all out for 64, not 60. Later, the scorebook was changed back to "Qamar Ahmed".

Ginny's middle-aged husband was an antique and art dealer who lived in a houseboat on the Thames and married her when she was 18: it was a blissfully happy marriage which lasted 30 years. They went to live in Romsey and she was a very popular figure in the town. Sadly she died of cancer at the age of 48 and hundreds attended her funeral. I went to it and counted the wreaths and other tributes. They came to 70. It must have been a record for any wandering cricket club scorer.

An eighteenth-century diarist wrote saying the Broadhalfpenny Down had a bleak look about it, and it certainly looked like it on Woody's retirement day on 22 July 2011. Heavy, black, slow-moving clouds drifted westwards throughout the day. But Chris Bazalgette, the man who is descended from Joseph of the same name who invented London's sewerage system and played a major part in the setting up of the Bat and Ball CC in 1993, assured us, "We shall certainly play, whether or not it rains. One of our rules is that the pitch should be pitched within distance of a six hit of a place serving liquid refreshment." Well the rain held off and with a 45-metre boundary on one side, we were soon able to take refreshment. The main bar of the Bat and Ball pub houses most of Hambledon's cricketing memorabilia. In these PC days there was no reference to Madge. The pub was built in around 1730 and served as pavilion and clubhouse. The landlord Richard Nyren, known as "The General", and his wife Elizabeth hosted plentiful dinners with venison and sides of beef washed down with "ale that would flare like turpentine – genuine boniface" followed by music with John Small, a legendary batsman, and his son playing the violin while Tom Suetter, the keeper and his longstop George Leer, tenor and counter tenor, sang duets.

Broadhalfpenny Down was a mile and a half from Hambledon, and most of the players had to carry their gear by foot and they found it very taxing, especially after a heavy night of eating and drinking. In the 1780s the club moved closer to the village and the last match of that era took place on the Down in 1792. In 1907 Edward Whalley-Tooker, the captain of Hambledon CC, thought it would be a good idea to build a splendid stone memorial opposite the pub dedicated to the famous cricketers of Hambledon, and it was duly built. It is very impressive. A year later a match between a Hambledon XII, captained by Charles Burgess Fry, took on an All England XII, skippered by Gilbert Jessop, and it was declared a first-class fixture, the only one ever to be played on the Down.

There is a plaque in the pub showing that the President – author Leslie Thomas who made his name writing *The Virgin Soldiers* in 1966 – used to play for the Brigands, which was founded in 1959, and remains President, though no longer playing the game. He worked for Associated Newspapers earlier in his career and one of his tasks was to write Sir Leonard Hutton's column in the *London Evening News*. "I learned a lot from Len but I soon forgot what he told me," he said. Being a Yorkshireman, Len never appeared to buy a newspaper. He borrowed other people's. Les was born at Newport, Monmouthshire, on 22 March 1931, and was orphaned at the age of 12 and was brought up in a Dr Barnardo's home. He is a remarkably cheerful man, always smiling and joking, but like many famous authors, his cricket ability was rather limited. In 2004 he became an OBE.

The survival of cricket on the Down after the 1920s was down to one man, Harry Altham (1888-1965), a war hero who was awarded the DSO and MC in the First World War, a highly praised cricket historian and the author of the MCC Coaching Book, Surrey and Hampshire batsman, chairman of the Test selectors and Treasurer and President of MCC. He was also a teacher at Winchester College and persuaded the college to buy the lease for the Down to save it from being turned into a ploughed field. He persuaded the Captain of HMS *Mercury*, the Royal Naval Signal School which was based at Leydene House, close to the ground, to take on the lease. Later the Admiralty assumed responsibility of it and after HMS *Mercury* was closed down in 1992, the Brigands and Winchester College created the Broadhalfpenny Down Association, a charitable organisation, to secure the Down's future. Each year 60 matches are played featuring clubs like the Royal Household (Windsor) CC, Hants *v*. Sussex under-10s, Rioteers CC, Geelong Grammar School, Hants *v*. Yorkshire Visually Impaired and Sons of Bacchus.

When the Woodpeckers arrived for the 2011 encounter with the Bat and Ball XI they found it hard to spot the pitch at the oddly named Broadhalfpenny Down. No doubt they had halfpennies in the 1700s, but why should they be "broad"? It looked just as green as the rest of the ground. "It will take a little turn," said Chris Bazalgette. From the start, the ball kept low – grubbers as they were termed in the eighteenth century – but I soon fell victim to one of the few deliveries which gained altitude as it arrived, with the ball flicking the top of my right thigh, the one which was operated on a few weeks earlier, and bouncing on to the off stump. A succession of batsmen fell to the slow lob bowler, John Balmer, and at 75-5 we were being bamboozled out by their pie throwers. Balmer (4-58) had a slight kink in his arm and there were no complaints about his action because the ball soared to such a height that by the time it dropped to the ground, any precipitation had worn off. The muscular Gareth Abbott (16) drove two sixes over the beech trees behind the pub, and Olly Mott (40) and Al "Oz" Clayton (34) hit one apiece in a similar region. The second lob bowler, Keith Ellis (1-70), was almost as slow in the air. Neither man turned the ball very much. Patience was required and Olly and Al showed plenty of it, almost doubling the total.

The rotund Rooke, an offspinner with more pace, bowled Al with his second delivery and POB was summarily bowled as well, second ball. When Motty was bowled, shamefully lifting his head in reckless abandon, last man Runky (0*) was left stranded. He left the wicket wearing a peevish expression. Motty's opening burst – 1-2 in four overs – soon restored his credibility and John Carr, our Beaconsfield-now-Ealing line and length expert, whipped out three of them. David Harris, one of Nyren's pioneers, was the first to suggest that the ball should be bowled on a length, instead of full tosses or bowling along the ground. He would have been proud of John's efforts.

Just before tea, a tall, suntanned blonde man of mid-twenties named Anthony Beddows arrived dragging his cricket bag from the car park across the road. There was a suggestion that he was ours, but Bazalgette, known as Baza, said he'd just been recruited for the Brigands by a Spanish agent. He had just flown in to Stansted from holiday in Almeria. He came in at 4 and defied the MCC Coaching Book, or any other coaching book. He stood at the crease with his legs so apart that a low-slung supermarket trolley could easily pass under. A left hander, his right leg was rarely in line and his first scoring shots were hoicks into the extra cover region.

By now the Brigands were fleeing back to the pavilion. Their score was a miserly 25-5 and the light was deteriorating fast. Big John reckoned he can only bowl six-over spells, and after taking 3-7 in six overs he made way for Old Tonbridgean Charlie Young at the end where there was a very small, moveable, metal-framed sightscreen situated close to the darkest of trees at the road end. Not having played for some time, Charlie hurled down some extremely short deliveries – mostly in his half of the pitch – and also tossed in a couple of beamers, but managed to take a wicket (1-19 in 2). He is a lawyer and looked a promising cricketer who needed a few nets.

Meanwhile Beddows, who came from Godalming, started to clout the ball very hard, too hard for Simon Anderson at deep extra cover who dropped him. Within minutes, as if to redeem himself, Simon dived into the line of one of his powerful drives, catching him painfully in the side of his neck. No damage resulted.

The gangly Ellis, at 7, was wearing a yellow cap with UK Tour on it under a small union jack. He whacked a six before POB (1-32) dismissed him with an lbw which the batsman thought was harsh.

"I nicked it before the ball hit my pad," he said. As he strode angrily away, the umpire explained to the fielders.

"Pad first, then bat," he said.

No. 8 Rooke joined Beddows at 56-6, and showed off the red marks on either edge of his sparkling new bat. "Yet to find the middle so far this season," he said. He played sensibly and what was an easy victory was quickly slipping away. The 100 mark soon passed. Runky was eager to show his lobs and he replaced Motty at the end where the best view is obtained – rolling hills and a rustic scene of the cows lying down for an hour or so before lazily getting up to return to their barns. Alas the Count, his equanimity disturbed by some fielding changes which he disagreed with, failed to strike and came off after five overs (0-33). A quick reference to the 1984 scoreboard showed that he was batting in the top five in those days and never took a five-wicket haul, like now in his dotage. He never admits his age but contemporaries reckon he is old enough to qualify for a freedom pass.

Suddenly we were in dire trouble. With a target of 20 at four an over and four wickets in hand, and Beddows belching fire, it seemed all over. The Brigands were about to snatch the prize. John Carr took over from POB and almost immediately struck gold. Beddows lashed out to extra cover off John's line and length delivery and POB charged round to his left, dived, and came up holding the ball high in triumph. What a catch! "Yes, I'd moved myself that way and when I saw it coming I knew I had to hold on to it," he said. Beddows went off totally deflated after scoring 81 hard-earned runs.

Rooke, no relation to Arsenal's Ronnie Rooke, famous for his ferocious shooting at Highbury in the late-1940s, caught the same bug. On 16, he swung his bat, striking the ball right in the middle and drove straight to POB off John's bowling whose final figures were a remarkable 9.3-3-18-5. An easier catch, but a vital one. Shortly afterwards, Balmer drove comfortably into POB's hands at mid off. Three catches in as many overs, by the same man off the same bowler. We were checking records: is that a Broadhalfpenny record, or even a record for first-class cricket? No-one knew. Maybe it was the first from a double-barrelled Browne.

Fourteen runs were needed by the last pair and it was too much for them. No. 11 Ellis was having difficulty running quickly and was run out. The Brigands were all out 146: a very meritorious win by 13 runs. POB showed concern about the way Ellis was dismissed, saying to him, "Were you impeded?"

"Yes," said Ellis, "by having to grab hold of my trousers to keep them up." But he had to go.

Could you imagine Richard and John Nyren and his mates, saying something like that 250 years ago? Probably not. But someone might have won money from a bet. Colin Blunstone played a few games for us around the 1980s and he might have been persuaded to write a song about the limping number 11. Colin was the gentlest, kindest individual who played for us, and he always insisted, "I'm not really a cricketer. I'm just here to make the numbers up." I put him 3 in the order in the 1984 match on the Down, recognising his musical talent rather than his cricketing ability. He went in at 2.54, played and missed several deliveries, managed to get a single and seven minutes later he was bowled by a youngster named Freeman, not John Freeman of BBC fame. He played another match at Ockham, in Surrey, and came in at 8 and was bowled for a duck by a man named Adams who bowled 24 overs without being taken off. They used to do that in those days ... when cricketers never trained and never went to gyms.

Colin's finest moment – certainly in a sporting context – came when he was fielding on the boundary at Dormansland, a small village in Kent, and a high-skewed off drive was coming down towards where he was standing, and all of us thought his fingers might be damaged, possibly ending his days as a guitarist. Hearts were in mouths, particularly his, but he managed to grasp the ball in front of his chest and was quickly mobbed by his fellow team mates and fans. "I've never caught such a catch like that before and it will probably be the last," he said. "A stroke of luck, I think." A totally modest man, Colin was born at Hatfield, Hertfordshire on 24 June 1945 and went to St Albans County Grammar School for Boys and was best known as a member of the pop group The Zombies. He is still appearing at gigs.

Simon Dee, the BBC radio and TV presenter, also played that season, without success. He was 48, past his best as a physical specimen. At Hertford Brewery CC I put him at 9 and he was swiftly bowled for a second-ball duck. He volunteered to field in the deep and managed to make a couple of good stops without reaching the keeper's gloves. Our total of 147-9 was on the low side and the Brewery was 23-4 when thunder and lightning struck, forcing the abandonment. The storm summed up Simon's career – he had a rapid rise, his life built up into violent noise and subsided into virtual obscurity. He was a garrulous, good-looking man, but we soon came to the conclusion that he would never be a good cricketer despite going to two of the outstanding cricket schools in the county, Brighton College and Shrewsbury. His real name was Cyril Nicholas Henty-Dodd and he had a very chequered life. He was called up on National Service in 1956 and took aerial photographs of the combat zone during the brief Suez Crisis. Shortly afterwards he was wounded in the face by a sniper bullet while in Cyprus. After a number of jobs, including sweeping up leaves in Hyde Park, he became a national figure as a disc jockey at the pirate radio ship Radio Caroline. He was soon signed up by the BBC and at one stage he had 18 million viewers for his prime-time show "Dee Time". He transferred to ITV where he had rows about his demands for an increased salary and departed, and not long after he was forced to sign on at the Fulham labour exchange to claim unemployment. He took a job as a bus driver and in 1974 he was imprisoned for 28 days for non-payment of rates on his Chelsea home. He died of bone cancer in 2009 at the age of 74.

3

The Batsman Who Locked Himself in the Loo

Alasdair Ross had a habit of locking himself in the loo when he played for the Woodies. He lived in fear of fast bowling and was a well-known football and snooker writer with the *Sun* who died at the age of 49. He helped to launch the English Press Cricket Association in the 1970s, a rival to the Cricket Writers' Club team for which I organised the club's friendly matches. His father John Ross worked as a football writer for a number of national newspapers and was based in Northampton. A Scot with a good sense of humour, John was a heavyweight drinker and was famous in sporting circles as being one of the first men to be taken to the wrong church in the wrong town for his funeral in the north of Scotland. The hearse had to make a big detour and arrived at the designated church well behind schedule. Naturally it caused a lot of confusion. Ally had similar traits and was also a big drinker like his father.

The best story I heard about him was about a rail strike. The sports editor of the *Sun* at the time rang him at his home in Cambridge and ordered him to report at the office at noon.

Ally said, "I can't, there's a railway strike."

The sports editor, "Well, I know that but use your car."

"I can't drive," said Ally.

"What?" snorted the editor. "Why have you been claiming mileage all these years when you haven't got a car?"

Ross Junior wrote about himself in a cricket tour brochure saying, "Surprisingly, his representative honours are limited to one appearance for Northants Cricket Association U19s, but I am now expecting to make the breakthrough. A keen golfer and dreamer, his ambitions include winning the British Open and hooking Dennis Lillee for six. A bachelor." Neither ambition was fulfilled and one of his touring colleagues said, "He certainly was a dreamer, a bit like a Billy Liar. If he saw Dennis Lillee approaching in his cricket gear, I'm sure his face would turn white, rush to the nearest loo and lock the door!"

Ally played a number of matches for the Woodies in 1976. At the Bank of England, when the home side didn't have a fast bowler, he was caught on the long on boundary from one of his golf-like straight drives for 96. After tea in the luxurious pavilion which the England football team used for training before internationals at Wembley, he took 3-30 with his mixture of good and bad balls, but was unable to take the last wicket with the Bank's side stealing a draw on 145-9. In the final minutes, he expressed some disquiet about our fielding. You never knew when he might explode.

A fortnight later I gave him a lift to the St Bartholomew's Hospital ground in Chislehurst and I told him he would be promoted one place in the order to five and he said, "Xxxxsake, I've just got 96!"

"We have four very good players ahead of you with big scores," I said. "You'll have to wait for your chance."

Tony Cozier, our West Indian broadcaster who played first team cricket in Barbados, was out first ball, caught at first slip off the express pace of Bruno Williams, a trainee doctor at the hospital, who came from Jamaica. Alan Wood, who was down at 4, said, "Rossi was first wicket down and padded up but when he saw how fast Bruno was bowling on a pretty quick, hard pitch, he rushed off to the loo saying 'I'm not coming out until that guy is taken off!'

"I said to him, 'Go on, you go in, they've brought the field up and there are some quick runs out there.'

"'There are plenty of quick runs in here as well!' he said. 'You (he meant me) were holding the fort, getting behind the ball when Bruno bowled straight and letting the other deliveries go outside off stump.'

"If you don't come out,' I said, 'you'll have to drop down to 11.'"

That made him change his mind. When the next wicket fell he walked out, padded up like a Michelin man, bearing the expression of a man on his way to the gallows, to join me. He looked petrified. Bruno tore up to the wicket, bowled ... and shattered his stumps. Rossi sloped off muttering oaths. The next two batsmen, Professor John Shepherd, a consultant at Bart's, and our Jamaican Elijah Franklin, were much braver and knocked up a few runs, nearly all behind the wicket. Eventually Bruno was taken off with figures of 13-6-16-4 and I declared on 146-8. We had the medicos reeling on 48-4 and I ensured that Rossi was kept in the deep field and not put him on to bowl. Bruno hit the winning run to win the match by six wickets. Alan told me later he played in a match with Andy Hooper, a former Kent player, and Hooper reckoned Bruno was one of the quickest bowlers in the country at that time.

The Woodies' Pearl Harbour took place on 4 September 1977 when we were bombed out for 25, our lowest total, on the village green at Ripley in Surrey. Ripley's cricket club was founded in 1749, and is one of the true pioneers of the game. Rossi was the first to show the white flag and we blamed him for our demise. It was a sunny, breezy day and Ripley were 129-9 when Dave Watkinson, our gentle teacher and medium-pace inswing bowler, tickled the bat of Ripley's number 11, six-feet-six-inch-tall Police Constable Chris Pinnock, and the ball appeared to drop an inch or two in front of the diving right hand of Rossi, standing at first slip. This was the time when Tony Greig was taking over the English team and introducing new methods of panicking opposing batsmen and umpires. Rossi was around 15 stone at the time – his weight rose in later years – but was fit enough to spring to his feet and hold up the ball in his right arm screaming "Howsaaaat" for several seconds. Most of our fielders had a good sight of the incident and agreed with me when I said, "Definitely not out!"

"What? It's out!" shouted Rossi.

Pinnock, a normally amiable young man, turned and said to him, "It bounced first, you git."

Rossi's face was contorted. "You're a cheat," he said.

"You're the one who has cheated," said Chris.

The home umpire duly pronounced, "Not out." Rossi continued to argue until I told him to shut up and go back where he belonged, the loo. Two runs later, the last wicket fell and as we returned to the Tudor-built pavilion, he was still cursing.

Tea was served from a hatch on the first floor and we had to come up some narrow, wooden steps to help ourselves from lots of plates filled with goodies on the covered snooker table in the raised part of the room. The lower half was where the players sit around small tables next to the bar. Our players collected our refreshments and sat in the snooker area while the Ripley players sat below. Fortunately this self-imposed segregation worked and Rossi was well out of range from Pinnock and his amused colleagues. I gave out the batting order and said to Rossi, "You're six." He grunted. Dave Barker, another of our many much-respected teachers, opened with me, and Pinnock, a fast left-arm bowler, marked out his 18-yard run. You could see that he was still seething about Rossi's disgraceful behaviour. Dave managed to survive the first over and in the second over, I was far too slow to keep out the fired up Pc's first delivery, a deadly yorker, and when I got back to the pavilion, I stood behind the scorers to see how the others would fare. Up on the balcony a couple of dozen or so players, drinkers and ladies clapped and cheered vigorously. They sensed it could be a revenge job. Jim Baker, our keeper, took guard and he too was bowled first ball. Pinnock roared in again and the new man, John Eade, heard the sound of the wicket being splattered by the hat-trick ball.

I moved upstairs to watch the destruction from the balcony and sent someone to go below to find out if Rossi was padded up. A minute or two later, my messenger came up the steps and shouted, "He's locked himself in the loo!"

"Get back there and tell him he's next in," I said. "Elijah Franklin has just been bowled!"

Four batsmen laid out and our total was 1-4. There was some delay and the Ripley players were joking with the umpires, claiming that the next man should be timed out. Pinnock said, "Don't do that. I'm ready for him. I'll knock his block off!" Rossi wouldn't have heard that, otherwise he might well have retreated to the toilet and turned the key. After a considerable time, he came out of the main door and began his slow walk out to the wicket. Hisses could be heard from the spectators sitting above. Pinnock deliberately waited after Ross was given his guard. His look was enough to make the batsman tremble, and he did. His long strides pounded the hard ground and as he went into his delivery stride I noticed that Rossi's right foot had retreated almost yard towards square leg. Crash ... the stumps were flying.

Five wickets in an over: it has only once happened in first-class cricket and I am indebted to my friend Steve Lynch of Cricinfo with this valuable information. He said, "In April 2011 South African-born Neil Wagner did it for Otago against Wellington in Queenstown and he took four wickets in the first four balls and another with the sixth delivery. The only other previous bowlers to take five wickets in six balls were Bill Copson (Derbyshire) in 1937, William Henderson (NE Transvaal) in 1937-38, Pat Pocock (Surrey) in 1972 and Yasir Arafat (Rawalpindi) in 2004, but their wickets were taken in more than one over." Like Pinnock, Wagner is a fast left-arm bowler who bowls over the wicket. Five wickets in an over may well have happened in village cricket but I have never heard of it. In its long history, the Ripley club is unlikely to have seen half a team shot away in just one over.

Having been 1-6 after four overs, our innings subsided to a new low of 25 in total, which included a club record of seven ducks. It lasted only 18.3 overs, with the Pc taking 8-17 in 9.5 overs. All of our wickets were bowled, another record.

Ashley Fraser Giles, the former England and Warwickshire left-arm spin bowler, made his first appearance for Ripley against the Woodies in 1986 when he was 13. He was well above average height and bowled reasonably fast for a boy of that age. The Test and County Cricket Board had no restrictions on overs for boys then, and Ashley opened the bowling and in his first spell of eight overs, had figures of 0-11. He came back for six more overs and finished 1-28. The two batsmen who took most runs off him were Tony Ward, our top-class keeper who played for Devon in the Minor Counties, and his son Ian, the Sky cricket presenter, who was also 13.

These boys had one thing in common: they were nice, polite boys and no-one predicted they would play for their country. Ashley played against us in three successive years and a back injury forced him to take up spin. He and "Stumpy" Ward – his nickname because of his lack of height – joined Surrey Young Cricketers, and he started out as a would-be tearaway bowler. He took the odd wicket but his batting soon developed and by the time he won a scholarship at Millfield, he had given up serious bowling and concentrated on his left hand batting. Neither Ward nor Giles had natural talent. They rose to Test class by determination and single-mindedness. Their fathers were good cricketers and a fair proportion of England cricketers have come up from the village green. The main breeding ground though is still the public schools. Elitism still reigns. Today elitism is looked down on but the meaning is "the choice, the best", and that is what they are: the top of the tree, irrespective whether their parents were rich or not. In both instances, Ashley and Ian came from modest backgrounds.

Ashley overcame a lot of criticism when he first played for England, but finished up helping to win the Ashes. I invited him to speak at our dinner and he spoke extremely well. He was still the same nice young man. Fame hadn't changed him. He was living in Droitwich and the Mayor named him an Honorary Citizen of the spa town and a year later, he was awarded the MBE. In quick succession, he became an England selector and the national team spin director, while becoming Warwickshire's Director of Cricket. He is now coach to the England One Day squads. "Stumpy" is six months older and he played in five Tests against Ashley's 54. Without hardly any training in television, he became a very efficient and confident sports presenter with Sky's cricket team. I salute both of them.

A year after our Pearl Harbor, Simon Dee turned out for us, and facing a quickish bowler, he stepped backwards and was bowled first ball. Alan Wood said to him, "That's an unusual dismissal."

"I wasn't wearing a box," said Simon, "so I had to protect the crown jewels!" I have to say Simon was probably the worst cricketer who ever played for us.

4

Chuckers We Have Known

The Woodies have played on some of the loveliest village grounds in England, and in 1979 we wondered how we came to visit Sydenham Gas CC in Beckenham in the Borough of Bromley, in South East London, where there were probably more proper cricket grounds per square mile than anywhere in Britain. A road named Copers Cope Road had six, all but one owned by banks. Now most of them have gone. Two more, the Gas ground and Charter Diamond CC, abutted it. The Bank of England still survive on their immaculately cut square at Roehampton, and the week before we managed to beat them by three runs, 106 to their 103. A batsman named Hoffman took 42 minutes for his 3. Was he related to the Hoffman of Northern Rock? We will never know.

The contrast between the Bank of England's posh ground and Sydenham Gasworks' couldn't have been greater. The Gasmen had a reasonable square but the ground was next to a gasworks and there was a shortage of trees and shrubbery. Around this time we had a number of Australians in the side and we were recommended to give a place to Graham Hillier, a teacher from Perth in Western Australia who had moved to London to gain experience of English schools before returning Down Under. Perth is famous for producing swing bowlers and Graham had a similar build to Bob Massie, the bowler who took a world record 16 wickets in the England v. Australia Test in 1972. The suspicion was that the Australians had used illegal methods. Not Massie, but someone else in the team was supposed to have a lip salve phial in his pocket, squeezing it on to one side of the ball, which swung alarmingly both ways. Nothing was proved but Bob only played six more Tests afterwards and was never picked again.

Graham looked a friendly, personable chap and I asked him what he did – bat or bowl or neither? "Both but mainly swing bowling," he said, "and I have a handy arm. You've got to have one on those big grounds in Western Australia."

"What about going in 6?" I said. We had a long tail.

"Fine," he said. I opened and had to stay there as long as I could because four wickets went down for 45. Graham strode in confidently and asked the umpire, "Centre please." Most Aussies take centre. Must be because of the way they like whacking the ball to leg. There was hardly time to assess Graham's potential before he stretched forward and was caught by the wicket keeper for 1 off the second ball he faced.

The Gasmens' over rate was poor and we had to declare at tea on 138-8 off 42 overs. Their innings mimicked ours – a reasonable start and then a swift collapse, brought on by the advent of our new signing. They were 44-0 when I gave Graham the ball, and he wanted an ultra attacking field – three slips, a gully, a short leg and a short mid off in the close field. He exuded confidence. His first delivery whizzed past the bat, thumping into the gloves of our keeper Jim Baker. "Very impressive," said Jim, "except that his bent arm suddenly straightens on delivery. It's a throw!" Jim knew what he was talking about: he was a qualified coach working part time at Alf Gover's indoor cricket school in Wandsworth at the time. Gavin's next ball disturbed all three stumps and sent the bails flying into the air. Again, the delivery was suspect. Neither umpire seemed concerned. In his next over, he bowled the opener and two overs later he had the other one lbw for 32.

The Gasmen were blowing a gasket – 68-5 and their remaining batsmen looked very pensive. Not only was he quick, but the ball seemed to make pace off the pitch, a sure sign that the ball was delivered by an arm which suddenly straightens. In his sixth over, three batsmen were thrown out. None appeared to want to take the matter up with the umpires. I said to him, "I don't think you can continue bowling like this. You've thrown every ball. Soon someone is going to say something about it."

"Don't worry," he said, "I can bowl without straightening my arm. I play a lot of baseball back home and that's the way I throw the ball. I thought they might allow that in England."

"'Fraid not," I said, "any qualified umpire would have taken you off and not allowed you to come back to bowl."

In his next, and final over, he bowled with a ramrod straight arm ... and bowled the number 9 for 0. The number 11, named Friend, declined to come in to face the demon from Perth so the Gasmen skipper declared on 69-9. Graham's figures were 6.2-3-11-7. We probably would have won easily even if he wasn't throwing, but the winning margin of 79 would have been smaller.

In the bar afterwards he bought a jug of beer to share around the players of both sides and I told the Woodies not to bring up the subject of illegality. The Gasmen didn't say anything about it either so foul cricket won the day.

The most written-about crooked armed bowler of all time was Muttiah Muralitharan, the first bowler to take more than 800 Test wickets, a record which is unlikely to be beaten. But not far behind in terms of headlines was the South African Geoff Griffin whose Test career started in the same year as my journalistic career in Fleet Street, in 1960, except that mine lasted 40 years and his Test career only extended a few days. The South Africans toured that year and 20-year-old Griffin, born at Greytown in Natal and educated at that outstanding cricket recruiting establishment called Durban High School, was chosen by the selectors when they knew that his bowling action was suspect.

On 2 May I carried out my first assignment as cricket correspondent of the *Daily Sketch* at Lord's, and E. W. "Jim" Swanton told me, "Watch out, the umpires will be looking at his action very intently indeed." Incidentally, the *Sketch* cost 2½ old pence, or one pence in today's money. The *Sketch* was absorbed by the *Daily Mail* in 1971, and now costs 60p. Egged on by a mad keen sports editor named Sol Chandler who knew nothing about the laws of cricket and hardly anything about the game, I had to write intros like this one, "Every time Geoff Griffin, the South Africans' pace man with the accident-bent right arm bowls in his first Test he is going to feel like a condemned convict walking down Death Row. One shout of 'no ball!' from an umpire and his Test career will never even start."

I asked Jackie McGlew, their even tempered captain, "Why doesn't he bowl with a straighter arm?"

"He's bowled like that all his life," he said. "He can't change now. He's double jointed, wristy and had an accident which gives him a stranger action than the average bowler."

A few days later I was at Alf Gover's Cricket School on top of a garage in East Hill, Wandsworth – now demolished and replaced by undistinguished flats – when Griffin turned up to undergo a day-long tutorial at the hands of former England and Surrey fast bowler Alf. I was welcomed in with an offer of a cup of tea but when I mentioned the *Daily Sketch* he asked me to leave. Alf referred to everyone as "old boy" and was renowned in the game for his joviality.

"Come on Alf, it's good publicity for your business," I said.

"Oh all right," he said.

When the first session ended I managed to get an opinion from him about the lad's faulty arm. "I know I can cure him, old boy, but I can only advise him and it's up to him," he said. In those days international cricketers were often barred from speaking to the Press without permission, so I was unable to ask Griffin what he thought. Always helpful, Alf confirmed that Geoff had a good day.

A week later Griffin was no balled 11 times against Nottinghamshire at Trent Bridge, and my column headed "By the Man with the Chopper" called for him to be withdrawn from action. Fifty years ago they did still have bylines like that! Today the international boards automatically suspend a bowler with problems with his action and film his action, suggest remedial solutions and then get the remodelled bowler back on to the field bowling without penalty. In the First Test at Edgbaston, Griffin was not once called for chucking in his 42 overs. Dr Gover had found the answer, or so it seemed.

The Australians sent a delegation to London around this time to attend an Imperial Cricket Council – now the International Cricket Council – meeting to talk about banning dodgy bowlers, and Don Bradman was the key spokesman. Tony Lock, no balled in Kingston in the 1953-54 tour for throwing, altered his action to avoid a repeat, but the excesses of Australian bowlers Ian Meckiff and Gordon Rorke had gone too far. Bradman's great friend Gubby Allen, the former England bowler who refused to bowl short pitched deliveries to Bradman and his colleagues in the Bodyline series in 1932/3, ably supported by Swanton, agreed with Bradman that, in the words of the Prince of Wales while visiting a Welsh colliery in 1934, "something has to be done". Their decision – stop chucking forthwith – was relayed to Sid Buller and Frank Lee, the umpires at the Lord's Test who took heed. I knew both of the umpires. Sid was a very kind, sympathetic man who died from a heart attack during the Warwickshire *v.* Nottinghamshire game at Edgbaston at the age of 61. This chucking business might well have started his heart problem because he was a very sensitive man. Lee was a bit of a card. He was born a few hundred yards from Lord's and survived to the age of 79. In the Test that followed, Griffin was no balled five times on the first day and six times on the second, all by Lee, for throwing.

On the Saturday Griffin responded by taking the first Test hat trick at Lord's by an overseas cricketer, to follow his record of being the first foreign bowler to be no balled for throwing. Overnight, the umpires obviously thought his arm had miraculously straightened while delivering the ball. He had M. J. K. Smith caught by wicketkeeper John Waite for 99 on the last ball of an over and then bowled Peter Walker and Fred Trueman while both men tried big swipes and missed, with the first two deliveries of his next over. Bedlam ensued with staid-dressed men jumping to their feet and clapping enthusiastically. It was also a blow for freedom, against the Establishment. England's captain Colin Cowdrey promptly declared on

362-8 to prevent a five or six wicket haul for Griffin whose figures were 4-87. In the second innings, Griffin was bowled for a duck by Brian Statham and the ball snapped the top of the middle stump.

I was there on the Monday, the final day, and a crowd of more than 20,000 weren't too happy about the prospect of being sent home with wickets tumbling. Fifteen minutes after lunch England won by an innings and 73 runs. The Queen and the Duke of Edinburgh were scheduled to arrive after the interval and the MCC high command decided to stage a 20-over exhibition game, the first time a T20 game has ever been played at headquarters, to make sure that both teams were introduced to them on the field before everyone dispersed. England batted first and scored 142 in 19 overs with Trueman almost clearing the pavilion with a towering six. Griffin came on to bowl just before the royal couple arrived and after watching his first two deliveries, Buller no balled him four times in a row for chucking. If this continued, with every ball declared illegal, we could be there well into the day.

McGlew spoke to the umpires and they suggested that Griffin should bowl under arm. Griffin did what he was told, an underarm delivery, and he was duly no balled ... for not informing the umpire about the change of bowling! Buller was England's number one then and acting like the Lord Chief Justice, he pronounced the death sentence on poor Griffin's international career. Not too many people know this but the royal pair were in time to see the final overs with the Springboks winning the exhibition farce by three wickets, with five overs remaining. Griffin was allowed to continue on the tour, as a batsman, and everywhere he went, he was cheered. The public thought of him as a scapegoat, a sacrificial lamb. A subsequent ICC meeting rather controversially decided to allow the Australian suspect bowlers to bowl on the 1961 tour while their actions were reported to the authorities and be considered later: a sop to the Aussies and a rap on the knuckles for the Springboks. But to their credit, their Australian Board decided not to pick Meckiff and Rorke for the England tour and peace broke out. Again, Bradman was the man behind it.

Forty-five years later I was on a tour to South Africa with the Forty Club and found myself omitted from the match at Durban High School. It turned out to be a very good decision: the Forty Club was annihilated by an all-Indian side, half of whom represented their State side. I met Patrick Compton, a journalist who is son of Denis Compton, and was highly impressed by him. A true Corinthian, like his dad. Another man you had to admire was David Magner, the Head who said he was descended from the Normans.

"I come from Escoville, near Caen," I told him.

"And I am from that area as well and my favourite actress is Audrey Tautou," he said. As my late wife was named Audrey, I was really bucked up to hear it.

Four days later I bumped into Geoff Griffin. He was playing as a batsman at Kearsney College, a private boarding school for boys in Botha's Hill, a small town between Pietermaritzburg, where Peter Roebuck had a home, and Durban. He greeted me as a long-time friend and he laughed when I told him that I was the person responsible for those huge headlines in the *Daily Sketch* under the code names of "Rex Brian" and "The Man With the Chopper".

"Well, that's what I got, the chop," he said, "but I'm not bitter. Life goes on. I played on for two more years playing first-class cricket in Rhodesia until I was no balled playing in a Currie Cup match against NE Transvaal at Salisbury. That was time to quit but I have kept playing in club cricket and became a coach. I've not bowled for years."

He introduced me to his second wife and their two children. He pointed to me and said, "That was my PR advisor, always telling me to quit. Perhaps I should have been allowed to give interviews to give my side of the story. When I was 11, I was riding my bike when a young black boy ran across my path and I was flung off my bike and broke my arm very badly. It never really recovered and that was why I bowled that way. If that had been properly explained, people might well have changed their minds."

He worked as hotel manager for SA Breweries and was hoping to start a new business. "I aim to write a book about my experiences," he said. "What about you writing it?" Sadly, I had to tell him that it was very unlikely that a publisher in the UK would want to publish it. I promised to send a synopsis to one or two, and I did, but there were no acceptances. Another Test cricketer, Henry Fotheringham, played against the Forty Club and scored 47. Geoff batted for half an hour for his 11, caught off a skier at extra cover. He was a very fit athlete in his youth, playing rugby and hockey at a high standard and was champion in the high jump, long jump, triple jump and pole vault for his State Natal. But the one part of his body which he couldn't use properly was his right elbow. He could have been another Mike Procter, Shaun Pollock or an Allan Donald but for that.

Kearnsey College was set in a beautiful, wooded area and walking around the back of the pavilion, I stopped to watch another match between two junior sides and a tallish, fair-haired bowler proceeded to take a hat trick. At the end of the innings I went up to him and introduced myself and said, "Well done, you've emulated the feat of Geoff Griffin, the first South African bowler to take a hat trick at Lord's in 1960 and he's playing in the other match here today."

"Thanks," he said, "but sorry I haven't heard of him."

Twenty-one months later I read that Geoff had died at the age of 67 ... from a heart attack, like Sid Buller. A month after I arrived home I presided over the Woodpeckers annual dinner and Ashley Giles was our speaker. He spoke well and our members agreed that he would make a career in the game when he retired. He did. I usually bring along some prizes for the raffle to pay for the expenses running the club and this time I had a collections of signed shirts and memorabilia and also two maps of the Zulu battlefields bought at the site of Rorke's Drift, now a museum. I forged the signatures of King Goodwin, the 20-stone Zulu King who stayed at the same hotel we stayed at, The Beverley Hills in Umhlanga Rocks, where the England cricket team was quartered a few weeks earlier. Well, a little skullduggery is permissible even in the game of cricket! Two girls each won a map and they were thrilled. I asked them where they came from and one said, "We're both from Durban."

On another occasion, I brought along a piece of equipment to treat soft tissue injures to give as a raffle prize. A few days earlier I was invited to a press launch at a restaurant in Soho and a company in Southampton was plugging their new cure-all equipment. After their presentation the man in charge said, "Would you like one?"

Having had a recent shoulder injury I said, "Okay, I can test it out!"

In the following days I strapped it on and when it didn't find the spot and I felt it was rather bogus. A week or so later I was short of items for the raffle and brought this one along to our dinner. After the speeches I said to Audrey, who was drawing the numbers from a bag, "Make sure John Peters doesn't win this one, he's won two prizes already!" In the confusion, she pulled out John's number by mistake and I had to hand over the goods. On the following week, the secretary of the man who owned the company rang and said, "Can you send it back to us? It was only lent."

I had to apologise and said, "I gave it to a friend and he took it back with him to Australia. I don't think I came contact him." She seemed a little upset. It cost £35.

5

Her Majesty's Servants Annihilated by an Indian Test Star

What do you do when you are about to play against the Royal Household Cricket Club – the employees of Her Majesty the Queen, the footmen, the courtiers and even perhaps the Footman of the Stool – and your fast bowler has just dropped out and there is no ready replacement? We need to find a stand in. But where? The RHCC was founded in 1903 and its ground is close to Windsor Castle, but you can't see it from the cricket ground. It's a beautiful, tranquil place to play cricket if there is a shutdown at Heathrow, because often aircraft fly in and out of the airport as though the Berlin Airlift had restarted, and they usually fly right over the Castle. In 1948/9, the Allies flew 200,000 flights in 335 days before the Soviets withdrew their blockade. It worked out that planes landed every four minutes. On a busy weekend in the height of the English summer, planes go over the Castle every three minutes. One of the locals told us that the Queen's quarters have double-glazed windows. Well, they definitely need them.

The Duke of Edinburgh, the President of RHCC, was captain of the first team at Gordonstoun, the school where spanking took place in previous generations. Prince Charles went there as well and he suffered from one or two unpleasant experiences like having his head shoved into toilets. The Duke played occasionally at the RHCC ground in his youth, and sometimes he is seen there driving in one of his carriages, or on foot. He was a medium pace cutter of the ball and the highlight of his career was taking a hat trick.

At one of the Royal parties at the Castle, a cheeky, middle-aged man once was purported to have said to him, "Can I ask you this question Sir?

Why did the architects let this place be built here when they knew that planes kept flying over all day long?" If that was true, the Duke would have seen the joke and chuckled. He likes a laugh. The Queen is the Club's Patron and one of her descendants, Edward VII, used to sit and watch the cricket in the circular turret at the top of the original pavilion, which was built for Queen Victoria's grandchildren. A new pavilion with a large, sunlit dining room next to the bar has now been built, and with more charity and corporate matches being arranged there, a large car park has been provided. It is much bigger than the parking area inside Lord's.

Over the years, RHCC have played around 50 matches every season, nearly all of them at their home ground. Their opponents included The Outlaws, the Barbados High Commission, Eton Cavaliers, British Airways (their staff probably brought their own ear plugs), the Honourable Artillery Company, The Fiddlers, Coutts Bank, Australia House and Old Pals CC. Our Woodpeckers fixture started in the '60s and came to a halt and resumed again in the '80s. This particular fixture was arranged for 25 May 1986.

You can't let the Royal team down, so I said to our Pakistan cricket commentator and writer Qamar Ahmed, a famed slow left-hand bowler who took 146 wickets at only 14.1 apiece in his 65 appearances with the Woodies, "Do you have any Test quick bowlers from the subcontinent hiding away in your part of London?" Impecunious young Pakistan Test cricketers sometimes stayed with Qamar in his flat in Shepherd's Bush.

"Yes I have," he said. "But he isn't Pakistan. He's Indian and he's over here on a short break."

"Can he join us?" I asked. He promised to ring me back.

Later in the day he called me with the good news. "I'll bring him along on Sunday," he said. I had to send a list of the names of the visiting players for security reasons the day before the match. There are always staff on duty at the Shaw Gate into Windsor Park and the public are not allowed in without permission.

"What's his name? Not Kapil Dev?" I said to Qamar.

"His name is Sekhar, Thirumalai Ananthanpillai Pallai Sekhar," he said. "He played two Tests for India in Pakistan in the 1982/3 series. He's very keen to play at such an illustrious place."

"I'm not sure whether I can write all that down," I said. "We'll have to shorten that to TAP Sekhar or Seks. We don't want to frighten the opposition. Don't tell them that he recently played for India otherwise they'll panic."

When Qamar's rickety old car drew up at the side of the ground three days later, the new signing stepped out and we were surprised to see how tall and thin he was – just over six feet tall with a shock of black hair and a moustache. Indian bowlers were traditionally on the short side, but these days some of them are giants. McDonalds have taken over their curry houses. Seks was very polite but didn't appear to be talkative. I noticed he was wearing an Indian Test team sweater. That was a bad sign. It might give the game away.

I was having a good run with the tosses and calling "heads" yet again, I followed our usual procedure of batting first. Seks said he would like to come in late in the order, 9 or 10. Clearly he thought he was playing in a good team. There was not much pace in the pitch and we didn't need him with the bat, and I declared on 196-6, leaving RHCC the same amount of overs. I asked Seks, "Which end?"

"Any end," he said. It's a flat ground, with a profusion of trees on the Heathrow side. The sun was shining and there was little wind.

Paul Davidson, our pocket-sized line and length bowler, said, "He ought to take the pavilion end, it's got a bit more lift." So Seks duly marked out his run of about 12 paces. I asked him about how many slips.

"I think two and a gully," he said. "Otherwise it's up to you. You know the pitch and the conditions."

There had been some rain during the night and the pitch was slightly damp. His first ball was little slower than a Stuart Broad opener, pitched just short of a length and the ball passed the batsman at chest height. Neither batsman was wearing a helmet. I said to Seks, "What about another slip?" He didn't disagree. By the end of the over his pace had risen to around 80 mph. The batsman played one ball safely and the others went through at the same height, giving a problem to our keeper Tony Ward, the former Devon player who is father of Sky linkman Ian.

Tony is well below height and he was taking the ball almost head high. In Sek's next over, he took a couple of paces back. So did the fielders. The third ball nicked the outside of the bat and Tony made the catch. The next batsman, also helmetless, displayed a degree of apprehension, like a pedestrian standing on the kerb looking one way and the other and weighing up the cars passing by.

"Right arm over the wicket ... and pretty nippy," said the umpire.

"Middle," said the batsman. Seks was waiting patiently. The next delivery, landing almost the same spot of the previous one, whistled past as the batsman took an involuntarily step towards square leg. By this time the whole of the home team knew that they were facing an Indian Test bowler. The incoming batsmen, mostly padded up, were sitting in a huddle.

Runs were hard to come by and most of them came from the edge of the bat down to third man. I always had a third man for quicker bowlers. If you add up the total of fours in current Test cricket to the vacant short third area it comes to a lot. Why do they persist with this folly?

Paul Davidson took two wickets and suddenly the remainder tumbled almost in a heap. Sek finished with 9.3-4-11-6. One of their older players named Richardson, down at 7, top-scored with 19 not out. It was a heroic performance by him, considering the quality of our bowling. RHCC were all out for 40, and our victory, by a margin of 156 runs, was a club record at the time. As the two batsmen departed towards the pavilion I noticed that there was no-one sitting outside the pavilion. Not a soul was on his feet ready to come out to clap us in. I said to Mr Richardson, "Where are the others?"

"I dunno," he said, "probably they've all cleared off. They weren't too happy about that guy's bowling. That's playing in the wrong spirit. Bringing over a Test player against our lot."

Tony Ward said, "I noticed that the marks where the ball landed were very close, just short of a length. He never strayed from that. That's the difference between a professional cricketer and an amateur." As a non-drinker, Seks went off home with his good friend Qamar for a curry. Now 56, he is still coaching, and was the coach of the Delhi Daredevils in the Indian Premier League. Oh, we weren't invited back the following year.

6

What's Happened To
Our Trophy?

Sarfrz Nawaz wanted two more short legs. "What for?" I asked, "you're doing enough damage already." The fiery former Pakistan and Northamptonshire opening bowler, now a politician and lobbyist, was opening the bowling for a Cricket Writers' Club XI against the US oil company Texaco. The match, or as it turned out, a mismatch, was to celebrate their sponsorship of the one day internationals between 1984 and 1998.

There had been some confusion before the start because our side contained two players whose journalistic credentials were questionable: Sarfraz, who once wrote an article for *The Northampton Bugle* before it went out of business and B. S. Chandrasekhar, the famed Indian spin bowler whose literary output up to then was insufficient to demand the services of a ghost writer. As captain of the journos I was in a dilemma. Just how good were the Texaco team? Their captain said they played regularly in a league and they certainly looked athletic and well attired in their bright blue baseball-style caps. It is a problem which faces anyone organising scratch games. Shall we lend them one of ours to make a game of it or shall we see how it goes?

I was happy to lend them Chandra whose speed through the air was around 65 mph, but not Sarfraz, who is six feet six inches tall, because he could be lethal. The pitch looked under prepared, I thought. The ground, vast and windswept, was a mile or so away from Plough Lane, at the time home of Wimbledon FC.

The Texaco skipper was adamant. "Thanks for the offer but we'd rather stick to our team," he said. "You keep your Test men. It will be a good experience for us." I won the toss and decided to bat. If they batted first they could be shot out and the game would be ruined.

Their bowling and fielding were impressive and we had to labour for our runs. Tony Cozier, the West Indian TV and radio commentator, scored a few. David Frith, editor of *Wisden Cricket Monthly* scored even more. And at the end of our innings, Sarfraz came in to play a typical one-day innings. His score, as I remember, was 35. He was quite pleased with that. "I haven't touched a bat for a long time," he said.

During the frugal tea, he forsook the Eccles cakes and chocolate rolls and went jogging round the boundary instead. As we prepared to go into action, he looked a little weary. "No, I'm fine," he said. "It is just that I have not had any exercise lately."

He pronounced that he was fit to take the new ball and started marking out his run of 30 yards. "I want three slips, two gullies and a forward short leg," he said. "And someone very close on the offside in front of the bat."

It was a confrontational field. His first delivery off his lumbering run was gentle in pace and passed by the off stump without the batsman having to play a shot. The next one was much quicker and shorter. It reared nastily in the direction of the batsman's unhelmeted head. Somehow the poor man managed to duck under it. From my safe position at first slip I thought it would be unwise to give Saff (as we called him), even an overweight, unfit Saff, too long a spell on such a menacing pitch. His third delivery, short on the leg stump, rose and bounced off the batsman's shoulder.

Now it was becoming serious (this was a time before Health and Safety was even thought of). Has a Test bowler, even a recently retired one, ever been taken off in the middle of an over? I posed the question and the umpire at his end seemed uncertain of what action to take. Perhaps he had heard that Saff occasionally became aggressive on the field and had to be disciplined. I saw an incident at Northampton when he was playing against the Australians. Jeff Thomson, the fastest bowler of that era, bounced him and Saff glared at him, swore in his native language and also in English and said, "Tomorrow I am going to put you in the local cemetery," and he pointed to the said cemetery. There were a lot of bouncers flying around that day! On the following morning, Saff gave Thommo a few tasters and each time the arrogant Thommo took evasive action. One up to Saff.

The Texaco batsman, though apprehensive, didn't seem to be too upset at his general line of attack so I let the assault continue. The next ball, again short, went harmlessly down the legside. Saff summoned me and said, "I am going round the wicket, and I want two short legs, not one." It was time to act. A serious incident might imperil the Texaco sponsorship, not only of the friendly press match, but the international matches.

"Do you think that's needed?" I said.

"Yes," he replied. "I can't get my line right."

I looked down the pitch to the batsman and I noticed he was wearing glasses. He was making no visible sign of protest. "All right," I said. Saff wanted someone just in front of square, three yards away and another fielder just backward of square, a few yards deeper.

Saff creaked up to the wicket again and delivered another short-pitched ball. This time it struck the batsman on the other shoulder as he tried to pull away from the line. "No, no, I'm fine," said the batsman. "No problem." He was either very brave, or very mad.

After the over was completed some of my colleagues urged me to withdraw this terror weapon out of the attack. How do you ask a temperamental fast bowler to come off after one over? What would Fiery Fred Trueman have said and done? Or Thommo? Or Dennis Lillee? I decided to give Saff one more over and kept my fingers crossed that he wouldn't kill or maim anyone. His second over was quicker, shorter and more dangerous. How the batsman survived was a mystery to all of us. Actually, he didn't. He was caught behind two balls later and the next batsman had his stumps shattered by the next ball. Off his last ball, Saff's third victim fell to a catch by the wicketkeeper. Texaco were 10-3 and I said to Saff, "Do you mind having a blow? We have a lot of bowlers and I want to use some of them and the way you are going, they won't have anyone to bowl at!"

He responded with grace and I asked Bhagwat Subrahmanya Chandrasekhar to take over at his end. Chandra, quicker than most spinners, was wayward and more costly. Three years younger than Saff, he contacted polio at the age of five and soon started profiting from his handicap. His bowling arm twirled round his right ear in a vertical plane and the ball fizzed out of the back of his hand, pouring out a baffling mixture of googlies, legbreaks and topspinners. He was often unplayable and took 242 wickets at 29.74 in his 58 Tests. He was one of the first mystery bowlers before Muttiah Muralitharan cornered the market. A charming man with a ready smile, he seemed to apologise a lot, especially when some of his bad balls were hit straight to a fielder. His figures were 4-28 and the match was over early enough (with the CWC team winning by more than 100 runs) for us to monopolise the copious amount of refreshment in the tent afterwards. Chandra only drank a soft drink and Saff, worried with his girth, settled on a couple of shandies.

I approached the captain and apologised for Saff's hostile bowling and I said, "I feared that we might be forced to drink in a separate bar." His response was unexpected.

"No, it was a pleasure to face him," he said. "We've worked it out that all ten batsman faced either Sarfraz or Chandra and it's been the highlight of their cricketing lives. They can die happy now that they've faced a great Test bowler." Saff's Test record was similar to Chandra's – 177 wickets at 32.75 in 55 Tests. There was a huge difference in their batting. Chandra recorded four king pairs and 23 ducks in 97 innings, and in one Test on the 1977-78 tour of Australia he was presented with a Gray-Nicholls bat with a big hole in the middle as a joke. Sarfraz scored 1,045 runs at an average of 17.71. Chandra worked for a bank for some years and I met him in Hyderabad some years later and he was in a wheelchair. A lorry crashed into him and left him with a permanent disability, but he was still smiling. On a subsequent tour I met him again and he'd been drinking too much.

I still see Sarfraz when he occasionally visits Britain. He has an impish grin and a good sense of humour, but he has upset a lot of people in the past, including Scotland Yard officers when he complained about not being interviewed about the tragic death of Bob Woolmer. Sarfraz claimed Woolmer was murdered and he wanted to give evidence. He was turned down.

It was also said that he was the man who invented reverse swing with his methods of treating the ball illegally, and when asked about it, he would always burst out laughing. David Gower has revealed the truth and speaking about the England tour to Pakistan in 1984 he said in his column in *The Sunday Times*, "Sarfraz was a very fine bowler and one of the first exponents of reverse swing, though I have to admit we had no inkling of the methods at the time. His new ball partner was Azeem Hafeez, the left arm quick with two fingers missing on his right hand, whose misfortune was fondly used by the Australian comedian Billy Birmingham in Australia in one of his 12th Man spoof CDs about a character by the name of Nafeez Handmissing!"

Who really invented reverse swing? In Chris Waters' fine biography *Fred Trueman* he quoted Ray Illingworth saying, "I know for a fact the bloody Pakistanis never invented it. Donald Waterhouse was showing me how to wet one side of the ball in 1947. Fine bowler, Donald Waterhouse. Took a thousand Bradford League wickets."

Texaco commissioned an expensive silver cup to be presented to the winners of our match and I had it valued. It was more than £500 in the late-1980s. They failed to renew the fixture for no apparent reason, and I kept the trophy at home. Over the years it looked rather tired and needed attention. When my wife Audrey died on Christmas Day 2000, my family and I thought it was a good idea to have it refurbished and given a new title – The Audrey Scovell Memorial Cup. It was presented to the person, preferably a lady, who did most to break the sex bar by persuading wives, partners and friends to join our jaunts to the country to poke fun at our Woodpeckers' stars. After four ladies were honoured, the trophy mysteriously disappeared. Now it is probably worth thousands of pounds. A reward was offered and so far, no-one has owned up.

Sarfraz played with Aftab Gul, the rebel students' leader, on the Pakistan tour of England in 1971, and I covered the series for the *Daily Mail*. The third ball of the First Test at Edgbaston, delivered by Derbyshire's Alan Ward, smashed into Gul's head, and he had to go off for treatment. After having stitches, he returned and scored 28 before Basil D'Oliveira bowled him with one of his gentle swingers. Most of the next two days, he and his colleagues watched Zaheer Abbas – the Tom Graveney of Pakistan in terms of style – totting up an elegant 274, then a record for a Pakistani against England. Zaheer was eventually dismissed by Ray Illingworth and I went to the pavilion to see Leslie Deakins, the Warwickshire secretary to ask if I could interview him. Being a gentleman, Leslie agreed. There was a short wait and I was conducted into the shower room of the Pakistan dressing room. Zaheer was stretched out in a steaming bath and the 15-minute interview may well have been the first to have been conducted in a bath in Test cricket, or even the last. These days the star performers are shepherded away to designated interview rooms, supervised by PR managers and exclusive reports are almost extinct. No-one is allowed into dressing rooms and certainly not shower/bathrooms.

When he was 21, Gul made his name throughout Pakistan with his stirring speeches as a law student at Punjab University. He became the first cricketer appearing in first-class cricket while on bail after being accused of inciting a riot. One source told me that the selectors were forced to pick him in Tests at Lahore, his home city, otherwise his supporters would turn up and torch the stadium. He played two series in England and I got to know him well. In 1983 I invited him to play for the Woodies at Hertford Brewery, a villagey-type ground next to a brewery in Hertfordshire. I picked him up at the house where he was staying in Wanstead, and he wasn't in a good mood. His mental state worsened when he was caught at first slip off his third ball for one. In the field later he was extremely disagreeable and sledged not just the home side, but ours. "Don't ever pick this guy again," said my opener Alan Wood. He was a captain's nightmare. Even before the first ball he said he wanted to make changes in the field. Every over he kept making suggestions. He never stopped.

Some years later I noticed a news story headlined, "Pakistan cricketer Aftab Gul arrested for having Sam missiles in his house." It came as a shock: a number of our Woodies players had peculiar habits but no-one was storing Sam missiles. Aftab gained a fearsome reputation as a political agitator campaigning against corrupt Pakistani governments, and later he became a successful lawyer. He was found guilty of being in possession of the missiles and the judge was lenient, not imprisoning him, but allowing him to go into exile abroad for 13 years. Today Pakistan still has corruption in high places with rigged elections, and if Imran Khan was voted in as President, with the support of the Americans, that wouldn't save the country either according to many experts. Meanwhile, Test cricket in Pakistan is still suspended after the attempted assassination of the Sri Lankan team in 2010, and there seems no chance of a reprieve.

On the day the Pakistan trio of Salman Butt, Mohammad Asif and Mohammad Amir were charged with spot betting, I was at the Media Centre at Lord's and noticed that my friend Qamar Ahmed was talking to Ramiz Raja, the former Pakistan Test cricketer, and several other former Pakistan Test players. I spoke to Mohammad Ilyas, who opened the Pakistan innings at the same time as Gul, and he said Gul was back home in Lahore still working as a lawyer. Illyas, who has lived in Essex for many years and married an English lady, had his Test career abruptly ended by the Pakistan skipper Javed Burki. I asked him how it happened.

"I made a comment about the hair style of Burki's son, "he said, "and Burki came up to me when we were resting at a swimming pool in Sydney before a Test and he upset me so much that I lashed out and knocked him into the swimming pool. I never played for Pakistan again."

A few weeks later the phone rang at my home in Bromley and a voice said, "Brian? This is Aftab, speaking to you from Lahore."

"Stop kidding me, I said, "that's one of Gavin's mates!" I thought someone was playing a trick on me, perhaps Billy Birmingham, the Australian comedian.

"No, really, it's me, Aftab."

I hadn't spoken to Aftab for more than 25 years. I said, "Is it true about the missiles?"

"Yes," he said. "But they were in the house next door, not in mine. I was arrested and charged but I am now back working with the appeal of the three cricketers about spot betting." When he later discovered the strength of the evidence against the three players, he decided not to represent Salman Butt and his colleagues and did several television interviews denouncing them for besmirching the reputation of Pakistan cricket. I saw the illustrated telescript and I noticed he still has a full head of hair and his eyebrows are magnificent, far superior to Bernard Ingham's, the former press officer who worked for Lady Thatcher for many years. Bernard lives in Croydon and is a cricket lover. Since then, I've heard no more from Aftab.

7

Marching Out to the Middle at Lord's

I am not one of those cricket lovers who dream of coming out of the pavilion at Lord's and walking out to the middle to the acclaim of 28,603 or so spectators. But it would have been nice if I had played a game on the main square, even if the ground was deserted. I have been ejected from the square and also the pavilion on the same day, so my name might have appeared in the MCC black book if they have one. My offences happened in 1990, the year of the hosepipe ban when Graham Gooch, England's captain, scored his monumental 333 at Lord's. The day before the First Test started, I was supposed to be interviewing Gooch and Mohammad Azharuddin, the charming 27-year-old Indian captain on the Nursery ground after practice. Instead, I was asked by the *Daily Mail* sports editor to call in at Highbury to see George Graham, Arsenal's manager. By the time George's press conference ended, I missed the captains' interviews at Lord's, but when I arrived I noticed Azhar was talking to some friends under the spaceship which passes for the Media Centre. I'd met him before several times and he was always polite and attentive. I interrupted – well, sports writers have to meet their deadlines sometimes – and asked him if I could speak to him for a few minutes. These days it is called a one on one and the game's rulers aren't very keen on those, unless the interviewer agrees to the party line and not ask awkward questions. They prefer controlled press conferences where the press officer can rule out certain tricky subjects.

Azhar couldn't have been more friendly. "Certainly," he said, "I'm going back to the pavilion. Why don't accompany me and we can talk?" We set off and soon I was treading on the not so lush outfield, banned territory for journalists unless they have special passes, like TV and radio people. Mick Hunt, the very sociable head groundsman since 1985, was on the square along with some of his staff, and he eyed me up rather suspiciously but said hello. It was unlikely that Azhar would be told to clear off, and me as well. The covers were off and we looked at the pitch. Azhar thought it was a typical Lord's pitch. Hardly a blade of grass could be seen. As we reached the other side he opened the small, white doors in front of the pavilion and said, "We can sit outside for a moment, if you like. Follow me." There was no-one in sight, and you don't turn down offers like that.

We sat on a bench in front of the windows and were talking about his hopes for 17-year-old Sachin Tendulkar, who had been given a barrage of bouncers by the Pakistani bowlers in Sialkot a few months earlier. "I have no fears about him," he said. "And except for Devon Malcolm, England don't have bowlers of that pace."

Suddenly I heard a loud shout of "Brian!" I turned and saw Lt Col John Stephenson, the MCC secretary, bearing down on me, peering over his glasses with an exasperated expression on his face. Everyone knew and respected The Colonel, and Azhar and I were somewhat taken aback by his agitated behaviour. "You know you are not allowed to be here," he said. "And you have walked across the ground and that is not on. I would have ordered you off. You must leave immediately."

"I've been invited by the Indian captain and we were just about to finish," I said.

"You must leave," he said.

Rather impertinently, I said, "Well, no-one is around."

"Well, there might be," he said. "You could be blocking the view of members in the Long Room." We looked round. There was no-one to be seen and I told him that.

"But you don't know," he said. "A member could appear at any moment." We had to smile and I got up to go. I shook hands with the Colonel and apologised, and every time he met me he would say to the others in hearing distance, "this is the fellow I had to throw out at Lord's!" I shook hands with Azhar as well, and I thought he had one of the weakest handshakes I've experienced, next to Gordon Brown's, whose handshake was like touching a soft-skinned turbot. The Colonel retired in 1993 and he did an enormous amount of charity work in Salisbury where he lived. I went to his funeral at Salisbury Cathedral in 2003 after he died of a stroke at the age of 72, and it was standing only. I was lucky to have a seat – a Press one, thankfully.

Azhar had been very helpful in my interview, but he failed to tip me off that he intended to ask England to bat first in perfect batting conditions. Gooch was dropped at 36 and England declared at 653-4 with two South

Africans, Allan Lamb scoring 139 and Robin Smith finishing on 100 not out. Azhar was slated over his decision, justifiably. Later he was implicated in match fixing: he confessed that he fixed three ODIs and was banned for life in 2000 by BCCI, the Indian Cricket Board, only for the ban to be lifted six years later. In the 2009 general election in India he won a seat in Parliament for the Indian National Congress party in Uttar Pradesh. As a cricketer, he was looked on as a right-hand version of a David Gower, all wristy and elegant, a master of timing. Many people who saw the Lord's Test in 1990 when he scored 121, after reaching his century off 88 balls, thought that was his best innings.

Some cricketers who are blessed with natural gifts also have bad luck, and Azhar was one of them. His career ended after 99 Tests, his top score was 199. His first marriage broke up and he married Sangeeta Bijlani, a former Miss India, and his son Ayazuddin, aged 19, died in a motorcycle accident. He could blame Hansie Cronje for leading him into crime. Cronje told investigators after his crimes were exposed that he introduced Azhar to crooked bookmakers.

Since the mid-1960s, I have run the Cricket Writers' Club team and it is a taxing job, although we only play two or three matches a year. We have around 350 members, many of whom played cricket or still do, and not many are available, especially now when the summer is filled with first-class cricket matches from early April to the end of September. In 1994 someone from the Royal Mail contacted me about playing against the Cricket Writers' Club team in a ceremonial match at Lord's. I felt a tingle of joy: an ambition might he fulfilled. I might be able to show off my latest sweep, copied from Alan Knott and Colin Cowdrey who used to shovel the ball to very fine leg up the eight-foot-six-inch slope at the Pavilion End. But soon it became clear that the match would have to be played at the Nursery Ground. I said to the man, "The Nursery is a postage stamp size ground, to coin a phrase, with boundaries no more than 50 yards. Can't we play out in the middle?" He was very apologetic. MCC wouldn't allow it. Harrow and Eton still played on the main ground at the time, but not Her Majesty's Royal Mail XI. He explained they wanted to commemorate the Summertime Stamp issue – a flimsy excuse I thought – and was assembling a team drawn from all parts of Britain.

The hunt was now on for our cricketing members from all round the world, and as usual, there was a shortage of volunteers. Richie Benaud was too old, Nasser Hussain and Mike Atherton hate playing these types of games and Derek Pringle, who appeared in a number of our matches after he retired, felt he wasn't up to it any more. Potential stars were dropping out almost daily. David Firth, the editor of *The Wisden Cricketer* and prolific cricket author, confirmed, and so did the talented all rounder

Eric Brown of the *Exchange Telegraph*. Tony Pawson, the former Oxford University and Kent batsman, who was chairman of CWC in 1980-81, was keen. He was 73 but he could still run fast with his short steps like Margaret Thatcher in her prime, and he didn't look his age. He died at the age of 91 in 2012. He was an international-class fisherman and a thoroughly good fellow. Brian Woolnough, formerly of the *Sun* and the *Daily Star*, put his name down as well. He was a useful all-rounder, and sadly died at the age of 64 in 2012. I was delighted when Malcolm Macdonald, the former Fulham, Luton, Newcastle, Arsenal and England centre forward known as Supermac, agreed to don his whites. Though not a member of CWC, we recruited him as a devoted cricket lover, and because he could bat and bowl and be quicker in the field than some of our over-fifties stars. Supermac never quite fulfilled his talents as a footballer, and after he retired with a chronic knee injury, he became an alcoholic and his business failed. He became teetotal in 1997 and now has proved to be a popular radio presenter. With 345 of our members not now available, I signed up Richard Gwyn, the Bromley CC swing bowler and one of my mates, to open the bowling.

Earlier in the day of the match I checked the weather forecast and learned that heavy rain was expected in London by 1 p.m. We had 11 men, five of them CWC members, ready and changed for an 11 p.m. start, and I called "heads" and said I would bat.

Their captain suddenly said, "You can't do that. We want to bat first. They've come all over the country and some of them are former county cricketers."

"Well some of my team has been gathered from all round the world," I said, "including Rohan Kanhai, and I think we can give you a good game, so let's leave it as it is. We'll bat first." He didn't know that Rohan was playing until then and wasn't happy.

The day before I heard that the former West Indies skipper was in town and short of top batsmen, I asked him if he could provide the side a half century to help things along. He was going to be 60 on Boxing Day, and his wonky knee was probably just as bad as Supermac's wrecked knee. He was 40 when he retired and had just scored a half century in the inaugural World Cup final at Lord's.

As David Frith and I were about to leave the dressing room, I heard a commotion. A friend of Vic Lewis, the famed musician, former bandleader and ex-manager of The Beatles, burst in and said Vic wanted to play because he was sponsoring the refreshments. For a time, Vic was the USA representative at ICC meetings and he knew all the secrets of world cricket. He once said, "Cricket is not just another sport. It's a religion, a way of life and a brotherhood." We had an XI, but I did a deal with the Royal Mail skipper that Vic could bat and one of our players would field. Vic had his own team and arranged countless charity matches with many of them played at the Royal Household ground at Windsor Park.

I was out early to their quick left-arm swing bowler, a former Gloucestershire player, and in came Rohan to loud applause from our players and a number of neutrals. Most of them were experienced MCC members who know where stars are playing in duff matches at the Nursery and they wanted autographs. They are like train spotters. And they are also on time. Rohan soon saw the left armer taken off and he was soon finding the gaps. Tony Pawson came in and showed Rohan how to scamper quick singles, but our star said, "Not so much of that. I've got a dodgy knee."

The 100 was up and we had plenty of batting left. Eric Brown, Wooly Woolnough and Supermac all kept the scoreboard busy and Rohan duly reached his half century. By this time clouds were gathering, and at 142-5 he gave a catch and walked in to be greeted with a standing ovation.

It was a declaration game and I could bat on for an over or two to allow Vic to come in, but I wanted 200. At ten to one, almost time for lunch, Vic's friend said, "Vic won't be able to bat unless you keep the innings going."

"Don't worry, someone will get out," I said. I shouted at our anonymous mate of Richard Gwynn and gave him the wind up sign and he obliged and got himself stumped. Eleven balls remained before lunch and Vic, a small man with short arms, blocked the first ball. The bowler was bowling offspin, and realising that our benefactor wasn't much of a batsman, he threw up a high full toss. Vic blocked it with a straight bat. The next four balls were patted back, all full tosses. Vic edged the last delivery for one, much to my annoyance. We still needed eight runs to reach 200.

As the field changed over I said, "Give it a go Vic, we want to pass the 200." Vic nodded. He proceeded to block all six deliveries from a medium pacer and I was forced to declare on 192-9. Ten minutes later rain started to fall and it lasted for the rest of the afternoon. Match drawn. The skipper wasn't overjoyed about not having batted first, but he made a nice speech and we were all presented with a gold commemorative medal which I still have in my trophy case. The way the pound is going I shall have to value it and sell it to one of these flourishing pawnbrokers. The last time I saw Vic was at a match at Windsor and he gave me one of his latest ties. He had a collection of 6,000 ties and I still have a number of them. Sadly he died aged 89 in 2010.

In January 2011 the Forty Club started their 75th anniversary season with a lunch at the House of Lord's, hosted by Lord Peter Brooke and Lord Michael Naseby, and I was wearing Vic's latest ties in honour of his death two years earlier at the age of 89. John Williams, a member of MCC and Forty Club, spotted it and said, "What's that ghastly-looking tie?"

"As you can see," I said, "it is dark blue, red, yellow, green, light blue and mauve, all very bright, and was the last tie Vic Lewis produced. It's made of pure silk, handmade and has the insignias of the Royal Household and three lions."

"It probably finished him off!" said John.

One of the more interesting matches I played in took place late in the summer in 2000 at Goodwood Park. I was invited, for some reason, to play in a Motor Racing Xl against the Duke of Richmond's Xl to start the Goodwood Revival, and the overs match was preceded by a lavish lunch at Goodwood House. I sat next to the Duke and he said he might well be available to umpire for a while, which he did. He was a charming man. I also met Jack Brabham, the only driver who has won Fl World Championships – in 1959, 1960 and 1966 – driving his own car. And that still applies now. He was 74 at the time and was hard of hearing. As we walked out the skipper said to him, "Where do you want to field Jack?"

"Slip," he said. I'd already been told to field there and as the bowler was about to bowl, I looked to second slip where Jack should have been and noticed he was standing right behind me.

"You've got to move to your right, Jack," I shouted.

"Oh no," he replied, "I'm quite happy standing here, out of the way!"

The final delivery of the opening over lifted on a slightly damp pitch and struck the top glove of the batsman and it lobbed high over my head. I wasn't able to jump high enough to catch it and turned to see Jack dropping it off an absolute sitter.

"My eyes aren't as good they used to be," he said, with a hearty laugh.

Umpiring at square leg was Murray Walker, the all time great Fl race commentator who joined in with the laughter. Wickets began to fall, mainly from bad shots from pretty poor cricketers. The innings closed on 121 and we repaired to the thatched pavilion for a strawberry and cream tea. Jack opened with me and was palpably lbw first ball, but Murray said, "Might just have slid down." Jack survived another over, managed a single, and was caught and had to depart.

Our innings followed the same pattern as our opponents, wickets tumbling to distinctly average bowling. I was caught for 15 and finished up second highest scorer. Just before our innings succumbed, there was a massive roar coming from the west – a Spitfire appeared over the trees on the left. It appeared to be flying at no more than a hundred feet, and the fielders, still standing, were ready to fling themselves to the ground if it happened again. The pilot zoomed up over some more trees and turned round over the Downs for another exercise seemingly designed to terrify the cowed spectators. Having seen Spitfires taking on German FW190s in the latter stages of the Second World War in the Isle of Wight, I knew that they were noisy, but at this short distance and height, this one was deafening.

The pilot swept over the cricket field at the same height and turned, and thankfully it headed back to base. "Hell's bells," said Jack. "I flew in the Australian Air Force and that brought back memories." Next day Jack crashed his racing car in practice and had to go to hospital. He'd been in accidents before but that was his first time he was put in hospital after one. Luckily the injuries weren't life threatening. The cricket match must have been fated. A week or so later I was told that the pilot, who was in his seventies, crashed in his Spitfire and he didn't make it. But Jack did and he is still alive.

8

A Famous Nine Year Old
Tells Them How to Do It

Qamar Ahmed, alias Q, one of the more distinguished members of the Woodpeckers, has one record which will never be beaten. When he first played at Broadhalfpenny Down against Hambledon he told us that he was the first and only Pakistan bowler to dismiss all five Mohammad brothers, Hanif, Wazir, Raees, Sadiq and Mushtaq. "You've lived on that back home in Karachi," one of our Australians told him.

Q has worked as a freelance journalist in 77 of the 105 Test match grounds and notched up 385 Tests, 721 ODIs and eight World Cups by St George's Day 2012. Geoff Boycott, who was born in 1940, was boasting about his many appearances in Tests as a commentator in the Dubai series between England and Pakistan, when Q, who is a little older, interrupted him said, "Sir Geoffrey, you can't come close to my record. You've not dismissed all the Mohammad brothers in Pakistan." Boycott had to agree. Richie Benaud has attended almost a third of the 2,000 or so Tests and he holds the undisputed Test appearance record, but he never captured the wickets of the Mohammads either.

In seven seasons between 1956 and 1963, Q dismissed the legendary Hanif Mohammad, Pakistan's Little Master, on two occasions. "He'd just come back from scoring the slowest innings in a Test in Barbados, when he made 337 in 16 hours and 10 minutes," said Q. "I had him caught at long on for 129." That record lasted 47 years before a certain R. Nayyar scored even slower, 271 in 16 hours 55 minutes, in 1999-2000. Q said, "The second time was just after when Hanif scored his 499, beating Don Bradman's 452 in first-class cricket. Then I got Mushtaq Mohammed out for 87 on his debut when he was 14. In 1960 I bowled Sadiq Mohammad on his debut at the age of 23 and I also took the wickets of the other brothers, Wazir, the eldest and Raees."

The Pakistan International Airways have been kind to the Mohammads and all of them played for PIA. Shoaib Mohammad, son of Hanif, played 45 Tests to the Little Master's 55, and he played for PIA, and now Shezhar, son of Shoaib, aged 21, plays for PIA as well. Mohammad Illyas, the former Pakistan opening batsman and recently chairman of the Pakistan selectors, said of Q, "He played at the highest level and was close to being chosen for his country."

In July 2001 the Woodies were short of players and Q told me at the Media Centre at Lord's that we should sign up Shezhar, Hanif's grandson. "He's nine but he's a very good little player," he said. We've had ten year olds, but a nine year old from the Mohammad family would, I thought, be a coup.

"He'll be the littlest of the little masters," I said.

I first got to know Hanif at Lord's in 1967 when he scored his dogged, unbeaten 187, and he had a limp then and still batted almost two days virtually on one leg. In 2001 he was still limping, more painfully, when we met again at Lord's. He gave me his address in London and said, "I am staying in a flat just off Oxford Street." We arranged to pick up Shezhar at noon, but I was held up by heavy traffic. I rang Hanif on his mobile to pass on the unhappy news and he said, "I'll be staying on the pavement outside to make it easier for you." Coming up Park Road towards Oxford Street, the traffic was almost at a standstill and I could see Hanif and his grandson. A car stopped and Hanif opened the front nearside door and ushered Shezhar into the car, which started to move off at a very slow pace.

I said to Nigel Phethean, my other passenger, "Someone appears to be kidnapping Shezhar. Hanif must be short sighted. He didn't see the driver properly. Hop out and try to find what's happened." Nigel dashed off and soon caught up the other car. He said to the driver, "You've picked up the wrong boy." Shezhar got out and Hanif finally caught up with the other car and apologised for the mix-up.

A few minutes later I arrived at the scene and Hanif, with a broad smile, said, "Here he is. He loves cricket and he won't let you down." Shezhar shook hands and he seemed much older than his years. "We'll be holding up traffic," I said, "so hop in at the back seat." He did so and had trouble to put on a seat belt. He looked so small: we ought to have provided him a small child's seat.

As we left Hyde Park corner and on to the Westway, I quizzed him about cricket and he spoke like a young man in his twenties, not a nine year old. I said to him, "What do you think of your grandfather's batting?"

"He was boring," he said. He spoke excellent English and soon convinced us that he had sound views about the game.

"And what about Geoff Boycott?"

"The same, he was boring."

His father Shoaib Mohammad played some very long, patient innings. "What about him? Was he boring?"

"Oh no," he said, "he played a lot of shots, particularly on the offside."

Crinfo described Shoaib as "short, occasionally strokeless, but with almost inhuman powers of concentration". Like his father Hanif. We asked Shezhar if he followed the family trait. "I like playing my shots," he said.

Mohammad Illyas had a different opinion about Hanif, and he told me, "He was as good as Sachin Tendulkar. If he was playing on today's pitches, not the uncovered ones of his day, he would have scored 20,000 runs not 3,945. He had everything. He was similar in size and style as Tendulkar."

Shezhar's debut was taking place at a village called Ockham just off the A3: the cricket club boasts on its website, "We are the friendliest cricket club in England." They play in the Surrey Downs League and on Sundays they only stage friendly games.

"Do they play overs cricket?" said Shezhar.

"They usually do, but we prefer playing declaration cricket," I said. "It keeps the interest up to the end. In overs cricket, the game can be decided too early because there is no draw."

"We play overs in Pakistan," he said. When we parked at the rear of the pavilion, he said, "Where will I bat?"

"Bit too early to say," I said, "but somewhere near the top of the order." He took out his mini bag with his gear and accompanied us to the away dressing room.

"Can someone bowl to me?" he said.

"I'll have to go out and toss up," I said, "but someone will give you a few deliveries to warm up." He had his own junior size ball. I won the toss and as I returned from the middle, he said, "Can I open?"

"Don't really think so," I said.

"They seem to have a couple of rather tall bowlers. Besides, Alan Wood and I have opened for more than 20 years and we're just getting on first name terms."

I started to change and seeing Alan arriving, I said to Shezhar, "This gentleman is my opening partner, and I've decided to put you at four." He didn't appear to be delighted with the news.

Before the Ockham team took the field he was ready with his boys' size pads on up to his hips and wearing a mini helmet and armguard. He was standing close to the square leg boundary as Alan and I walked out to the pitch. Within minutes, I was stumped for a duck and John Murrin, a six-foot-seven-inch former rugby player, joined Alan in the middle with the score 10-1. Shezhar was bending over on the boundary like a 100-metre sprinter about to answer the starting gun. A second wicket fell at 10, with Alan being bowled for 10. The tinytot was halfway out to the middle before Alan passed him on his way to the dressing room.

John told him, "Have a look at it." There was no response. The fielders were smiling among themselves at seeing such a disparity in size between the gigantic John and the pint-sized little boy. Most of them hadn't seen anyone so small playing in a seniors' match at the historic Ockham, which is mentioned in the Domesday Book (in 1086). Shezhar said confidently to the umpire, "One leg." He made his mark and looked around the field to check the positions of the fielders. All were close in.

One major concern emerged from the very first ball he received. The bowler wasn't quick and the ball passed outside the off stump, level with his helmet. I reckoned Shezhar was around four feet eight inches in height, and technically speaking the umpire could have called no ball. Nothing happened. The second ball went down the leg and he swished and missed it. He played a Boycott type forward defensive shot to block the third delivery, which ended the over. One expected the senior batsman would have taken the initiative to talk to him about the state of the pitch, the quality of the bowling or even the weather, but Shezhar was the first to react and strode up to John to give him some advice. "Keep your head down," he said. John struck a four to leg and followed with two singles. When he played the ball to deepish mid on he called "No" – obviously thinking that Shezhar's little legs might have caused him to be run out. Shezhar shouted, "That was a single! You ought to run."

Shezhar nicked a single behind square leg and after pushing another single, this time to backward point, his over-confidence cost him his wicket – caught behind for 2. As he came off he was greeted with sympathetic applause. At 18-3 the Woodies were in trouble. Shortly afterwards, John was caught behind for six. We were 32-4 and in dire straits. Robbie Wood, son of Alan, was then bowled for 1 on 38-5. Time to think about talking up next year's fixture, if there is one! Next man was the tall and handsome Mark Edwards who went on two Press tours of India under the leadership of Mihir Bose, and knew the cricketing wiles in the subcontinent. Mark started off with a straight six and soon followed with two Dhoni-style fours.

Inside the small pavilion, Shezhar took off his gear, packed it away and volunteered to help the side by umpiring. Neither side had a paid umpire and the players of both sides took turns. No-one liked doing it.

"Are you sure you know all the laws?" I asked him.

"I know them all," he said. "I can do it."

The other players were aghast. How can a nine-year-old boy be a key figure in a game of grown-ups? I said, "Sorry Shezhar, I think it might cause problems with the home side."

He said, "So can I do the scoring?"

The young man who was doing the score – our number 10 and opening bowler Michael Robeson, known as Larry, said, "Let him do it. I'm sure he knows all about it." Rather reluctantly, I let him take over the team pencil.

Odd players and supporters were coming up and asking Shezhar the score and they helped to put the scores up. He did the scoring alone, without help from anyone else. In little more than an hour, 138 runs were added by Mark and our actor John "The Bill" Peters. The debonair Edwards was approaching his century, which would have been his first for the club, and fours and sixes were cascading merrily along. Mark spends much of his time working in finance and he always knows his own score while batting. He thought his tenth four brought his score to 100 and was mystified that no-one applauded. He thought to himself, "They're taking the mick." That has happened in the Woodies in the past. Next ball he called for a single and was run out. Someone put up 97 against the Last Man and the normally mild-mannered Mark looked rather peeved as he came towards the pavilion. "I thought I'd got a ton," he said.

Shezhar said he was sure that he only made 97 and Mark had to accept his word. When he cooled down over a pint of bitter, he said, "I'm certain it was a hundred, but we had to give way to the boy and take his word. We can't offend the Mohammads!"

Anyway, a total of 189-7 after being 36-5 was some achievement. After a typical village tea – not all the cakes were from Tesco – we were ready to restart. Shezhar piped up, "I can bowl you know. Which end can I bowl?"

I had to quieten him down. "We've got two top-rated bowlers to start with and I'll see if I can give you an opportunity later."

As the players approached the square, he raised the subject of his fielding position. "I can field anywhere," he said. "Mid on will suit you very well," I said to him. Mid on is one of the places fielders can hide and never having seen him in the field, I wasn't taking any chances. The possibility of Shezhar bowling was soon removed, with Larry ripping out Ockham's top order batsman with Bothamesque figures of 10.5-6-12-6. Ockham were out for 84, giving us victory by 105 runs. Shezhar had little to do in the field, but he did a lot of talking.

Later in the evening our scorebook was checked again and there were several obvious omissions, including a four which went to John Peters, and not Mark. Ah well, we don't want to make a fuss about it, we thought. The Mohammads are one of cricket's great brotherhoods. As I drove him back to his grandfather's flat, I asked him how long he was staying in England. He said, "A couple of weeks and I can't play next week, but I'm all right for the following one." By the beginning of the second week we were struggling for players against the Avorians, a Surrey League club just across the M3 at Cobham. I had to report the England *v.* Australia Test at Lord's and Alan Wood was captain. Q supplied two more Pakistan players, Utahayashankar and another Mohammed, no relation, and Shezhar made a third.

It was a steaming hot day, which pleased our Pakistan contingent. With the Test finishing early, I was able to do the umpiring, denying Shezhar a possible opportunity to cause an international crisis. The bowler Mohammad bowled seven accurate overs to take 3-26, and Larry Robeson had figures of 16.4-4-50-4. Shezhar kept handing out advice, but when he chased the ball towards the boundary, some of our fielders shouted, "Get on with it, they're about to run a fourth." He reached the ball before it went over the boundary and returned a presentable throw to the keeper. Not many of our players would have bettered that. The Avorians were all out for 180, not a lot to get on a flat pitch.

Woody gave the opening spots to John Murrin and his son Robbie, and they put on 88 without much trouble before both of them were dismissed. The unpronounceable Uthayashankar fell for 9, and the wickets started to fall against two rather elderly bowlers.

"Where am I going in?" said Shezhar.

"Eight," said Woody. He looked glum. Within two minutes Woody changed his mind. "I need some experience so can you swap with Larry? You're now 9." More glum and despondency. After slogging a cross-batted 4, Larry was bowled and Shezhar came in to partner his skipper. They started a revival and Shezhar played several correct shots which, understandably, had little pace. They brought him two 2s and four singles. Trying to drive wide of mid on, he lifted his back leg, missed the ball down the leg side and was stumped for 8.

"I'm in," he said to the umpire.

"'Fraid not," said the umpire. "On your way sonny." The innings ended on 165 – 15 runs short. It was like one of those Premier League football matches: one side dominates in the first half but after the break, they tire and then collapse in a heap. Lack of a curry between innings might have been the reason for our frailty.

Q met Shezhar early in 2012 and he reported back, "He's tall now and he bats high up in the order for PIA, occasionally keeps wicket and sometimes bowls offspin."

I emailed back, "Does he umpire and score as well?" Just a joke, really.

He made his first-class debut against Lahore Shalimar at the age of 17 and scored 70 and held three catches. In 2010 he made two ducks in the game against Sailkot.

Mohammad Illyas said of him, "He has a chance to get to the very top as a wicketkeeper-batsman. He is very tall and knows the game." We knew that. We wish him well.

Shezhar had his 21st birthday on 12 November 2012 and if we had his address, we would have sent him a greetings card. It must be a tough job being the third generation in Pakistan's most famous cricketing family. If he ever returns to England we'll always keep a place for him in the Woodpeckers side. On the other hand, he might be in the Pakistan Test side, and in which case, that wouldn't happen. Anyway, he's likely to be in charge whatever happens.

9

Geoff Lawson Shakes up Mitcham, the World's Oldest Cricket Ground

Most of our fixtures came from recommendations from friends, but in 2005, the year that Andrew Flintoff wrecked his knee and career to help regain the Ashes, we had to call up the Club Cricket Conference which specialises in arranging games when matches are cancelled. July 17 in our fixtures list wasn't filled and Mitcham, a Surrey League side, hadn't a fixture, and I took it. I realised they could be stronger than our usual type of opponent and Gavin, who was working on the Test series for Channel 4, said, "We can get Geoff Lawson to play. He likes playing the odd game." When Lawson, nicknamed Henry after an Australian poet, learned that Mitcham boasted having the oldest cricket ground in the world, he was very keen. He was 48, and still able to bowl at a reasonable speed.

Most records of English cricket indicate that Mitcham Green staged the first organised match there in 1685, and there is a plaque hidden across the road which confirms it. Another plaque in the pavilion claims that Admiral Horatio Nelson occasionally watched cricket at the Green while he lived at nearby Merton House. Lady Hamilton, his mistress, bought the mansion on his behalf for £9,000 in 1801. Now it has been demolished and a block of flats occupy the land. In Nelson's day, the cricketers changed in the Cricketers Inn 30 yards from the boundary, and the scorers sat in a balcony to do their work. The original inn was bombed during the Second World War and was replaced by another building in 1958. These days the players still change in a rather shabby two-storey wooden pavilion built in 1904, close to the Burn Bullock pub, and they have to cross a very busy road before reaching the ground. The steps up to the first floor are so worn by the studded footwear of players like Andy Sandham, Tom Richardson and Ken Barrington, who lived in Mitcham for much of his life, that someone slightly tipsy might have a bad fall.

Our new fixture on the Green took place on a scorching day, the kind of dry heat Lawson knew when he grew up in Wagga Wagga in New South Wales. When we arrived we found that we were locked out of the away dressing room and we had to wait for someone to turn up with the key. The dressing room was very cramped. Up to ten coffins occupied most of the floor space and the players found it difficult to change. Lawson didn't seem to mind. He was one of the boys, not a prima donna.

When we won the toss and decided to bat, he opted to go in at ten. Jim Maxwell, the eminent Australian broadcaster, wanted to play as well, but had to work so we were one short. Our opener, Tim Percival, a PR for npower at the time, who sponsored the England series, hit a beamer high into the air, and it started coming down towards an oncoming top of the range Mercedes with an open top. The ball landed on the bonnet with a loud bang and bounced high into the air before it fell on the pavement and finished up in the gutter. The car pulled up with a jerk and the smartly dressed young man at the wheel, sitting next to an attractive blonde, jumped out.

"Who's running this place?" he said. Someone pointed to the stairs to the pavilion.

"Up there," the man said. Leaving his car in the road and blocking the westward traffic, the driver bounded up the stairs and shouted at one of the older members, "Who do I sue about this?"

The man said, "Is that car insured by you?"

"No, I'm afraid I'm not insured to drive it."

"I think you had better drive off quick before the police catch you," said the man. The deflated driver left after accepting the advice. The bill was probably in the hundreds or even thousands.

Mitcham used seven bowlers and four of them, Anish, Azim, Afzal and Amar, indicated to us that they were wily, but not too threatening. Geoff Lawson brought out the first jug of orange squash for drinks after Tim was given lbw for 31. It was another record for the club – the first Test player from Down Under to act as the drinks waiter. The heat seemed to affect the middle order batsmen and it was left to Gavin, who has played cricket in India, Pakistan, Sri Lanka and Bangladesh, to crash on, and he was 140 not out when the innings was declared on 263-6.

The Australian pace bowler, coach, writer and broadcaster opened the bowling and failed to take a wicket in his first ten overs. His frustration built up after a Pakistan-born teenage umpire kept rejecting his lbw appeals. I asked him if he fancied having a break and he said, "No, I'll stay at that end until I get that bastard out." He was referring to the batsman who kept being hit on the pad, sometimes plumb in front. He bowled around 70 mph and moved the ball both ways from a classic high arm.

In his next over an inswinger struck the batsman in front of the off stump and he appealed vigorously. The umpire raised his finger slowly like a Billy Bowden, with the utmost caution. As the batsman departed, Lawson shouted to him, "Well batted mate, I enjoyed all five of your innings, now fxxx off!"

The batsman spun round. "What did you say?"

"You were out five times, but the umpire has only just acknowledged the last one," said Lawson. An argument started, but realising Lawson is one of the toughest and tallest (six feet three inches tall) of the caustic bunch of former Australian Test fast bowlers, the batsman ended it by trudging off, still mouthing words of indignation.

Not long afterwards, the young Pakistani umpire turned down another appeal from our profusely sweating Aussie, also for lbw, and Henry said, "You xxxxxxx xxxx, that was out!"

The startled umpire began waving his arms in the direction of the pavilion and shouted, "Skipper, can you come out here?" The home captain came on to the pitch and there was an earnest conversation between them before the captain announced, "I have taken over the umpire's duties." The umpire, somewhat relieved, walked off. A civil action might well be looming.

Unfortunately for the club's lawyers, if there were any, no more trouble ensued. Lawson's figures were 17-2-71-1, a testament to his fitness, but not to his temper.

None of our wicketkeepers were available so we called up Tom Rawshorne, the *Daily Mail*'s investigative writer, and he took a personal best of four stumpings, all off the slow lobs of our actor John Peters. I should have asked Geoff to make way for him earlier, because JP's innocuous bowling was more potent than his in these subcontinental conditions. Like most of the Terror Thomsons of Down Under, Lawson was very genial off the field, and he was soon talking to the Mitcham players about the Ashes Test and England's chances of winning the next one. Our guest spent an hour or more over several rounds of lager with players of the home side, including the captain, but not the Pakistani umpire, who had disappeared.

Just over two years later, Lawson was appointed coach of the Pakistani team and they had the best record in ODIs of all the major countries in that period. Eighteen months later he was sacked. "I got on very well with the players," he said. "It's the selectors and officials who caused the trouble." Ijaz Butt, the madcap chairman of the Pakistan Cricket Board, decided not to renew his contract saying, "We have no use for Lawson."

Henry was dismissed in a despicable manner. A bell boy shoved a letter under his hotel bedroom and he opened it to learn he was no longer in charge. During the row about ball tampering at the Oval Test in 2010, Ijaz Butt put the blame on the England team and threatened legal action. He should have been dismissed immediately, but it took some months before he was sacked.

Another official who was in power at the time when Lawson was fired was Salahuddin Mulla, the chief selector who later went the same way, out the door. He was the same Salahuddin who played five Test matches, and I signed him up for the Woodies at the age of 20 during the Pakistan tour of England in 1967.

I was covering the series for the *Daily Sketch* and I had a good relationship with the team manager and I said to him, "I notice Salahuddin is not playing Essex in Colchester, and I wonder whether you could let me have his services. My team called the Woodpeckers have a re-arranged game at Hampton Hill CC to commemorate an anniversary and we need a star to help things along." To my astonishment, he agreed. You couldn't see that happening today!

I picked up Salahuddin at the team hotel and he appeared to be a well-behaved, well-educated young man. He stayed at our home in Croydon, not far from a school where D. H. Lawrence taught, and my wife Audrey, who had just given up her job with ITN as a production assistant, ready for the birth of my daughter in several weeks, cooked a curry which he liked. He explained he was a Muslim and needed to pray five times a day and it meant getting up in the night and early morning, but that didn't disturb us.

"Actually I was going to play for Beddington's third team at Wallington tomorrow, which isn't too far away," I said. "Do you fancy playing in that game as well? It would be a nice warm up for the big one next day. The standard won't be too high."

He readily accepted the offer, and when we arrived at Wallington's fenced-in ground in the suburbs no-one took notice of his Pakistan cap and sweater. I opened with him against Wallington's third team and he scored 89 to win the match. As non-drinkers, we didn't stay for the celebrations, and we had another curry that evening, stronger than the previous one.

Later in the evening the boss man of Hampton Hill rang to check about the match. "Are you sure you have a good enough team to take us on?" he asked me. "It's a big occasion for us and we don't want to let people down. The Mayor is coming and some of his friends." I assured him the Woodpeckers would give his lads a fair contest.

There was a goodly crowd at Hampton Hill's beautiful ground in Bushey Park, close to Hampton Court Palace, a home of King Henry VIII, and Salahuddin was very impressed. "It is a much better ground than the ones we play at home," he said. "So green." There was some confusion when we arrived because Hampton Wick Royal CC were next door, and they were considered as the big boys. We had to check whether we were on the right pitch. The Hillites were playing their strongest Sunday side and nowadays their website stresses the fact that the club is a non-discriminatory organisation. From Wallington Thirds up to this level was some leap. Mick Hogan, our 18-year-old Irish version of Ian Botham, would match their best, but if Salahuddin failed, we might collapse with our elderly batsmen quailing against anything above 60 mph.

The pitch looked a good one and I decided to bat. Their captain wasn't happy. Looking around our team, he obviously thought the celebration match might be over by lunch. "Don't worry," I said. "We have several good 'uns."

Salahuddin opened with one of the old brigade and his partner soon departed, bowled middle stump. Seeing me limping out to the middle must have caused more concern for the Hillites and its caterers. But Salahuddin soon showed his class and we began purring ahead. His cap was embellished with "Pakistan" and also on his sweater, and like the day before, no-one asked him about it. A lot of English cricketers are like that: they don't take much interest in the opposition. But they should! At lunch we were 150-1, Salahuddin 125 not out, and me on a turgid 15 not out. I sat next to the man in charge and said, "This chappie is a pretty good player, as you can see."

"Arrr," he said, "but if our darkie had been fit, he wouldn't have lasted long. He's really quick!" These days, the club is sponsored by an Indian and a lot of the players are Indians, Pakistanis and Sri Lankans. Times have changed, thankfully.

As we were about to go out, Salahuddin said, "Shall I give my wicket away?"

"I'll be out soon and you can see how it goes," I said. But when we resumed, he gave a high catch and was caught on the same total. He was thinking of his colleagues: what a nice man.

We declared on 249-8 and the Hillites were 100-6 when I brought him on to bowl his off breaks. He took four quick wickets and it was all over. The top man shook hands when we left, but he didn't suggest another fixture. Len Hutton once described Salahuddin, "The worst opening batsman I've ever seen in any international side." Perhaps he was right. He only scored 117 runs in his five Tests, with an average of 19. He took only 2 wickets. The highlight of his career might well have been at Bushey Park.

One of the best pieces of sledging involving an Australian Test cricketer in our low standard of cricket came at a game at Wandgas CC in New

Malden. Lawson and Michael Slater both played for the Woodies. Slats opened with me and I said to him, "There's a bit of green on the pitch and the ball will move about and they have a very good quick left armer, Greg Palmer, who sometimes plays for us."

"Don't worry," said Slats. Disregarding the inside information, he started hitting out into the air and after scoring only 8, a Sri Lankan in his fifties proceeded to fall backwards at mid off and just as he landed on the ground, the ball fell miraculously into his right hand. It was a flukey but marvellous catch. "Haven't caught one like that ever," he said.

Some elderly spectators were sitting in front of the pavilion and as Slats came in, one said, "We know why Justin Langer was preferred to you in the Aussie Test side – you're useless!"

Slats fumed. "What do you mean?" he said. "I'll sort you out." He soon realised it was a joke and eventually, took it in the right spirit. Slats became a very popular commentator in Australia after retiring at the age of 30. He played 76 Tests with an average of 42 and maybe he was in too much of a hurry. He was a batsman who wanted to dominate, but he had the assets to become a Bobby Simpson.

Jim Maxwell, the ABC radio commentator played in that match for us and managed to go into double figures before he was caught at extra cover. He is a very popular man in Australia.

We played Wandgas a year later and when we drove into the ground we saw a huge bough of a tree which had fallen near to where cars were parked. It could have landed on one of ours. We decided not to renew the fixture for Health and Safety reasons.

10

Carried Off by Ian Bishop at Marlow Park

Trinidad has produced some very fine whirly bowlers like Sonny Ramadhin and Willie Rodriguez, but in 1995 Ian Bishop, a born-again Christian, was well on the way to become his country's first great fast bowler until he pulled up lame like a flat race champion. Up to then he'd taken 83 Test wickets, with an average of 20.46 which rivalled Malcolm Marshall's average of 20.94. He was 26 and in his prime and none of the West Indian fast bowlers were quicker than him at the time. Then a cracked vertebrae in the lower back put him out of action for a second time and he needed a year's rehabilitation, mainly spent swimming and praying.

His prayers were answered and he went on to play in 43 Tests (1988-97), taking 161 wickets at 24.7 apiece to make him the tenth most successful West Indian bowler. But another injury, to the Achilles tendon, the part of the body which does most damage to bowlers, forced him to retire in 1997. A very big, cuddly man of six feet five and a half inches and weighing almost 16 stone, he found his size a handicap and at the age of 30 he quit. He had the same build as Angus Fraser, who bowled at least ten mph slower than him. Later he became a TV cricket commentator who spoke sense in well modulated English. In 2004-05, he gained an MBA at the University of Leicester in between commentating jobs.

The Woodies caught up with him in the summer of 2004 and Gavin invited him to play for us against Marlow Park CC at one of the country's most beautiful and alluring areas, right on the Thames. It's a rowing centre which has produced Olympic champions, and Sir Steve Redgrave has a statue not far from the boundary. Not having any gear with him, we managed to find an outsize pair of white flannels, a vast shirt and a pair of size-11 cricket boots for him. Another cricketer with a well-known name, Vermeulen, was playing for us as well. Roger Vermeulen is a brother of Mark who played for Zimbabwe and was banned for life after setting fire to the Zimbabwean Cricket Academy in Harare. A month earlier, Mark lost his temper playing for Werneth in the Lancashire League and hurled a cricket ball into the crowd, narrowly missing a young girl, and he compounded it by going up to them and brandishing a boundary spike. He was banned from playing in the League for ten years. Two years earlier, he was hit by a bouncer and an Australian doctor had to put titanium above his eye and he reckoned the injury affected his brain. The wealthy son of a dentist, he made amends by paying for a new Academy building and was allowed to resume his cricket career in Harare.

Roger didn't have the same class of brainstorm, but he had a mild one in this friendly match. Coming in at first wicket down, he hit wildly at a straight delivery and was bowled for a duck. He was distinctly unhappy and told us so in strong language. Soon, the duck virus spread to two more of our batting stars. Gavin was caught after 15 minutes of scratching around for 0, and our ex-rugby player John Murrin was bowled by a man named Field – the same bowler – at the same miserable total. Being 34-4 on an excellent pitch in front of more than 500 spectators was embarrassing. Marlow always draw a crowd on a sunny day, with many of them walking around the cricket ground on to the towpath to watch the rowers and the river boats. The top club in posh Marlow is Marlow CC, just behind a narrow unmade up road next to Marlow Park CC, which is rather looked down on, but their multi-racial team does well in the League on Saturdays and enjoy a social romp on Sundays.

Our mad romp was initiated by the curse of Vermeulen, with everyone losing their heads. When our *Daily Mail* investigating journalist Tom Rawstorne charged down the pitch and was stumped for 38 with the score on 52, we were wondering why a West Indian Test cricketer who once scored a hundred against Yorkshire at Scarborough was coming in at nine.

"No, no," said Bish, "nine is fine for me. Eleven would be better!"

Shortly afterwards, our number 6 batsman Johnny Kydd, the actor, was run out for 12, and suddenly collapsed to the ground. He stayed down and was obviously in distress. Not having a St John's Ambulance team on hand, we called for someone of medical experience. No-one responded. But Bish said, "I'll go out there and see what's happened." To everyone's astonishment, he picked up him up and gave him a piggy-back ride to the pavilion at some speed, and deposited him into one of the leather armchairs in the pavilion. It was an extraordinary performance, especially as he'd had back trouble for some years. We ribbed him about it and he said, "I'm not really fit for all this."

When the seventh wicket fell at 73, I told him, "Get your head down and you'll get a 50!" Except for the players, no-one would have known that he was one of the world's best bowlers. He took guard and the bowler, named Hatch, was slowish in pace and his first delivery passed the bat and struck the off stump. Bish's "shot" was too tentative. The Marlow fielders, mostly middle aged, were ecstatic. As Bish came in his face had a sheepish look about it.

"Sorry about that," he said, "went down the wrong line." The Woodies were all out 88. Abysmal.

The innings was over so quickly that tea wasn't ready and Marlow went in to bat for an hour. Bish said he preferred to bowl from the river end and measured out a 20-yard run up. Our keeper wanted to know where he ought to stand. Our skipper said, "Well, he's 37 and he's not likely to bowl at 90 mph. Fifteen yards would be ample."

There were three slips, a gully, a short leg and only two fielders in front of the bat. Bish ran in briskly and his first delivery, slightly over pitched, was driven for two. His final ball in the over beat the number 2 opener Barlow, and knocked back the off stump. Our spirits rose: their target of 89 was in jeopardy, we hoped. Bish will shoot them out! In his next over, our spirits tumbled. Slater, the left handed opener whom we reckoned was not far off qualifying for a Freedom Pass, took a 4 and a 3 off his second over. Clearly rattled, Bish retaliated with a very fast bouncer which flew over the heads of both batsman and wicketkeeper for four byes. The stocky Slater showed no sign of being intimidated – so far. Nigel Phethean, our grandfather slow medium bowler, came on to have Ellis caught by Vermeulen for 9 on 2-21. Tea was taken at 45-2 and we were quaking. If Bish can't get this veteran out we will lose, we thought.

The pavilion is wooden, small and old, but with its large leather settees and chairs the main room looked like a men's club in Pall Mall, bearing a slightly stained appearance. An immense amount of food – sandwiches, sausage rolls, Scotch eggs, tomatoes, fruit, and several cakes both homemade and from supermarkets – were laid out on the covered snooker table. We urged him to hold back on the pasties and as we went back on to the ground Charlie Risso-Gill, one of our players who worked for the Channel 4 coverage of Test cricket with Gavin, said, "Get at 'em Bish!"

Refreshed, our new signing conceded just two more runs and began a run of five successive maidens. In the fourth maiden he tried to unsettle Mr Slater with another bouncer. The batsman tried to hook it, missed and the ball hit him on the top of the forehead, knocking him to the ground. Bish rushed up and said, "So sorry, are you all right?"

"I'm fine," said his victim.

"You should wear a helmet!" said Bish.

"Never wore one and it's too late to start now," said the batsman with a smile. Two overs later, he pulled a short ball from Bish which went to the direction of the square leg boundary for two and his team mates were on their feet yelling and cheering.

Bish bowled his ninth and final over, a maiden, and said he was exhausted and needed a rest. He hadn't blasted them out as we hoped, but he had presentable figures of 9-6-11-1. Two of our slower bowlers came on and went, and I brought on Vermeulen, working on the theory that he might have some venom to unleash on Mr Slater. Alas, there was none, and after being smacked for three boundaries, one of which nearly hit a spectator, he was sent back to the deep field. I tried seven bowlers and Tom Rawstorne, who tweaks an odd offspinner, settled the matter giving away 15 runs off his final over. After hitting the winning single off Risso-Gill, Slater 43* was rapturously cheered in by his colleagues, "I thought I'd never play against a great Test bowler and certainly not come out on top," said the proud batsman. We'd been smashed by eight wickets in 27.1 overs and it was only four minutes past six, almost an hour and half before the normal close of play. Jokingly, I suggested a ten-over exhibition match to fill the time, and Bish was the first to object. We ate the remainder of the tea and passed the congratulatory jugs of beer and lager round before setting off back to South London in the Sunday night traffic. A teetotaller, Bish had a soft drink.

As far as I know, he has never played again. He now sticks to his commentaries and is rated second behind the Caribbean's doyen Winston Anthony Lloyd Cozier, to give him his full name. Tony has been one of my best friends from 1963 when he first toured England with the West Indian side as a junior radio broadcaster and journalist, and his cricketing knowledge is unsurpassed. When that Test match was abandoned in Kingston on the first day because the pitch was too dangerous, he did the bulk of the commentating for some time after the game was cancelled, reeling off facts which even the statisticians had yet to find in their records. He has won nearly all the honours Barbados can bestow on their citizens, and he was rightly honoured by the MCC early in 2012. He is very honest in his opinions and is not afraid to criticise both administrators and players if it is justified. When the heat is turned on him, he sometimes jokes about being called – wrongly – "a black bastard". One of the 5 per cent of white people in Barbados, he comes from Scottish descent and when black men descended from former slaves tell him he isn't entitled to be there, he always says, "We got here 150 years before you lot!"

Tony was a fine opening batsman and wicketkeeper and played for the Woodies on 19 occasions, scoring 526 runs, average 29.2, with three half-centuries. He was one of my favourite opening batsmen because he was rather bulky and preferred hitting boundaries to running short singles. When we opened at Alleyn Old Boys in 1973, the scorer had him down as "Crozier". We put on 56 for the partnership and his contribution was 22 in only four overs. In 1976 we put on 127 for the first wicket against Slade Green, in Kent, with him scoring 73 and me 79 (I seem to remember mine took much longer).

In that year, Dave Sexton, the former Chelsea manager, played for us at Brighton University at Falmer. He was a fine all rounder and coming in at 7, he top-scored in our innings of 146, which was soon overturned by the students who only lost two wickets. Next year I promoted him to 3, and he scored 21 and later took 2-27 and we held on to a draw. He had a longstanding knee problem and didn't play again. He was outstanding coach and a thoroughly nice man. I attended his funeral in Kenilworth on 24 November 2012 and the packed congregation included Roy Hodgson, the England manager, and many other eminent managers. He lived a full life of 82 years, only marred by the onset of Alzheimer's on the last lap.

The next fixture, at Bethlem Hospital in Beckenham, which specialised in treating mental problems, we were watched by the biggest crowd we've ever encountered in the beautiful surroundings of masses of rhododendrons and various trees and plants. After the second wicket fell, hundreds of patients arrived and sat all around the boundary, jabbering away. They took hardly any notice of the cricket, but one man picked up the ball and refused to throw it back. We had to persuade him to give it back. After an hour, they all stood up and walked back to their various wards for tea. It was a case of the vanishing crowd, but 30 years later, I was checking the scorebook and discovered that the page containing the Hospital's innings had vanished as well. It must have been a souvenir hunter, or perhaps he wanted to read something.

Tony's son Craig, who makes his living from writing about cricket and being the Frindall of the West Indies in terms of stats, is also a good cricketer. He hits the ball further than his father, but is more laid back. On one occasion he was supposed to arrive early in the morning from Barbados and we wanted him to play at Headley, a top ground on Box Hill in Surrey. The ground is long and narrow and has a gentle slope down to the pavilion. Some of the boundaries, particularly next to a road, are no more than 50-60 yards bordering a wood, but the number of lost balls is surprisingly low. Usually there are more passing vehicles struck by flying balls than balls lost in the wood, and in 2010 the club had to erect high nets to minimise these incidents. They feared a rash of insurance claims with drivers claiming the effects of the dreaded whiplash.

By midday, Craig hadn't arrived in London and I joined the other players at Headley for a 1.30 start. We batted first – we usually do to get in batting time in brighter conditions – and wickets started falling. I rang Audrey back at Bromley and asked him if there was any news about Craig.

"He's in bed, fast asleep," she said. It was 3.30 and we were five wickets down.

"Goodness me," I said, "we're facing a catastrophe! Can you wake him up and get him over here?"

Audrey woke him up and he was somewhat aggrieved about being disturbed. It took 45 minutes for the journey and when he stepped out of our Honda Legend we were 85-7 with 45 minutes to go before the tea interval. The tea urn was about to go on and they serve a magnificent tea. I tossed him a pair of boots and a box and as the next wicket fell, I asked him to go out there and show the Bajan spirit.

Tall and lean, he took some time to shuffle out to the middle. He asked for "centre" and Jim Baker, our former wicketkeeper-batsman who holds the club's wicketkeeping record and was umpiring at the time, nodded and action commenced. The veteran bowler at the far end tossed up a legbreak, Craig swung his bat aiming to attempt a six over the road, and missed, and the ball hit him on the front pad.

"Howzat?" screamed the bowler, but not the keeper.

"Out!" said Jim.

One of our players was umpiring at the other end and he said, "This man has just flown nearly 4,000 miles to come here from Barbados and you've given him out lbw first ball!"

"Well," said Jim, "he's out, that's all I can say." Worse, Craig had to field after tea, bowled poorly and was distinctly unhappy on the ride home.

Willie Rodriguez, the former West Indian all rounder from Trinidad, had an equally galling appearance for the Woodies in 1972. I've known him since he toured England in 1963 and he is a good friend. He had cartilage trouble in his knee before the First Test, but was able to open the batting in the final Test at the Oval, helping to put on 78 with that wonderful man Conrad Hunte. Like most Trinnies, he has a great sense of humour and is revered in his country for his work with youngsters, and for being the last of the double internationals – cricket and football. But for injury he would have played more than his five Tests. He bowled fizzy legbreaks and googlies and often dismissed top batsmen in the midst of some loose deliveries.

His debut for the Woodies took place at Beddington Park near Croydon against the local club which boasted Peter Loader, David Halfyard, Arnold Long, Ernie Clifton and others, all professionals.

There is a sewage works nearby and Willie said, "What's that smell?"

"The wind is blowing the wrong way," I said, "it comes from the sewage farm." That wasn't a good start.

The batting order I gave to the scorer had to be altered in eight positions because Willie thought 3 was too high for him. "I haven't touched a bat for ages," he said, and moved himself down to 5. When he came in at 77-3 he was wearing a West Indian cap, which no-one noticed. He played some attractive shots before George Dolby, the Godfather of the Dolby cricketers from Beddington, had him caught and bowled for 14.

Coming in at 6 was Chris Lander, the *Daily Mirror* cricket writer and great walking friend of Ian Botham. His colleagues called him "Crash" – for obvious reasons – and this was another crash. He was out for a duck. We used up 57 overs to reach 153 on a very low, slow pitch. I needed Willie to get on early and he came on at first change in the tenth over. His first three deliveries, all legbreaks, turned a lot and beat the bat and we expected to see him run through the Beddington side. But his fourth and sixth deliveries were full tosses and both went to the boundary.

Suddenly, Willie started rubbing his groin. "It's gone!" he said. "I'll have to take my sweater." He stayed on to field at slip but it was a blow losing his bowling, variable or otherwise.

I brought on "Crash" to engineer a collapse, but his legbreaks were no more accurate than Willie's, and he couldn't find a googly to surprise their batsman either. "Crash" completed five overs and bowled their number 6 for an analysis of 1-26. We lost by four wickets.

The greatest West Indian all rounder of his time was Lord Learie Constantine, and though he never played for the Woodies, he agreed to become our President. I got him to play for the Cricket Writers' Club at Great Burstead in Essex when he was 67. He hadn't played for some years but I persuaded him to make a comeback. He came in at 4 and smashed six sixes in his brief innings of 62. "Just failed to beat my age," he laughed. He was much loved. In 1942 he broke the colour bar in Britain when he successfully sued a hotel in Russell Square after he was refused a room because of his colour. A qualified barrister, he conducted his own case. Learie's Presidency didn't last long: he died five years later and his beloved wife Norma died two months later, from a broken heart we reckoned because they were so devoted to each other. If he had been born in 1991 instead of 1901, he would now be a superstar in T20 cricket with his sensational hitting, dynamic bowling and dazzling fielding, earning more than KP's £1.2 million.

Khalid Ibadulla, the Pakistan all rounder and coach, played for the Woodies in the 1970s. He made his Woodies debut at Beddington in 1974 and helped me to put on 87 for the first wicket before being stumped for 60. He came on second change with his medium-paced cutters to take 4-18, and we avenged our earlier defeat by 47 runs. That day the wind was the right way and there was no stink. Universally known as Billy, he was a very dignified and genuine man. He scored 17,039 runs in his first-class career (1952-72), played in four Tests and featured in a number of records in his seven seasons with Warwickshire.

He later became a first-class umpire and moved to New Zealand where he became one of the country's finest coaches. He was 39 when he played for us and in his second appearance he bowled 15 overs for figures of 2-50 on a very hot day at the Courage and Barclay Sports ground in Hayes, Kent. The home side had some mean seasoned players and batted for 57 overs for their 226. They were very talkative as well, and Billy wasn't too keen on them. We had three Dutchmen in our side and that might have upset them. I must have bored them stiff because I batted for two hours for my 44, and we were bowled out for 105. The fixture was not renewed, understandably.

Two years earlier another of our Test stars, the Pakistan opener Alimuddin, the youngest cricketer to play for the Ranji Trophy at the age of 12 and 73 days, played for us on the same ground and only scored 5 and took 2-39 in a five-wicket defeat. In the Pakistan tour of England in 1962, when I first met him, he opened with Hanif Mohammad. He was a stocky, powerful man with a broad smile. He was proud to tell us that he faced the first ball delivered to a Pakistan batsman on their first-ever Test at Lord's in 1954. He played in two other matches with us at the age of 42, taking 3-58 in 15 overs and scoring 14 at Ripley, and scoring 22 and taking 3-64 in 15 overs at Hertford Brewery. He only took one wicket in his 25 Tests, but managed to rustle up eight wickets playing for the greens (the Woodies cap is dark green, similar to the Pakistan cap). He stayed on to live in London working for PIA at Heathrow and was last seen at Lord's watching a Test. He boasted he hadn't missed a Lord's Test match for decades. A bachelor, he died on 13 July 2012 aged 81.

11

Fun and Games at Frant

Frant is a very small hamlet 5 miles south of Tunbridge Wells in East Sussex: it has just 1,367 inhabitants, and the number is falling every year. You could drive down the A267 southwards and you wouldn't notice it. There is a pub, a church and a church school ... and a very unusual cricket ground built on the side of a hill. The fall from the top, where the tiny pavilion is situated, to the road below is almost 40 feet, four times the slope of the Lord's cricket ground. It is ideal for cricketers with one leg shorter than the other. Once the batsman strikes the ball down the hill, particularly at times of drought, no fielder can catch it up. More likely they might tumble to the ground, cursing their luck. In the seventeenth and eighteenth centuries, smuggling was the major industry, next to the iron industry, before iron dried up. Hill climbing, rather than the noble sport of cricket, is more appropriate in the present times.

There is photographic evidence, verified by experts at Reading University, that cricket has been played at Frant since 1860. After the twelfth century the name Frant appears in records as Fernet, Fenth, Ferthe, Vernthe, Fanthe, Fraunt, Feruthe and Fant, and the name derives from the Anglo-Saxon meaning "place of fern, or bracken". The man who brought cricket to the village must have been bonkers: how do you play a proper game on the side of a pronounced hill? Some of our players love playing on quaint grounds and are not deterred by having to make a two-hour journey from Wandsworth, Clapham and Battersea on a Sunday to these outposts. But there were others, especially unmarried ones, who were less keen, and Frant was one venue where we would arrive 15 minutes before the start without a quorum of players. Sometimes we had to borrow young sons of the home players to make the numbers up. Some years ago we had four fit players, two boys under 12 and two mothers.

Tom Ryder, the then captain of Frant, said, "Are you sure you've got enough players?"

"Don't worry," I said, "they'll all turn up eventually."

As I was about to come up with an excuse, an open top MG sped round the corner and went down the hill towards the main road. A woman in her late twenties was driving and she slammed on the brakes, got out and walked purposefully towards the rear of the vehicle, shouting abuse at a man still sitting in the passenger seat. It was difficult to hear and against the noise of the traffic on the A267, but the woman's feelings were clearly shown when she opened the boot and started hurling out the man's gear on to the side of the road. The man stayed where he was and a few four letter words were exchanged. A pair of white flannels flew through the air and Tom said, "Is that one of your players?"

I had to say, "Well, he doesn't look like a Woodpecker, but he's certainly qualified as a Henpecked One. You never know. We sign up players anywhere, in pubs, bus queues, in toilets, anywhere."

Once we were short of four players for a match at St Lawrence CC, the club in Canterbury, and I noticed an oldish guy was standing at a traffic light in Greenwich. The lights went red and I opened the window and said, "Do you fancy a game of cricket in Canterbury this afternoon?"

He said, "I've got nothing on and as it's a nice day, yes, put me down."

We had a convivial chat on the way and I forgot to ask about his cricketing prowess. On arrival at the ground, I fixed him up with a white shirt, flannels, a pair of socks and size-9 boots and a cap. Everything fitted perfectly. We were in the field – by now we were nine in strength – and I said, "What about fielding at mid on?" He seemed perplexed. "Over there," I pointed.

"Oh," he said.

Three balls later the opening batsman drove the ball straight at him, not very fast, and he let it go through his legs. It cost us two runs and the bowler was furious. I said to the man, "When did you last play cricket?"

"'I can tell you," he said, "52 years ago when I was at school." Well, I thought he was in his sixties. You get these things wrong sometimes.

Back at the slanging match at Frant, the angry woman in the MG, arms gesticulating, came round to the other side of the vehicle, ordered the man to get out and opened the driver's door and got in and drove off. The man bent to pick up his clothing and shoes and walked round the corner. I said to Tom, "I don't think it was to do with cricket. Must have been a domestic upset and he's certainly not one of ours."

In another game at Frant, Gavin was scoring a lot of runs in a very short space of time, and he and his partner had to keep shouting out "Watch out!" or the more favoured exhortation, "Fore!" because the boundary near the school was less than 50 yards from the playing pitch.

A chest-high full-toss came towards him and he swivelled round and pulled the ball at a low trajectory into the path of a small, red car, which was going down the road close to the children's playground. The ball never rose higher than ten feet, and on its present course, it would hit the car. Sitting in the back seat were two young children. Gavin screamed, "Look out!" The woman driver didn't hear his warning and we were holding our breath: someone might be killed. It was a fearful moment as the ball crashed into the rear of the vehicle through an opened rear window. Realising what had happened, the woman braked and the car came to an abrupt halt. Gavin and one of the Frant fielders were the first on the scene.

"Are they all right?" he asked the woman. She stepped out of the car and looked unflustered.

"Don't worry," she said. "It missed them and neither was hurt." We expected her to complain about flying missiles and risk of accidents. A normal mother might well have called up a lawyer within seconds on her mobile phone. "Don't fret," she said, "I am married to a cricketer. I know these things can happen." After a brief, friendly chat, she got back into the car and drove off.

This is a date to remember at Frant – 14 September 2008, the anniversary of when the Gregorian calendar was adopted in Britain in 1752. We needed Gregory and some of his mates to play because we were three short when Tom and POB walked out to the grassy, sloping pitch to toss up. POB lost on the call and as a gentleman, Tom said, "As you're a bit short, you can bat." We learned that the peculiar pitch hadn't seen a roller for five weeks until the day before, when one of their members rolled it for three hours. All that did was to bring up more moisture, ideal for their seam and swing bowlers. Back at the pavilion, POB was begging our frightened players to don the pads, but none of them showed any interest. One said, "Got a bit of a niggle. Number six should suit me in these conditions."

POB asked me to open. "If no-one wants to I'll do it," I said. "But I need a runner. My hip has flared up again. Can't walk, let alone run."

POB went outside to see Tom, who was sitting outside about to open the scorebook to record the names of his bowlers and said, "Brian has a problem with his hip again. I know it happened in 1943 but it still haunts him. Is it all right for him to have a runner?" Tom was perfectly agreeable.

By this time I was padded up and had strapped on a chest protector, which was bulging out my sweater. It was a pre-Patsy Hendren version: nothing like today's thin, stylish variety.

"We've forgotten the team helmet," I said.

"You won't need that," said POB with a grin.

I said to him, "I'll try to block the other end and give the lads a chance to hit up a few runs." The bowler from the top end played for Tonbridge School and he was fast and bowled short of a length. The odd delivery stopped and reared towards the head, but most of them shot along the ground. The other bowler, 14-year-old Tom Pearson, was the better bowler, swinging the ball towards the packed slips and after five overs he had to be taken off – the ECB rule forbade lads of that age to exceed five overs at the time – with impressive figures of 3-6.

We were told that he was being schooled by a top coach at nearby Bells Yew Green CC, part of the parish of Frant, which has 400 boys in their colts section with their mums all paying subscriptions to the club, and as a result the club is booming. Bob "The Cat" Wilson, the famed sports comedian, raised £20,000 to start it off when he arranged a big, full-house dinner at Tunbridge Wells, and the chief speaker was Ian Botham. In his mid- to late-sixties, "The Cat" often skippers the Sunday side and still takes wickets – but not catches – with his slow lobs. The next generation of English professional cricketers comes from these nurseries of the small clubs and most of them are sons of cricketers. It's self-perpetuating and very reassuring.

Mark Prendiville, from the loneliest part of the Southern Hemisphere, Perth, was our chief hope to make a score before he migrated to calmer financial houses in the Far East, namely Singapore. He'd just recovered from nose surgery and risked more damage to his face when he stepped back to pull a short delivery. He miscued the ball and it went very high into the air before falling out of the hands of the fielder at mid on. Suddenly, and surprisingly, Prendi was walking back to the pavilion.

"He stepped on to his wicket," explained Tom Ryder, who kept wicket and insisted on standing up.

I managed to nick a full toss towards the fine leg boundary for two, doubling my previous score after nearly an hour at the crease. My first runner soon had to make way for the first batsman to be dismissed, and none of my six runners stayed too long. They were bored stiff watching forward defensive shots ad lib, or the elegant raising of the bat to let the ball through to the waiting gloves of the keeper. Several shooters managed to be blocked, and there were several polite mutterings of "well played" from the fielders. Seven wickets fell in quick succession and our total only just passed the number of overs – 48 runs from 39 overs. It was stoical, absorbing stuff. Once a beamer struck me in my bulbous chest protector and I waved away the close fielders.

"I know Brian Close," I said, "he always did that. Never show pain."

POB shouted from the pavilion, "Time to get a move on." I intimated to him that reckless batting wouldn't help the side. Someone had to stay there.

Trying to play an extra cover drive, I failed to connect with the centre of the blade and there was a loud appeal from Tom for a catch behind. I stayed where I was and looked the umpire – Cam Pearce, our mad Australian quick bowler – in the eye and Cam said, "Look, I don't know mate." At least he was being honest. The young bowler, an excellent slow left-arm bowler, appealed again, and this time Cam raised his finger. I showed no sign of leaving the wicket. My runner was in a quandary.

"You've been given out," he said.

Tom said to me, "Did you hit it?"

"Tom," I said, "I can honestly tell you that I didn't. The sound you heard was the bat hitting my 35-year-old left boot."

"In that case, I'll withdraw the appeal," said Tom.

I long for the day when a Test wicketkeeper does that at Lord's and the announcer says, "Bloggs (or whoever) has agreed to withdraw his appeal!" You can imagine the 28,066 capacity crowd on their feet cheering.

I got my head down again, but my chance of hitting a single boundary was thwarted when numbers 10 and 11 were speedily removed. All out 65 in 46 inglorious overs. What do you do when you come in after two and a half hours and you haven't played a single shot? Do you apologise? The Frant fielders broke into muted applause as I limped up the hill towards the crowded pavilion. Not every cricketer bats through the innings. As I came in – half of the Woodies were hiding out the rear – I said to the scorer, "Did I manage to squeeze into double figures?"

"Sorry mate," he said. "You got 7, no fours, no sixes, one two and five singles."

It brought back memories when I was 15 and was put in at 11 for the Ventnor second Xl at Parkhurst Prison's hugely sloping ground, not too dissimilar to Frant's when "Brisher" White, the captain, took one look at the fearsome pitch and the long grass and said, "I've changed my mind. Can you open the batting? We need someone to stay there."

My previous five innings brought five ducks and they all took up a lot of deliveries. "Brisher" thought I had the makings of a young Boycott, executing beautiful forward defensive shots. I agreed eagerly to his unusual request: only Wilfred Rhodes, I think, later became an England opener after he started his career as a number 11. Like the innings at Frant, Ventnor's odd assorted batsmen came and left in quick succession, but I remained defiant. After an hour I was on 2 not out, completely strokeless. Nine wickets went down for 62 runs after two hours, and I decided to open up. A full toss appeared and I edged it down the hill to third man, and with the gully fielder overweight and unable to run very fast, I managed to run 3 valuable runs. I had a stiff right leg after a bombing raid by two Focke-Wulf 190 fighter aircraft at the end of the Second World War, and in those days I was able to sprint just as fast, or quicker, than anyone in the side.

Next ball our number 11 was bowled and I came in with 5 runs against my name and the total, 65, was perfectly defensible in these hazardous conditions. At tea, the home side secretary – not a lifer, but a prison warden – arranged a raffle for the club funds and I won the box of chocolates, and the man who handed it over, the Assistant Governor, said with a laugh, "You ought to be locked up, you little scoundrel!" We had the last laugh because we won by ten runs and I took 3-10 with my tricky Chinamen.

At Frant their innings had collapsed to 38-7 with our Aussie pace bowlers, Prendi and his chippy sandgroper mate Cam Pearce, producing a host of different deliveries from shooters to potential killer balls, which rose off a length. For no particular reason, Cam started sledging their number seven Dave Pearson, who now runs the club, and Dave, clearly ruffled, hit back by heaving a gigantic six over the A267, almost shattering the slates of a roof of a very expensive property. Dave took 12 more runs off the over and the match was virtually over. Two overs later we lost by three wickets and came off to be greeted by joyous applause. Cam was suitably upbraided for his stupidity. If he had kept quiet, we would have won a famous victory.

Afterwards we repaired to The George Inn in the elegant High Street, no more than 200 metres in length, for the inevitable inquest. Chris Tooley thought my latest effort might well be a world record – the first batsman to bat through the innings with a runner from the first ball, and use six runners.

The next morning I checked with Bill Frindall, the great, late scorer, and he said, "It might be a record for someone scoring under 10, but Graeme Fowler did it twice in the same county game at Southport in 1982. He strained a thigh muscle and David Lloyd ran for him in the first innings and he finished with 100 not out. In the second innings, Ian Folley was his runner and Foxy (Fowler) scored 128 not out, and it must have been a different type to the Frant one! I can understand your colleagues being reluctant to act as your runner. Rigor mortis might have set in!"

Opposing captains can object to a runner – and Andrew Strauss did that once when Graeme Smith complained of cramp – if the batsman wasn't hurt during play or taken ill, but a court case in 1993 changed the thinking when Ian Harris, a batsman playing for Veryan CC in Cornwall, had his leg amputated after a farming accident, and when he was fitted up with an artificial leg, he resumed playing cricket for his club. The opposing side objected and the League decided to ban him. The Court found in favour of Mr Harris and the case was referred to MCC, and John Stephenson, the then secretary, ruled that a permanently disabled batsman is entitled to have a runner, otherwise no disabled cricketer would be able to play the game. I agreed with that, naturally. So let these runners run.

Around this time the ICC were about to outlaw the use of runners. They thought too many batsmen were feigning injury and cheating. There was a famous occasion when Gary Sobers needed a runner in the 1969 Test at Lord's and Ray Illingworth, who had a very high respect for Sobers, agreed to let him have one. The opener Steve Camacho, not the fastest of runners, donned his pads for a third "innings" in the match to help Sobers to score an unbeaten 50, watched by Her Majesty the Queen and Prince Philip, who were also fans of Gary through their shared interest in horse racing. Always a gambler on and off the field, Sobey set a perfectly reasonable target of 332 runs in as many minutes. To everyone's astonishment, he opened the bowling and bowled unchanged for 16 overs, mainly with his spin. With Geoff Boycott taking two and a half hours to reach 50, England fell behind the rate and Illingworth called off the chase. England ended the match on 295-7.

Forty-two years later I rang Illy at his home in Farsley and he said, "At that time you had to allow a runner if a batsman is injured. I wouldn't have stopped Gary and you could see he was limping. I'm not sure it's a good idea to ban runners when a player is genuinely injured. A better way to do it is to get the batsman to resume his innings in the last three positions of the order, 9, 20 and 11. They should stop more important things, like the 12th man and others coming on every few minutes. It slows down the over rate and people don't want to pay a fortune to see these antics. In social cricket, I'm all for having runners if the batsman is hurt. It's down to honesty, but I am afraid some of them today tried to take advantage of it." Nowadays having a runner in first-class cricket has been outlawed.

According to Steve Pittard in *The Wisden Cricketer*, runners were introduced in 1805 when special dispensation was granted to the poet and writer Lord Byron, who had a club foot, to have a runner in the Eton *v.* Harrow game. His Lordship didn't detain his opponents, scoring only 7 and 2 in his two appearances at the crease.

By 2009 the Frant fixture was under threat. POB thought it was too far for some of our City bankers. Dr Harvey Pynn, our Army doctor who has served in Iraq and Afghanistan, had to withdraw because a second child was imminent and two other banking Aussies, Ross "Swampy" Marsh and Greg Palmer, dropped out. Our ageing force had to use a Dad's Army pair to open – Chris "Godfrey" Rossi and Brian "Jones" Scovell, both in their seventies. A more appropriate name should have been the Grand Dad's Army. I first met Chris in 1958 when I worked for the *Norwich Evening News* and the *Eastern Daily Press*. I was there for only three months and most of the summer the newspapers were on strike, so I played three or four matches a week. Chris – younger than me but looking older – opened with me at the Barleycorns, a side packed with members of the Norfolk Minor Counties side. Why we were given the honour to start the innings was never explained. Possibly the skipper thought we were expendable, as indeed, we were at Frant.

Fifty years later Chris and I met up again and here we were marching down the hill to take up the challenge. Neither of us wore a helmet, but we did have our chest protectors on. Another member of the Pearson family – 13-year-old John Pearson, son of Dave, now promoted to Frant captain in place of Tom Ryder – opened the bowling, and he swung the ball prodigiously. Not fast, but not easy to handle on a wet pitch, he whacked Chris on the gloves and in the chest before he dismissed him for a plucky 0, which occupied half an hour of rearguard fighting. For some reason I changed tactics, playing a number of square cuts off the front foot and two went over the boundary. When 17-year-old Tom Gibson from Bethany School tried to bounce me I succeeded in doing a Dilshan, flicking the ball over the keeper for 4. My entertaining cameo ended when Tom bowled me for a fast off cutter, for 14. Well, it was twice as much as my laborious 7 of the previous year, and much faster. Tris Sheehan, also in the banking business, arrived late and was striking the ball well until he missed a lollypop from a slow bowler who failed to turn the ball. With a top score of 30, all from extras, we managed a creditable 144-9.

One of the reasons why some of us loved playing at Frant was their teas. This time four wives laid on a tea which included ten different types of homemade cakes – surely a club cricket record – and there was more cake than sandwiches, which I have to say, were top class as well, far better than The Ritz tea, the costliest in London, now £80.

Larry Robeson, our swing bowler, scored 25, three short of his career best, and POB entrusted him with the top end. It proved to be a mistake. Larry failed to hit his usual probing length and kept moaning about the state of the ball, a sure sign he was in trouble. Seventeen-year-old Tom Pearson, son of Dave and brother of John, wasn't fit to bowl at his customary pace, and took up batting instead. He started like an Adam Gilchrist, bashing the bowling of Larry and POB all over the hill. POB bowled him for 32 and there were major setbacks when Tom Ryder was dropped twice by the venerable Nigel Phethean at mid off. Fourteen-year-old Olly Gower, grandson of Nigel, bowled Mr Ryder for 50, but Dave Pearson soon took up the run chase with gusto.

We noticed that there was a blood stain on his bat and asked about it, he said, "Two months ago someone bowled a beamer and I tried to hit it and deflected it on to my nose, like Mike Gatting when he was struck by a bouncer from Malcolm Marshall. Sometime later, an interviewer asked him 'where did it hit you?' and Gatt pointed at it. I held my nose and it seemed all right but when I took my hand away, it was like a river of blood everywhere." It's not a bad idea to have blood stains on your bat: it shows you have been in a battle and still keep playing on regardless.

No drinks were served on the field, but with three overs left and with Frant in a good position to win, the ice cream man turned up with his van. A dozen or so young children, including some who played for the home side, sped off to make their purchases, and POB told our youngsters to remain at their posts. Three boys were loaned to us and ten-year-old Sam Jones from Hook Green, who was four feet six inches tall, was asked to bowl as a last, desperate fling.

Asked about his style of bowling, he said, "I am a spin bowler who turns the ball both ways." His first delivery, a legbreak, landed on a length and his second, a big turning off break, beat the batsman. Startled by such precocity, two of their batsmen hit catches to AOB at deep mid wicket, and in his two overs, Sam had 2-8. The match ended on 146-7 when his father, who was batting, tried unsuccessfully to put him over the A267. A three-wicket defeat was perfectly acceptable. Perhaps POB should have brought Sam on much earlier.

This is the best of village cricket – with young lads growing into good cricketers to take over from the current teams – and it will survive. It must do. We had a convivial time at The George, and in these close-knit communities word spread, and my old mate from the Fleet Street days, Nigel Clarke, the tennis and football writer of the *Daily Mirror*, *Daily Mail* and *Daily Express*, turned up. He used to live in Chislehurst, near the caves, and moved to the High Street of Frant.

"Much prefer living here," he said. Nigel was famous for saying at a press conference in the start of the 1990 World Cup, "I'm here to fry Bobby Robson."

With Brian Woolnough of the *Sun*, these two were ordered by their sports editors to make life difficult for the England manager and they did. But Robson came close to winning the Cup, but for two missed penalties in the semi-final shoot out in the San Siro, and next day they went up to him and apologised.

"Robson was such a great bloke that he accepted our apology," he said. "On our next football trip, he invited us out to a hotel in Eindhoven and he picked up the bill. It showed what a great man he was." It was 8.47 with dusk falling when our last three players, and skipper Pearson and his sons, plus mini Sam Jones and his dad, left for home.

During our annual dinner a consensus of members agreed to cancel our visit to Frant, and as fixture secretary, I had to ring Tom Ryder with the sad news.

"Never mind," he said. "I know some of them think it is a long way but it's worth making the trip. We've always enjoyed our games with you."

12

Our Chance to be Presented to the Queen

A telephone call from Stephan Lazarczuk, fixture secretary of the Windsor Great Park Cricket Club on 21 April 2011 left my heart fluttering. The previous year we played the servants of Her Majesty the Queen and were downed, vociferously, by nine wickets. Some of Stephan's young players were very boisterous, even louder than ours, but we must have made a reasonably good impression because he wanted the fixture to continue. He said to me on the phone, "We have some good news. I told you last year that the club was formed in 1861 and this year it is the 150th anniversary. We asked if the Queen could come to one of our matches and we are now told that she would be available on 26 June. She often visits the church in the Great Park and will come along when the service ends. Both teams will be presented to her and the wives, partners and children can come along as well."

I fell short of making a whoop but wow, what a prospect! The wives and partners would be rushing to the King's Road to buy new outfits. Our players would have to shave and learn how to shake hands with the Maj – and don't speak until spoken to. The Duke might make a witty, provocative comment about slit eyes. We have no players of Chinese extraction, although we did have one some years ago.

Stephan suggested that we might have to improve our team and bring in a couple of big names. I said, "We've had plenty of Test players playing for us and I am sure we can call on one or two." Not too many professional cricketers have the chance to meet the Queen, only a few occasions when she is presented to the two teams in Tests at Lord's. They would be queuing up to see her. She meets plenty of jockeys but not so many cricketers.

Our inaugural fixture against Windsor Great Park last year fell on the day England needed a victory against Germany to stay in the FIFA

World Cup, and Stephan wanted a 12.30 a.m. start to ensure the players could watch the 3 p.m. kick off. We agreed but by this time there was a bad smell about England's campaign in South Africa and some of us were unenthusiastic about watching sub-standard football in a sweltering, noisy bar. Steven Gerrard and Wayne Rooney were under attack from the tabloid newspapers about sex scandals, and the England players appeared to have lost confidence in Fabio Capello, the Italian manager who still hadn't mastered learning English. Some time ago I went up the lift at the FA offices in Soho Square with Fabio and asked him whether Sepp Blatter wanted to have a fourth term as FIFA President, more than any US President. He smiled broadly, but he didn't obviously know what I was talking about. Communication in football is essential, and it made me wonder how the FA appointed him.

Windsor Park's employees use the large building known as the York Club as well as a cricket pavilion, and there were two large screens in the bar. After playing cricket there for 150 years, they have yet to name the pavilion in honour of a cricketing personage – unlike Dominica in the West Indies. Their government named their Windsor Park ground after Billy Doctrove, the West Indian umpire, after officiating in just 29 Tests. Billy was the umpire who kept mum when Daryll Hair was drummed out of Test cricket after the ball tampering affair in the England *v.* Pakistan Test match in 2008. Astutely, he kept out of the row and stayed on as an Elite List umpire.

The residents of Windsor call England's 5,000-acre park "the Great Park", famous for its large population of deer, which is owned and managed by the Crown Estate. The Duke of York has a residence in the Royal Lodge, which is not accessible to the public for obvious reasons. In the 1930s the Crown Estate built The Village to house the Royal estate workers, and it has a shop. You could see the chimney pots sticking up above the trees on the western side of the cricket ground. At the latest count the WGP cricket club has 74 members and seven of their players were all from the same family, the Lazarczuks, who originated from the Ukraine. At the end of the Second World War, the Four Powers, England, France, USA and Russia, agreed to repatriate the displaced people from various European and USSR countries, and the Lazarzuks found themselves in London. One of today's grandparents applied for a job at Windsor Castle, and was accepted, and the rest followed. Their children and grandchildren are still there.

When some of our WAGS arrived, one of them said cheekily, "They've brought a tasty lot of birds here." He wasn't meaning Her Majesty's swans who appeared later in the day, but our revered ladies. That was the only light relief in a very harassing and hot day. Some of our best batsmen were still on the road, and their captain sportingly agreed that we could bat first on the hottest day of the year (30 °C). POB, our harassed skipper, was forced to put four men in the top five who normally contest the low order positions, which put extra pressure on Gavin Scovell who opened.

Stephan Lazarczuk described his club as "medium strength" in the Club Cricket Conference book, which lulled us into believing that we had a good enough XI for the day. Two of their side played in the Windsor 1st XI on Saturdays, and one scored 201 in the previous week, and another took 7 wickets. We were rather mugged!

Wickets were cascading and at 23-3 on one of the best pitches we have played on for some years, we were facing a hiding, but Gavin reeled off nine successive boundaries on a lightning fast outfield. When John Peters, our character actor now hobbling after damaging rugby injuries, was dismissed for 7 at 64-4, we feared that the contest would be over in time to see the kick off from Cape Town. Just in time, our missing stars Toby and Tris eventually hove into sight, 40 minutes late, and warned that they needed to play themselves in. Both did, and Toby (45) helped Gavin to put on 90 for the fifth wicket. Toby played the shot of the innings, an extra cover drive, and he stood still for a second or two to see the ball sizzle to the boundary with his bat high and horizontal: reminiscent of Colin Cowdrey at his best, with more oomph. It was a dogged, courageous stand by both men, because we felt their four quickies overdid the bouncers against helmetless batsmen.

George Gould, aged 17, had to be warned by our umpire for snatching his cap at the end of one stormy over. George, son of England's Test umpire Ian Gould and a good friend of Gavin, was twice no balled and each time complained.

Trying to be friendly, I said to him, "I know your dad."

He replied, "Yes, every xxxxing geezer knows him too." Charles Dickens would have termed him "a disagreeable young man". But he is a fine bowler, several times beating Gavin with late inswingers.

One of Gavin's most spectacular straight drives ended in a pond and the ball wasn't recovered. The home skipper produced a ball which looked as though it had been doctored for a previous match – rough on one side, and on the other, smoother and slightly damp, helped by the application of moisture. Noticing that a large bottle of Evian was lodged behind the talkative keeper at both ends – prohibited by the laws – and seeing the skipper wet the ball, I faced the dilemma: should I warn him? Perhaps thinking that we might lose a good fixture, I kept quiet. The Anglo-Lazarczuk XI was certainly playing it hard. When one of Toby's towering sixes fell out of a fielder's hands on the long on boundary, I saw the fielder on long off, almost level, signalling a six. As I started to raise my arms, the captain said, "That's four." I signalled a diplomatic four.

The over rate was so slow it would have been impossible to complete the 40 overs in two and a half hours, and the captain and POB agreed on 35 overs. Two overs later, the captain announced it would now be 30 overs. Gavin had to change tack abruptly, but it was too late. He'd ricked his back in the third over, and when he was caught behind for 72, Tris ended a promising knock of 15 by being run out in a needless mix-up with POB.

"Never a run," said POB, trying to justify himself.

Predictably, the tail flopped and we were all out for 178 in 29.3 overs. Good scoring rate but an appalling rate of wicket falling. Russell Cox, the skipper, bowled cleverly, using arm balls, rolled offspinners, and the most dangerous of all, the straight one. With a helpful ball in his hands, he finished with 4-17.

A wide ranging dinner-cum tea was served by a foreign lady on paper plates in the bar as we settled down to see the misery on the screens, and after the third German goal went in, the players of both sides got up and went out to resume our match. A result of England 1, Germany 4 was one of England's biggest defeats in the World Cup. Gavin wasn't able to bowl and he had signed up two young Indians, both quick and keen in the field, but their bowling wasn't too accurate. Ben Pugh bowled a corker which almost took the opener. He was also dropped later, and with luck running with him, the batsman finished up on 80 not out. John Peters, with his high lobbers, made them think, and with more fieldsmen on the boundaries, he might have had more than his one wicket – a stumping by Tris. Our hero in the field was Hugh Miller – hurling himself into the concrete-like surface to bring off some incredible retrievals on the boundary – "Good practice for playing rugby in the Southern Hemisphere," he said.

The man who was stumped, Mick Lazarczuk (59), helped Ben Morris to put on 131 for the first wicket. Earlier our umpire sent out a message to tell young Gould not to sit in front of the scoreboard, as he was doing. One of the older players went over to him, put an arm round him and suggested he should move. Eventually he did. When he came in to bat, he and Ben kept up a constant line of patter. He chugged along to 25* until Morris, still jabbering away, told him to block it out until the thirtieth and final over, seemingly for a laugh. Only two runs needed to win and I stopped that nonsense by calling two wides, and it was all over in 28.3 overs. Beaten but not disgraced by nine wickets.

After the BBQ that followed, Stephan explained how his family got to work for the Queen. "In the War we had to fight for the Russians, otherwise we would be shot, and when it ended, we were called Displaced People," he said. "The Allies needed to clear up afterwards and my father, who was a carpenter like me, came to England. He saw an advert for a job at the Great Park and we've been there ever since."

I suggested he should ask the Duke, who was soon to be 90, to come along to cut a ribbon with the Queen. Or even bowl an over. "Well," said Stephan, "I know he once took a hat trick. He was an offspinner."

I refrained from asking, "Did the Duke 'doctor' the ball as well?"

Early in January I contacted Stephan about renewing the fixture – we were intent on putting out a stronger side and gaining revenge – and he agreed. Checking on my diary, I discovered these words on 21 April, the birthday of Queen Elizabeth II, "Stephan rang to say the Queen has agreed to attend the game against the Woodpeckers." In the following week Prince William married Kate Middleton, and on the 26th, three days before the wedding in Westminster Abbey, I walked past Buckingham Palace, struggling to thread my way through thousands of people, mainly visitors from abroad, on my way to see my implant dentist Leslie Howe at Wimpole Street. On the way back, I stopped for some refreshment at the newly built Duke of York Plaza off Sloane Square. All good omens.

The next day Stephan rang and said, "I have some bad news. The captain and the vice captain and one or two of the other members of the committee decided to cancel your game and give the fixture to the Australian Crusaders. They already have a fixture against us on 10 July but the man who organises it, Swan Richards, cancelled his game at Chester at the start of their tour and said he was now available to play on your date, the 26th." I have never been gazumped while being about to buy a house, but I felt the same as someone who had – awful, let down and a victim of a dirty trick. Stephan said he was so upset that he decided to resign as fixture secretary.

I met Swan Richards a few times when I organised several fixtures for the Cricket Writers' Club against his Crusaders, and the last two were in 1997 and 2001 at Longparish CC. He brings a party of young promising players and a preponderance of veterans on his tours. Now in his late-seventies, he calls himself "a scrubber at the game" after scoring eight ducks in a row playing for the Prospect 6th XI in Adelaide. His full name is Robert Milton Richards, and he explains the name "Swan" by saying, "They said no-one had made so many ducks so gracefully, so they called me Swan." He now promotes Newbury bats and probably has more signed bats as memorabilia than any Australian. He started the Crusaders in 1977 with David Richards, the former ICC chief executive, and Ray Steele, the former President of the Australian Cricket Board – both of whom I knew well, very decent men – and the first meeting took place at the Windsor Hotel in Melbourne. His Wikipedia says, "They have been represented by more than 2,500 players, in more than 1,500 games, toured England and Europe 11 times and, through Swan's incredible capacity to get things done, forged enduring relationships that extend all the way to the Prime Minister's office." As we learned to our cost, he really is good at getting thing done.

In 1997 the English Cricket Writers' team played the Australian Crusaders again at Longparish, a small, attractive village, where John Woodcock, the former editor of *The Wisden Almanack* and cricket writer of *The Times* lives in a seventeenth-century thatched house named "The Old Curacy", where his father grew up. The ground is only a few hundred yards from John's house. Our side featured Gavin, who was their star, Geoffrey Deane, the erratic fast bowler who works for *The Times*, Chris Martin-Jenkins, John Etheridge of the *Sun*, Brian Murgatroyd, the former ICC press officer famous for running headlong straight into a sightscreen at a Press match in Guyana, and Vic Marks of *The Observer*, who top-scored with 129 in our total of 253-8. Derek Pringle of the *Daily Telegraph* bowled accurately despite his girth. For some reason, the Crusaders had an extra six overs and they won by seven wickets, but we parted amicably. They had one or two younger and better players and deserved to win.

In 2011 I met a 30-year-old Australian cricketer from Melbourne who played against the Woodpeckers on another occasion, and he knew Swan Richards well after going on some of his tours. "He's a bit like a bull in a china shop," he said, "and he charges around and gets what he wants. They're very well organised tours and he has played a big part in the development of young talented Australian cricketers. I went on a tour of England once with him and we played at the Royal Household ground in Windsor and the players of both sides were presented to the Queen." It's a great shame that the Woodpeckers could not have been given their chance when the Crusaders had already had the privilege.

Stephan told me the Crusaders have played four matches at the Great Park in the previous eight years, and in the past they also played against the Royal Household CC a few miles away before the series was ended after a row.

Next morning, Dean, the vice captain, rang me to say the decision to ditch the Woodpeckers won't be changed.

"We'll see about that," I said. "You are not dealing with an ordinary fixture secretary. I ran the Woodpeckers for 43 years, I am now Life President and have been fixture secretary for many years, and I have links with the Royal Family. As chairman of the Cricket Writers' Club, I asked the Princess of Wales to present the Young Cricketer of the Year trophy to David Lawrence in 1985, I met Prince Charles in Pisa in the same year, and in recent years I have written the Handbook of the Forty Club, which has 2,500 members who play against schools and who pass on the message to the next generation about sportsmanship and fair play. Prince Philip is the

Patron and I expect to see him at the club's 75th anniversary dinner later in the year, and I will tell him about this shabby business. He once wrote 'cricket is a wonderful game but it can only be enjoyed when it is played by civilised people with the highest standards of sportsmanship and good humour.' ... I worked for the *Daily Mail* for 40 years writing about cricket, and when this story comes out, I am sure some newspaper columnist will jump on it."

Later in the day the captain called and apologised saying, "I know this has left a very bad taste." He mentioned the possibility of having both away clubs being invited on the same day, competing in two Twenty/20 matches, and I told him that might work. But he said, "Both your club and the Crusaders will be bringing along 40 or more people and that would cause security problems."

I said, "The three teams, say 45 people including officials, are the only people who will be presented to the Queen, and that is no different from the occasions when the Queen meets the Test teams at Lord's." He seemed a reasonable man and I urged him to approach his committee and come to a compromise. Later I set out our views in a letter and posted it with a new, higher-priced first-class stamp. I asked for a quick response.

Nearly three weeks went by, despite leaving several messages, and on 28 May I wrote to the club secretary Carl Kneale saying I was intending to write to Christopher Geidt, the Queen's Private Secretary about the matter. My letter crossed with the one written by the captain, dated 9 May, and it arrived at my house in Bromley on 28 May. I knew there was a new boss of the Royal Mail, a lady earning £500,000 a year, and she might have made some cuts in the service, but this was ridiculous – 19 days is almost as long as the time the British Navy despatches from Cape Trafalgar reached the Admiralty in London in 1805.

The captain's letter said:

I have now presented your letter to our committee and regrettably, I have to inform you that they wish for you to respect their decision to play Crusaders on June 26. Whilst they understand your disappointment, there has been an unfortunate error on our fixture secretary's part which has given Woodpeckers CC false aspirations. Our committee do not feel that this decision has anything to do with sportsmanship and fair play, moreover that it is WGP's 150th anniversary celebrations and that they should be able to choose what celebrations should happen for their club without confrontation. Like I stated, it was always our intention to celebrate the proposed visit of our guest with a match between us and the Crusaders as we have built up some very strong relationships with them over recent years and they are our highlight fixture of the season. Our club also very much appreciates the efforts of Mr Richards to re-organise a complex itinerary to bring his squad to Windsor from Manchester the day they arrive in the UK in order to play us. We hope you understand and respect our decision and hope that you can be part of our future fixtures. If you are still interested in playing us from 2012 onwards, please do contact myself.

I wrote back saying, "I am afraid I have to tell you that our members certainly do not want to play your club again." It wasn't quite up to the incendiary standards of the Bodyline row when the MCC and Australian cricket exchanged heated cables in the early 1930s, but it is worthy of a footnote in cricket's low form of insulting behaviour. We just hoped the Queen would have an enjoyable day. Mr Geidt had been a very busy man that summer and we decided not to contact him.

13

The Clash of the Cricket Covers

The Count – Neil Runkel of many cricketing clubs and a surfeit of coloured blazers – was responsible for fixing up a highly prestigious fixture in City Road in the City of London, the day before the 10th anniversary of 9/11. He is a member of the Honourable Artillery Company CC, although he does not have any military experience, and he thinks the pitch is so slow that he finds it hard to turn the ball. His bowling figures, on occasion, are horrendous, which is why he defects to the Woodies on a regular basis.

Because of a worldwide warning suggesting that Al Qaeda was threatening a terrorist attack, roads were closed and others were cocooned by thousands of red and white cones as the utility services tried to meet Mayor Boris Johnson's schedule to smarten up the place ready for the 2012 Olympics. We were assured if we supplied our car registrations in advance, we would be allowed to park inside. Alas, that turned out to be false. When I turned up at midday, ready for a 12.30 start, a young man in the entrance building said, "You can't park here." I pointed to my Blue Badge and he said, "Oh, all right then." Everyone else had to leave their cars some way away, which distressed some of our members who had late sessions the previous night before going on to nearby pub The Artillery at breakfast time to watch the England *v*. Argentina World Rugby Cup punch-up from Dunedin. Olly Mott fell asleep and missed most of the match, including the foul language used by James Haskell, which shocked the nation's TV watchers.

The Honourable Artillery Company is the oldest regiment in the British Army dating back to 1537, and it first moved to the present site in 1641. Cricket was first played there in 1725 at the behest of rich bankers and traders in the City who wanted to while away their time betting on the matches. In 1744 the first Code of Law was drawn up there by certain noblemen and gentlemen after City fathers banned the new sport because it was looked upon as a disreputable activity. Not long after they changed their minds, and the cads who were responsible for most of the excesses were drummed out.

Shortly afterwards, our star Aussie all rounder Mark Prendiville texted from Singapore, announcing the arrival of a third Prendi child named Edward Patrick. We sent them hearty congratulations: young Edward also bore the name of our skipper! The 6-acre HAC site is next to the Bunhill Fields Burial Ground where thousands of victims of the Plague were buried. Soon there was no space left and the remaining bodies were shipped down the Thames and buried next to Greenwich: the area was called Blackheath, now famous for kite flying, Bank Holiday fairs and gridiron traffic jams. The HAC is the second most expensive piece of turf in the world after Kowloon CC. Our veteran Chris Tooley from Oxford University, who volunteered to turn out for the Woodies but finished up playing for the HAC, said, "it works out £150,000 for every blade of grass." Possibly a slight exaggeration.

Lee Fortis, the tall 30-year-old Yorkshireman, who was the chief groundsman, was driving the roller up and down two other pitches. The one which had been selected for our game was firm with light coloured grass. He appeared to be disgruntled. No wonder – at the advertised time, hardly anyone had arrived. There were seven pieces of artillery pointing straight down the pitch – five from the Napoleonic War and two from Second World War vintage. The Union Jack and the HAC flag were flying from the top of the Armoury House, which was built in 1735, and we were unable to find a flagpole tall enough to raise our Woodies flag. So our flag was still in the boot of someone's car.

The match started late at one o'clock, with James Ladner opening from the Chiswell Street end, opposite to where the victims of the Black Death were interred. Off the first ball, Tris Sheehan charged like a Lord Cardigan down the pitch, missed, and was struck on his leading pad.

Ladner screamed, "Arrgghhhzaaat!" Quite deafening! As our umpire, I had to take into account the yardage which the batsman had advanced, the late inswing and also the height of impact, and after considerable thought, I said, "Not out." James, being brought up properly, didn't argue volubly, but he did show some concern about the decision.

"Did too much," I said.

"What?" he said, "where to? Looked pretty straight to me."

"Well my son is in charge of the TV coverage at the Sri Lanka *v.* Australia Test series," I said, "and he is involved with Simon Tauffel in coaching off-field umpires about examining replays and make right decisions. A lot of lbws are guesswork. The technology isn't 100 per cent. You still have to rely on the umpire's judgement."

"Have I met you before?" he said.

"I spoke at the HAC CC dinner over there in the Armoury House on 4 November last year and after 20 minutes of hilarious anecdotes and pungent comments about the state of the game, I discovered that your President, Judge John Gallagher, put a note in front of me which said 'Time has run out. Can you sit down?' I continued for several minutes to talk about my book about Brian Lara, a copy of which was auctioned for your club funds. It raised a meagre £50."

"Oh goodness me," said James. "I'm sorry I didn't recognise you under that Dubai Shopping Week cap!"

The club pay £4,000 a year to rent out the ground which is also used for hockey, rugby, football and corporate events of all kinds. In 1995 Brian Lara turned up for a corporate personal appearance and was turned away by stewards. His agent eventually persuaded them to let him in.

Tris told me later he thought he was out first ball, and I might have shared his view, but I gave him a tweeny-weeny benefit of the doubt. A few balls later there was another deafening appeal from James, almost sounding like a howitzer going off.

"Outside the line," I told him.

He smiled. "It should have been referred upstairs," he said.

Tris began crashing his shots over mid off and extra cover and his batting was brutal. Chris Rossi, cast in the role of the wooden horse, was soon shot away for a duck – with all three stumps being knocked out of the ground. The scorebook showed the name of the bowler as Enzyme, but it turned out to be Mark Vonzon, a Kiwi who came up to the wicket like a sergeant major giving a spirited demonstration of speed walking to a group of squaddies. His bowling wasn't particularly fast, but the groundsman had poured water into the holes. That's what happens at Test match grounds – it gives the public the impression of high-speed bowling, careering the stumps into the air. Very spectacular.

James Cudd, hobbling on a seriously damaged knee, soon matched Tris's all out bombardment on all sides, and we wondered just how many windows would be broken. The ground is almost completely surrounded by seventeenth/eighteenth-century Grade One buildings, some elegant four- or five-floor block of flats, and a mixture of stylish, massive banking offices and several hideous ones. It was difficult to estimate the total number of windows, but it was in the hundreds or even thousands. One pull from Tris dropped against the concrete wall of a building just missing one of the four-by-three-feet windows at a height of around 22 feet.

Richard Webster, the keeper who is the HAC fixture secretary, missed an easy stumping of Tris, and POB, our skipper, ran on to the pitch carrying the red blown-up armband with a view to handing it to him. The Woodies had a spell when mistakes in the field were rewarded by having to wear the armband as a form of penance. As a penalty, they were forced to throw in with their weaker arm and retain the armband until the next mistake occurs by another player. But here Richard didn't see the joke. He looked aghast. As POB approached, he said, "I don't want that. Take it away." POB had to retreat back to the small marquee.

The scoring rate was up to 10 an over for a while and The Count, skippering the side, brought on his son Adam Thompson, who normally takes wickets for the HAC with his legspin. Adam had Tris dropped twice, and Cudd once in quick succession. Tris's final charge was his last: he was bowled by James for 53. Alex Collier started out with a straight drive back over James's head and the bowler said, "Christ, they all seem to be all crash bangers." Tris hit only two sixes and Alex beat him to it with three in his quick-fire 58. An element of T20 crept in with Alex and Ross Marsh, with 4, both being caught off the bowling of Ben Fulton, the Bickley Park first-team batsman who sometimes plays for the HAC. Ben's email starts "gogobenny..." and he soon showed how true that was!

When the Count invited him to become the second slow bowler, Ben said modestly, "I'm not really a bowler you know." He managed to pitch some of his leggers and off breaks, and managed to prise out four batsmen at a cost of 51 runs. The Count held himself back, sensibly, but soon took himself off again after his three overs conceded 30 runs. Our New Zealand left-hander, Mike Wraight, was hit on the right ankle on the full by James on 4, and the bowler, still labouring on, was relieved to see the finger going up. As he went off, Mike seemed to indicate that the bat had caught the edge of his bat, but there was no evidence of that, as verified by both bowler, keeper and umpire. He was not a happy Kiwi.

There was a flurry of boundaries from the bat of Motty, who scored 19, and a slightly hung over Al Clayton who ran himself out for 39, with 38 of the runs coming from legside heaves into cow country at the deep mid wicket boundary. He ignored Motty's call of "No," started to run like a dervish for almost ten yards, stopped, turned, and found himself short of breath. He was well short of the popping crease at his end, but he did hit three sixes, and none of them struck windows. Amir Kavinga, our import from Colombo, batted interestingly for his 12, and James bowled 17 overs in a row on a very humid day to take 4-80. The total of 267 from 43 overs looked formidable, but if someone had played a Jonathan Trott-type innings, without giving easy catches, it would have passed 300.

The bulk of the tea was provided by The Count, who earlier exclaimed, "Dearie me, they've taken off the covers of the sandwiches and they'll soon be crusty." Hugh Miller's mum brought along some of her homemade salmon pasties, especially for the umpires.

The HAC's innings was almost a replica of ours with their number 2 being cast in the sacrificial role. The slingy Amir was entrusted with the Chiswell Street end and he went off like a Hyde Park firework display – explosive high-flying bouncers and dam-busting wides on either side of the wicket. When he pitched one on target, the batsman heard the sound of the stumps ripping out of the ground. Ben, first wicket down, adopted the Shivnarine Chanderpaul stance – facing mid wicket – and soon he was out-bombing our big hitters.

Motty kept bowling down the legside, apparently being distracted by the ladies who attended the wedding which was conducted in the Armoury House. After the ceremonies ended, the lead performers and their guests spilled out to pose for pictures and one of the home side said, "The reason why they keep cars out is to avoid mucking up the wedding pictures with parked cars." One bridesmaid, dressed in green, caught Motty's eye, and between overs he had a few pleasant chats with her at deep fine leg, close to the sightscreen. POB kept waving his arms, trying to move him 20 or so yards away from the screen. Motty pretended he didn't hear him. When there was a break in play, he sat cosily with Miss Green on a bench. "Her name is Green," he announced. These weddings cost up to £3-4,000, depending if someone is in the regular army or the Territorials, otherwise he or she receives a handy discount.

Amir conceded 43 runs in 5 entertaining overs and Windy Miller took over from him and helped the HAC run rate, giving away 55 runs in six overs. Eating too many of his mum's salmon pasties! POB relieved Motty at the troublesome end and moved him to deep mid off. He was the most accurate of the bowlers (0-37 in 5). Fulton's thunderous hitting continued unabated, and with Chris Tooley batting the Trott way, HAC's total flashed past the 100 mark and then 150. Four runs later our only spinner Meddy Edwards was summoned, and he had Chris lbw for 49 well down the pitch. Chris looked quizzically at the umpire, but didn't make a fuss. It probably saved him £50 on a celebratory jug of champagne. Another 61 runs came mainly from the flailing Newberry bat of Fulton, before Meddy broke the stand, having Nick Crendall lbw at 234-4. Only six runs an over were required and the Woodpeckers were looking nonplussed.

Desperate for a breakthrough, POB called up Swampy Marsh, who is not really a bowler, and he produced his grenade ball. Fulton, on 113, missed a very high full-toss, which dropped on to the bails. By the time the ball passed under the level of the shoulder, there was no chance of the umpire calling a no ball, seemingly.

"Failed to pick it up from the top of the Armoury," Ben said. "The screen wasn't high enough!"

Motty returned to have the chubby, rugby-playing number six caught at long on by the agile Amir, and now we were in a better position to win with the clouds building up as the light began to fade. Haines, the number 7, a former lance-sergeant in the Territorials, was blocking, and his partner James confessed that he'd never scored a 50, "but this could well be the moment".

Erratic throwing, leading to several overthrows, dropped catches and a flood of wides (33 in all) all helped the HAC to have a chance of winning a match which the Woodies ought to have won by now. Perhaps the early start to the City, and the lager, was bringing them down. Haines clouted some lusty runs and Richard Webster had his stumps cruelly dislodged by Motty for o. Twenty runs needed, three wickets left, and was the rain going to intervene? A few minutes later, it did rain, and it fell with an unpleasant velocity. Harry, HAC's pro umpire from Willesden, was questioning whether he should call a halt, but both sides wanted to continue. Suddenly the groundsman started pushing the first cover towards the square while the game was still going on.

The Count, agitated, even distressed, shouted, "Come on, take that back! The rain has almost stopped." Mr Fortis, the groundsman, took no notice. Chris Tooley said, "You expect to see the Lord's cover come on, but not in a friendly club game!"

By this time the advancing cover was in position on the square ready to be pushed on to the pitch and the groundsman, a six-feet-three-inch tall Yorkshireman who lived on the premises, strode agitatedly back to bring on a second cover. There were four in all, so the whole operation needed time for him to complete the total coverage of the pitch. Umpire Harry began walking towards him and POB and The Count started pushing the first cover back to where it came from. The groundsman shoved and heaved to move the second one towards the square, only to see the first one crashing into it. The groundsman pushed his, the Woodies pair pushed the other one in the opposite direction, and it was like a shove of war of the covers. It was probably the first time this type of incident has ever happened in the history of cricket, certainly at the HAC ground. The groundsman was shouting, "I am in charge of this ground and I've got six more matches to play this season. The game is over."

Oh no it wasn't. POB told him the rain had stopped. The Count was waving his arms and shouting. Harry, the calmest person on the field, pointed out that the umpires were the sole judges of the state of the weather and "my view is that the game should restart". After a minute or two of bluster from the groundsman, he conceded. With a sour face, he pushed the number one cover back beyond the boundary. The game then restarted. Even Dickie Bird wouldn't have been able to conjure up a story of this quality and originality! It would have made a wonderful TV scene.

Sadly there was no happy ending for the Woodies. Ten runs were needed in the final over and Meddy's first four balls went for 2-2-4-2, all off the blade of the joyous Haines, and HAC were the victors by three wickets. Meddy bowled superbly for his 3-39. Should have come on earlier. Afterwards the groundsman was seen to be having a long chat with one of the HAC's higher ups out in the middle as the light closed in. His behaviour appeared to be rather odd, but good groundsmen treat their pitches like a favoured child. They treasure them.

On the way home most of us would have noticed that it was a full moon, and I reflected on the HAC's motto – "Armed Strength for Peace". At Lord's on Sunday I met Alec Stewart for a signing session of my book *Thank You Herrmann Goering – The Life of a Sports Writer* and told him about the groundsman's conduct.

"I know him well," he said. "He worked for Surrey at the Oval for three years and I can tell you he is one of the best groundsmen around. Those pitches at HAC were in a poor state when he took over. He's done a good job there."

Alec spoke at our dinner in 2002 when Gavin was Woodpecker of the Year. I asked him if fancied a game for the Woodies, or even the Cricket Writers' Club team, and he said, "I've only played once, in Perth, since I retired. I won't play another."

There was a happy sequel. Seven months later Surrey CCC appointed Mr Fortis the head groundsman at the Kia Oval, succeeding a number of outstanding groundsmen there, including the legendary Bert Lock, Harry Brind and Bill Gordon. Richard Gould, Surrey's CEO who went to Exeter University at the same time as Gavin, said, "It's not an easy job, but in Lee I believe we have a found a formidable candidate who will be able to provide consistently world class pitches for many seasons to come."

We would echo the use of the word formidable!

14

We Nearly Forgot
Our 75th Anniversary

Earlier in 2011, hardly any of the Woodies' High Command noticed that this year would be the 75th anniversary of the club. No plans were laid and there were only cursory mentions at the dinner which took place, as usual, at the Alma pub in Wandsworth on Friday, 15 April, more than two months late. We have had a host of England captains speaking in the past, including Gary Lineker (well, he did captain the England football team once and played a few second XI games with Leicestershire), John Emburey (solid, good on strong opinions), Graham Gooch (surprisingly funny), Nasser Hussain (full of pungent views) and Alec Stewart (some of us thought he was the best) and others who also entertained us were Gus Fraser (very sensible, with a dry sense of humour), Mark Ramprakash (the ladies loved him!), Mark Butcher (nice, unassuming with a liking for a drink and a song), Ian Ward (one of our former players who has now became one of the stars on Sky, a terrific guy), Ashley Giles (who played against us when he was in his mid-teens, one of cricket's top yeomen), Nick Knight (lovely man who exudes niceness) and finally, Simon Hughes, the TV cricket analyst and writer.

I leave Yosser (his nickname) to the end for several reasons. When he turned up at the 2004 dinner, I reminded him that almost half of the audience would be ladies. "It's not like rugby thrashes," I said to him. He proceeded to tell some very risqué stories, laced with four letter words, and after a short time there were mutterings among the ladies. Soon the most responsible of the men began expressing their disquiet as well.

When he sat down there was muted applause and I noticed that Richard Nowell, one of our ex-players who had a brief spell with Surrey as a slow left-arm bowler, was fast asleep with his head resting on his left forearm. He'd had a tough drinking day. I rose and said, "I have just seen Richard sleeping on my left and he obviously missed Yosser's speech so I'll wake him and we can ask Simon if he could repeat it." There were frantic cries of "no, no" from all round the first floor room overlooked by Wandsworth Town Station. Being a decent fellow, Simon said afterwards, "Sorry about that. I got it wrong. Apologies to the ladies."

From 2008 we dropped the idea of inviting famous cricketers – our leading actor John Peters of "The Bill" and countless other programmes and TV ads, recited some of his stories that year, and others contributed short pieces. It was good fun, but perhaps we should have asked Graeme Swann, the funniest among the current England squad, to come along and talk. He could have told us how he managed to get off from a drink drive charge by blaming his cat for being trapped under the floor of his house. In his evidence, Swann said he had to go to a supermarket to buy a screwdriver to remove a strip of wood to free the poor animal. On the way, he exceeded the speed limit. As he has an agent, he probably would want a stiff fee and/or expenses to address us, and until then we had no treasurer and no kitty. All the previous speakers came without asking for readies, which is highly unusual.

Nick Knight was living near Birmingham and two hours before the start of the 2007 dinner he rang me and said his wife was ill, but he wouldn't let us down.

I said, "If you want to stay with her, don't worry."

"No, I said I would go and I'm now on my way," he said. Rain was pelting down throughout his trip down the M40, another reason for him to stay at home. He arrived half an hour late, after spending some time finding a parking space among the parked black 4 x 4s, spoke eloquently and earnestly and answered every question without dodging any tricky ones. We sent his wife a huge bouquet of flowers. Nick is a gentleman and I'm glad to see that he has established himself in the Sky commentating team, despite receiving some flak from one of KP's more irrational tweets.

If we knew the exact date when the Woodies started out in 1936 we could have arranged a big event to celebrate it, but we had no records before 1968. Glancing through Christopher Walmsley's *Cricket Through the Year – A Day by Day Account of Cricketing Events 1598-1984*, I was hoping to select a date from 1598, but the only reference was, "Who in 1598 said in a court hearing that he played 'krickett' at Guildford?" The answer was "John Derrick". Geoff Boycott pronounces the word "cricket" as "krickett" in his Yorkshirese, but it wasn't him, so I chose 18 July by chance. That date marks the birth of W. G. Grace, G. S. Sobers and D. K.

Lillee, probably the greatest trio of cricketers to be born on the same day. WG was born at Downend, Bristol, on his mother's 36th birthday in 1848, and was known as the greatest cricketer of the Victorian age. I do have an affinity with him because I am one of the few people who has visited his grave in Elmers Cemetery, Beckenham, not once, but several times. As editor of the annual *Handbook of The Forty Club*, I have written several articles about him.

Henry Grierson, the founder of the Forty Club, was once told that WG's house was about to be demolished in 1939. Knowing that his doorstep was inscribed, "This stone was once the threshold to the home of Dr W. G. Grace at Downend Bristol – Laid July 19, 1910", Murray Witham, the eccentric Head of Wellingborough School, drove to the house, nicked the stone and installed it in front of the school's pavilion. It was duly consecrated in 1940 by Grierson, and it was said to bring good luck to all batsmen who stepped on it. That might apply to some batsmen, but not all of them as Grierson discovered later.

In 2011 I spent a very happy day at Wellingborough School to write about the 75th anniversary of the Forty Club's inaugural game there. A pretty 17-year-old girl named Emily Ablitt captained the school and had an eventful day, bowling her inswingers with relish, dropping a sitter in the field and blocking out the final over to ensure an honourable draw.

The Forty Club, along with MCC and Gloucestershire CCC, Grace's first county, still maintain Grace's grave. In 1993 the white marble edifice needed a facial, and the club raised £2,065 to restore it. Howard Smith, the latest curator, said, "It's in a pristine state but so far since I've looked after it, no-one has visited it which is sad. They think he was buried in Downend. It needs to be publicised. People go to Highgate Cemetery to see the grave of Karl Marx but not the Greatest Cricketer's grave."

WG was a bit of a cheat, often putting the bails back when he was bowled, claiming the bails had been blown off by the strong wind. Invariably he batted on and he drove a hard bargain about taking money for appearing in matches. A lovable rogue, you might say. A few yards from his grave lies the remains of Thomas Crapper (1836-1910), the Yorkshireman who invented the modern loo. One of his patents was a spring-loaded seat which rose automatically – ideal to lift WG's 17 stone – but it was soon withdrawn with a host of unfortunate people claiming injuries. With today's problem of gross obesity, it might be a good idea to bring in a similar shoot-up seat.

Garfield St Aubrun Sobers was without any doubt the number one of all the all rounders. I wrote his autobiography in 1988 called *Twenty Years at the Top*, one of several autobiographies in his name over the years. I always thought mine was the best and he didn't disagree. Through my friendship with Lord Constantine – Learie Constantine, the man who was the first great West Indian all rounder – I asked Sir Donald Bradman if he could write a foreword. Sir Don wrote it himself – he never used a ghost writer – and he said, "I unhesitatingly rated Gary the greatest all rounder I ever saw and the best stroke I ever saw was his straight drive in 1971. I was sitting behind Dennis Lillee as he delivered one of his thunderbolts but Sobers unleashed the most wonderful straight drive which hit the sightscreen almost before the bowler's forward momentum had finished."

Adam Sisman, then an editor with Macmillan, arranged a signing session at Waterstone's in Bromley Market Square, close to my home, and 50 people turned up. It would have been more, but at that time there were very few West Indians in the whole of Bromley. Gary was a perfect gentleman, signing every copy with a quick chat with each purchaser. The day after the Woodies had a game at Hertford Brewery and the Woodies had eight men.

"You'll have to play Gary," I said.

"Not me," he said, "I'm 52 and my knee is shot to pieces."

It was: it was crunched in the crash on the A34 at Stone in 1959 when the car he was driving ran into a ten-ton cattle lorry at 4.45 a.m. Two other cricketers were passengers in the vehicle and Tom Dewdney, the fast bowler, survived and Collie Smith, Gary's best friend, died three days later from spinal injuries. Collie had kept his mate on the right path, but after that tragic accident Gary drank and gambled too much for a while, nearly ruining his life. He was found guilty of driving without due care and attention and was fined £10. In those days, no-one thought about having seat belts. Front seat belts were first introduced in the UK in 1967, well behind the USA and most European countries, and it wasn't until 1991 before it became law to wear seat belts in rear seats.

Gary was living a calmer life after being knighted by the Queen, and on his visit to Bromley, the birthplace of H. G. Wells, he was accompanied by his latest girl friend Nicky, a top-class English squash player, who was half his age. She was supremely fit. Not so long after, the affair broke up and he now has a new girl friend. When he joined Nottinghamshire two years later, a dispute arose about the spelling of his first name. His father, a seaman who drowned when his ship was torpedoed by a German U Boat in 1942, named him after the US film star John Garfield. Suddenly a boot supplier printed "Garry" on his patented bowling boots, and a rogue publisher also used "Garry" on the front cover of a novel, supposedly written by Gary, and from that time on it was always two Rs. How can Garfield become Garry? Not in my book!

Peter Presence, the recently deceased owner of First Features and a sometime Woodies very slow legbreak bowler, persuaded Gary to put his name to a weekly column written by me and distributed to more than 20 newspapers around the cricketing world. Getting hold of Gary was almost impossible before the days of the mobile phone. Lady Prudence, his first wife, an Australian lady of distinction, rarely knew where he was, and my job of translating his views into reasonable English turned out to be a difficult one ... but also an enjoyable one. The contract lasted seven years before he got the urge to go on to something else. On my frequent visits to Barbados he always greets me saying, "You never ring me Brian! What's happening?" He says that to most people.

As 2012 wore on Patrick Owen-Browne, who went to the Dulwich College preparatory school, made plans for a club game to celebrate the anniversary at the college – Poms (English-born Woodies known as Prisoners of Her Majesty's Service, mainly because POB and his family spent some years in Australia) against a Rest of the World side comprising Aussies, Kiwis, Welshmen and a Prussian (Count Neil Runkel). The cost of hiring the school ground was £1,500. When the Woodpeckers started in 1936, you could buy a ten-bedroom house in several acres for that.

POB wanted a four-innings match of 20 overs, with a long lunch break after the first innings of each side. Five prominent Old Boys of the main school were Trevor Bailey, who set a number of records when he was at the senior school, Pelham Grenville Wodehouse, KBE, the eminent English humorist, novelist, playwright and lyricist, Raymond Chandler, the big-selling US crime writer, C. S. Forester who wrote the Captain Hornblower sea stories, and England cricketer Eoin Morgan (who had a brief spell). Like Bailey, "Plum" Wodehouse has his name on several cricket team boards in the pavilion, and there is a museum on the premises of the school, founded in 1619, dedicated to him. Bailey went on to become one of England's finest and most stubborn all rounders, whereas "Plum", though a useful batsman, was a mere mortal of the game. He wrote lovingly about his favourite sport and kept pouring out work for more than 70 years. He reckoned to write an average of 8,000 words a day, an immense amount, after doing 45 minutes exercise each day when he got up.

"Plum" Wodehouse made a fortune in America, and in 1934 he became a tax exile living in Le Touquet. When the Second World War broke out, he was interned and taken to Toszek in Poland and then Berlin, and the Nazis persuaded him to do humorous radio broadcasts for an American market. He was called a traitor in England and libraries banned his work. He never lived in England again, settling in Remsenburg, New York.

Nowadays he was looked on as rather naive for working briefly for the despised Joseph Goebbels, the German Propaganda Minister, and the Establishment eventually forgave him in 1975 by appointing him a Knight Commander of the Order of the British Empire. He wasn't fit to travel to London to have his shoulder touched by the Queen's ceremonial sword, and died at his home six weeks later, aged 93. Incidentally, Goebbels read Archibald Macdonell's book *England, their England* in 1938 and found it totally repugnant. He reported to an aide, "These people ought to be the first to be exterminated!"

On the day of the Woodies game, the Wodehouse Museum was closed, otherwise we would have been able to read from "Plum's" best cricketing work during the luncheon break, featuring that mythical character Percy Jeeves. Well, the wives and partners might have welcomed it, but not so much the cricketers. Wodehouse pinched the name Jeeves from a real Jeeves, a Yorkshireman who played for Warwickshire between 1912 and 1914. Wodehouse was walking in Wensleydale when he saw a cricket match at Hawes, and Jeeves, who bowled fast medium, the same pace as Trevor Bailey, was playing for the home side. He was the professional at Hawes CC. *The Daily Mail* cricket team made three tours to Hawes, and I stayed once in a hotel there where Jeeves had a winter job as a gardener. He's still a big name in Hawes. He was killed in the Battle of the Somme in 1916.

I must have been on ten *Daily Mail* tours under the inspired leadership of their chief reporter David Williams, who is universally known in the trade as "Chief", the name given to Alfred, Lord Northcliffe, who founded the *Mail*. They were all very entertaining and their almost-all-through-the-night celebrations were legendary, not that I managed to see out any of them, being a teetotaller. One was in Dorset and Billy Bonds, the most popular footballer ever to emerge from West Ham, was playing for the Plush CC where he has a second home in the small village. Plush was so secluded that it was impossible to use a mobile phone, and that suited Bill. It's close to the River Piddle and has a lively music festival. He opened the bowling and bounced me a few times on a slow pitch, but I managed to bat through the innings for 67. Bonzo played for and managed the Hammers (1990-94) for 27 years and was sacked, after two promotions and a relegation in his five seasons as manager, in a most despicable manner. His former friend Harry Redknapp was appointed in his place and the two men never spoke again.

I got to know Trevor Bailey in the 1960s when he was doubling up as the star all rounder of Essex and acting as secretary – all as an amateur. Actually he probably earned more than the professionals. He was born in Westcliff-on-Sea, a quiet town near rowdy Southend, with hardly anything to commend itself except for having two theatres and one of the largest casinos in England, and he lived there all his life. His father was a civil servant who worked at the Admiralty, and he was a useful cricketer. He knew Denys Wilcox, a former Essex captain who taught at Alleyn Court Preparatory School, and that explained why a boy living in Essex found himself at Dulwich College. His father wasn't wealthy enough to pay school fees and his son was granted a sporting scholarship.

He was 14 when he first came into the 1st Xl side and headed the batting and bowling averages in 1939 and 1940. He became captain in 1941 and topped the averages in his last year. At 18 he was commissioned as a Second Lieutenant in the Royal Marines without going to the front line, and when the War ended he read English and History at St John's College, Cambridge, graduating in 1948. He won Blues for both cricket and football and played at centre half, inside right, and on the wing for Walthamstow. In 1952 he was on the winning side in the FA Amateur Cup at Wembley, watched by a crowd of 100,000. He also played in the two matches against Manchester United in the FA Cup when Walthamstow drew 1-1 at Old Trafford, before losing 5-2 in the replay at Highbury.

"Oh yes, I was pretty useful," he told me. "Not as quick as some. Never thought of being a professional. Too rough!"

Doug Insole, his best friend, once said he was rather boisterous when he was younger, but soon calmed down. Trevor could rival C. B. Fry as a complete all rounder, except he wasn't able to emulate Fry's successes in the high and long jumps: he might be subject to being charged as overweight. He reported on football for the *Financial Times*, wrote several weighty books and was a punchy analyst on BBC's Test Match Special for 26 years. He had a posh accent and spoke in short sentences. I asked his opinion of a certain player once and he said, "Not good enough. Too much right hand." He was the same when he appeared on the radio – short and snappy, unlike today's verbose former sportsmen who lack the gift of economy. He was always helpful to young journalists like me, and was never frightened to answer a sticky question. As his temperament cooled, his girth increased substantially. But he was still turning out occasionally for Westcliff CC in his sixties.

I skippered the English Press Cricket Association tour of Barbados in 1976 and Trevor was the manager. The tour was heavily sponsored: one sponsor was Gilbey's, and a large consignment was stored in his suite in the hotel on Accra Beach, with another consignment lodged in Ian Wooldridge's room. Trevor celebrated his 53rd birthday during the visit, and not wanting to play cricket, he preferred to have big thrashes. There were thrashes of the other kind administered on the field as well, but near the end I said to him, "How's the booze situation? Much left over for the last night party?"

"Well," he said, "I have to say it's nearly all gone. Greta and I have had a very enjoyable time! And Woollers is in the same state."

Woollers didn't play either. Ian wrote in the brochure, "My appointment as spiritual adviser and director of discipline to our baptismal tour will come as no surprise to those acquainted with my abstemious habits and monastic mode of living." When some of our players staggered out on the tarmac to board the aircraft, Woollers fell head first on to the ground without damaging himself. He was unique: a brilliant writer who got to the heart of sport for almost 40 years, turning out twice weekly columns for the *Daily Mail*.

With the help of Trevor we invited Geoff Boycott to become our sponsorship superstar. Boycott seemed interested, but two months before our departure to Barbados he withdrew, so we signed John Jameson, the England and Warwickshire batsman who proved to be an outstanding tourist before he became injured. Not many people like Boycott because he is considered as self obsessed, but after I spoke at one of his benefit dinners at Honour Oak CC in Dulwich in 1974, he wrote a letter of thanks by return of post. Not many beneficiaries do that! He wanted me to ask Gary Sobers to put his name to an article which I was about to write. The piece ended with Gary saying, "I don't think we will see him pottering on into his forties in county cricket." Gary got that wrong. Boycott's first-class cricket ended when he was 45. A good friend of his told me, "He's been kind to many people, including the Bairstow family. After David committed suicide, Geoff paid for holidays for them." Boycott recovered from cancer of the throat and people who knew him recognised he was a different man after his close call.

Most of the matches in our tour were rained off – yes, rain does fall in November in Barbados – but the most exciting encounter, in the opinion of some of our players, was against an Essex village side Belhus of North Stifford near Thurrock at the Bridgetown Oval, the rebuilt Test match ground which has risen from the wreck of the previous one. They struggled to reach 130 and we only needed five runs off the final over to beat them. Whether it was because our batsmen were still hungover I don't know, but we succeeded in losing four wickets and the match was tied. As we came off, a gnarled old man who obviously had seen all the great players at the Oval, looked up and said, "Man, that's the worst game of cricket that's ever been played here!"

The second half of the tour was a wash out and John Jameson said, "There wasn't much to do except drink, but we arranged a game on the beach at Accra between us and the ladies and lo and behold that was rained off as well!"

Trevor was a devoted and loving husband, father and grandfather – his grandchildren called him "Poppy" – and he was still caring for his invalid wife on the morning of 10 February 2010 when he stuck a piece of bread into the toaster and went out to open the door of their flatlet in a residential home. When he returned the bread had caught fire and the room was enveloped in smoke. He died from inhaling smoke. He might have chuckled when he arrived at the pearly gates and asked his age – "Eighty-seven, that's the bad luck score for our great rivals the Australians!"

I attended the funeral and it was a jolly day. One of his sons, Kim, started his address saying, "It is Red Nose Day today but we don't want to see red eyes." The Boil, or Barnacle as some called him, had a cracking innings, played in the right spirit.

Some of our Woodpecker players appeared to be slightly worse for wear when the 75th anniversary match started at Dulwich. One was woken at 3.53 a.m. in a flat in King's Road by a text from Toby Owen-Browne saying, "I am decelerating." A fleet of mini buses transported the players to Dulwich College at 11.30 and on arrival Toby opened Chris Rossi's crate of ales to continue decelerating. Luckily the historic pavilion had three large fridges, ample room for the copious amounts of food and drink. The two innings of the Rest of the World totalled 189 with the talkative Australian Greg Palmer top scorer. He had to retire on 53 (50 was the limit). Our anonymous match reporter wrote of the halftime BBQ, "It was epic – lamb shoulder, snacks, steaks, burgers, salads, cold veg all washed down with endless of Pimms and Polypins of Rossi's ale." We have a cake mistress, Kate Anderson, who provides exciting homemade cakes for most of our matches and she brought a lemon drizzle cake (awarded 8/10) and an almond pavlova (a solid 6) and Gemma, Rossi's daughter, chipped in with a Betty Crocker Choccy Fudge number (9 but reduced to a 7 when we heard Betty was involved).

The World side captured three quick wickets until Toby came in and slammed 28 of an over from skipper Ross "Swampy" Marsh. He was accelerating for a change. Count Runkel picked up Toby's wicket and the game was still in doubt until the Scovell father and son partnership changed things round with a stand of 45.

"Where's your lid Gav, Whitey's (Kiwi Kieran White, whose last appearance was 180 at Outwood CC several years earlier) fired up today?" was the sledge from Greg behind the stumps. He should have directed it at the Life President (me), who nearly came a cropper, ducking under a Kieran beamer. It reminded me of Withyham in 1978 when a beamer cost LP six teeth and huge dental bills. Kieran bowled offspin at Outwood but was bowling pretty fast this time and I was relieved to avoid injury. I wasn't wearing a helmet and never have. Bowed but not beaten, I retired on 13. Gavin retired on 54 and with Mark "Meddy" Edwards scoring an unbeaten 49, the Poms won by four wickets with 15-year-old Olly Gower hitting the winning run after taking the Bowler of the Day award, a large bottle of coke.

The report ended, "We retired to the Alma where we drank until ejected with the winning skipper celebrating with an Indian take away. Her name was Priyanka!"

15

The Fearsome Colin Croft
Misses Out

The first thing that strikes you when you are about to go up the top steps to both dressing rooms at the Oval is the narrowness of the steps. You couldn't imagine Colin Milburn, all of 15 stone, climbing them without difficulty. When the Cricket Writers' Club team took on the Giles Clarke's English Cricket Board XI there on 26 September 2011 we didn't have an obese player, but Geoff "Buffer" Dean of *The Times* is six feet four inches tall and has lost weight, otherwise he might have encountered a Health and Safety hazard.

The CWC squad were advised well in advance to make their way to the home dressing room, but one of several emails from the ECB GHQ conveyed a contrary message saying, "you are now in the away dressing room". Relegated already! That was the other thing you noticed – the away dressing room is much smaller than the home one. You can imagine towering giants like Curtly Ambrose, Courtney Walsh, Joel Garner, Ian Bishop and Colin Croft bumping into each other in the West Indies dressing room in their heyday.

Croft was one of our late call ups for the ECB match. Nowadays he is a cricket commentator and writer and in the past he has played for CWC. On the last occasion he failed to show up without an apology. But at the 65th anniversary lunch of the CWC, held in the Long Room a short time previously, I asked Vinny Codrington, the Middlesex CCC secretary, if we could borrow a young Middlesex quick bowler because our veteran opening bowler Ralph Dellor was unfit. He said the players were having their farewell party the same night, but he would provide one. As he finished I heard this roar from the right – "Brian Scovell, you are not still fixing friendly matches! Here I am, put me down!" It was Colin Everton Hunte Croft who had a high ratio of success as a terror bowler, taking 125 wickets in his 27 Tests at an average of 24.6 and cracking the odd skull. Of all the express West Indian bowlers of that era, he was the one who petrified more tail-end batsmen than any of the others. He gave me his card. "Ring me with the details," he said.

"Okay, you're in," I said.

The young Middlesex players may well have had an uproarious night or were about to be going on holiday. The first rule in selecting wandering teams, as distinct club sides, is to recruit the first available good cricketer and not wait until the last day. We shook hands and I told Croft he would be bowling at the end where Michael Holding took most of his 14 wickets at the Oval in 1976.

Four days later he emailed to me saying, "Hi Brian, I have decided not to play on Monday. I have much to do and not much time to do it in. But pencil me in for next year when the West Indies are here. Thanks, cheers, Crofty." The joy of emails is that you can fire one back within minutes.

"Please reconsider: it's only three hours in a T20. Make an effort!" I replied.

Next day he was back – "I really do not have that 3-4 hours. I have very much to do, that is true!" He should take up poetry. So I signed up Robbie Williams. Not THE Robbie Williams but the one who was on the Middlesex staff, and he turned out to be a extremely nice young man with tousled hair who arrived on time and showed no sign of a hangover. He bowled from the Holding end and several of his high arm deliveries, around 80 mph, flew down the legside for one-day wides. Croft, at the age of 58, might have struggled to get anywhere near to that speed.

One of the features of the away dressing room are the handwritten notices on the white, plain walls about leading Test players who have done well at the Oval. I noticed one on the right side concerning Croft. Next to it someone had rubbed off the notice about another player. It was suggested that we should have removed Crofty's one, but the idea was soon dropped. The dressing rooms of the Kia Oval are not like the ones at Lord's where the details are carved and painted in on posh mahogany boards. The Oval, despite its resplendent £25 million OCS Stand at the other end of the ground, still retains a bit of its working-class image set against the high polloi of Lord's. The night before the West Indies managed to beat England in a T20, rather unexpectedly, and the current players were much shorter and less bulky, so they probably didn't complain about lack of space in their dressing room. The most comfortable of the home dressing rooms of the England Test grounds is at Cardiff. Glamorgan bought some swish chairs and settees where the players can sprawl out and have a nap. The largest, and best sited, is at Edgbaston, and the neatest, at Trent Bridge.

At Old Trafford they have installed a hydrotherapy pool for the players' use. After their exertions, they can jump in and walk, or sometimes run, through the water to ease aching muscles. Neville Cardus always wailed about the amount of rain that fell at Old Trafford, and in the ruinous, soaked summer of 2012, he probably would have jumped out of his coffin in protest.

Earlier in the year when I met Jim Cumbes, the Lancashire CEO for yet another staging meeting about the new media centre, I asked him, "Have you thought of having a Wimbledon-type roof?"

"Yes," he said, "and it would have cost £18 million so the answer was No!"

There are 15 of the 400-odd members of the CWC who played for England, but for several appearances by Vic Marks, Mike Selvey and Gus Fraser, none of them want to play for the club. There are many more former Test players, like Nasser Hussain, Michael Holding, Alec Stewart, Michael Vaughan, Mike Brearley, Geoff Boycott and Ian Ward, who could play but don't which is a pity. Most of them don't like to be shown up or pull a muscle. In the latest ECB match, Steve Elworthy, the Director of Marketing, skippered the side, and he played four Tests for South Africa, and Charlotte Edwards, the England women's Test side captain, opened the batting. We included Simon Hughes, of Middlesex and Durham, and he has been our most loyal former professional cricketer.

Our squad of 13 for the T20 at the Kia Oval – two were floaters who turned up in case anyone was unfit – assembled in the refurbished Long Room promptly at 1 p.m., ready for a 2 p.m. start. William Powell, the CWC archivist and fourth-choice wicketkeeper, asked a female member of the staff, "Are we in the right place?"

"I'm not sure," she said, "all I've done is to lay on some tea and coffee." Another member of staff said, "the tea and coffee isn't for your lot. You are in the away dressing rooms and you'll have to walk out to the front and go up the stairs on the left."

Simon Lister of *The Cricketer* said, "I can't imagine the England players dragging their coffins round the front."

The man explained, "That door is locked so that's why you have to go outside and possibly get wet!"

We vacated the Long Room and took our coffins and bags up the long route to the third floor, where tea and coffee was laid on, but no biscuits or muffins. We needed some Indian baggage men: a porter in the subcontinent can pile up several coffins and bags on his head and carry them to the passengers' destination without any of them tumbling to the ground.

At 1.50 there was no sign of any of the ECB XI. Geoff Dean had been speaking to Bill Gordon, the long serving groundsman and now consultant, and he said, "They think it starts at 3." A quick call to one of the staff at Lord's confirmed the alarming news. More disquieting news arrived from the same source – "Giles Clarke, the chairman, is injured and won't be leading the side." We were banking on Giles playing and using up a few dot ball overs to give us a chance of winning. It was the time for me to announce that our leader – me – was also out of action. "My artificial right hip has suddenly become loose and now the ICC have banned runners so I, too, am unable to play," I said. There were muffled cheers. I said, "Andrew Miller, the top man on Cricinfo, is taking over and he'll do a great job, better than Alastair Cook." There was a ripple of applause.

In the inaugural match at the Nursery at Lord's in 2008 Giles put himself in at 5, and I did the same, just to be matey. Mike Gatting, OBE, Managing Director of Cricket Partnerships, was a few minutes late and went straight in at 3 and stroked his way to a very safe 50, mainly hitting the ball along the ground with a straight bat. When I moved fielders back to the fence – which isn't too far on that tiny ground – he started chipping the ball into the air to tempt me into bringing them in again. I didn't fall for it. It was a T20 match and he was performing like a recalled Test cricketer. Two wickets fell and he was still batting on with less than half of the quota of overs remaining.

"It's about time to retire Gatt," I said to him. Giles and I hadn't agreed on batsmen retiring at 50 and Gatt seemed reluctant to depart. He scored a few more runs and probably slightly embarrassed, he started to walk off. We clapped him in for his sportsmanship.

Giles took over and without being critical about his batting prowess, I had to say he wasn't another Gatt. He played and missed a couple of times and dot balls were appearing, causing dismay to the younger ECB batsmen lined up on the seats below the Indoor School, mostly padded up. I told our bowlers, "Don't try to get him out. That's are only chance of winning." When Gavin batted earlier he suddenly collapsed with a severely torn Achilles tendon after taking a quick run and had to be carried off. They sat him down on a bench and he was advised to go to hospital. Not long after, an ambulance arrived which whisked him away to St Mary's Hospital in Paddington where Alexander Fleming invented penicillin.

We didn't have any reserves except for a non player who fielded at fine leg both ends, but noticing that Qamar Ahmed, our Woodies hero of the previous generation, was standing over by the Nursery Pavilion, I rushed over to him and said, "Can you take over, we need a quality spinner?"

"I haven't played for nearly 20 years," he said.

"Don't bother about that," I said. "I'll get you an England kit, trousers, shirt and jersey and you can keep it."

"I don't have any boots," he said. "I'm wearing my brown mocassins."

"No time for that," I said. "Wear your mocassins. You'll be the first cricketer to play at Lord's in brown mocassins."

Within minutes Qamar was ready to go on. I put him straight on at the Indoor School end. "Don't get Giles out," I said, "we need him to stay out there and stop their hitters coming in."

Qamar laughed. "I don't think I can get anyone out these days," he said. He looked slightly nervous. His first ball, straight on line and length, was blocked by Giles with an elegant forward defensive shot.

"Well bowled," I shouted. "Keep that going. Don't start spinning it!" Next ball was slightly quicker. It pitched 6 inches outside the off stump and curved beautifully in like a bowls wood and knocked back the off stump. There was jubilation all around, but not from the skipper.

"Oh no, you've ruined the game," I told Qamar.

And so it proved, with the ECB winning by five wickets with three overs left. In the bar afterwards a very attractive middle-aged lady went up to Qamar and said, "You're the man who ruined our day by getting my husband out!" and laughed. She was Judy Giles, a former gossip writer for one of the national newspapers.

Before the start, I had to call in John Stephenson, the Director of Cricket at MCC, to stiffen our batting, and he struggled in our innings of 141-9. "They left the covers off overnight and it was a bit damp in the first few overs," he explained.

Nick Compton, grandson of my hero Denis, also played and he made a cautious 32 without hitting any sixes. Nick isn't a member of the CWC but he has been trained to be a TV personality and with his good looks and manner, he will eventually get there. In 2012 he scored 1,494 runs with a Bradmanesque, with an average of 99.60, and but for missing a month through a back injury and playing in the wettest cricket season since 1812, he might well have matched some of his grandfather's gargantuan feats.

I was at the CWC lunch at the magnificent Plaisterers' Hall in London Wall when he was presented the trophy to the Best Championship Player of the Year and I reprimanded him for not wearing a tie.

"Your granddad wore a tie when he was honoured," I joked.

"Someone said it was casual wear," he said.

Before the ceremony, I asked him if he had a call from Geoff Miller, the chairman of the selectors, telling him he was included in the England squad to tour India. He laughed and said, "I've got it in my pocket, cocked for action." Later Joe Root, the Young Cricketer of the Year, was asked the same question by David Fulton, the presenter, and the naive Joe said, "Yes."

That was greeted with roars of laughter because Joe had inadvertently broken the embargo about announcing the squad next day.

Nick has never tried to copy Denis's flamboyant batting style. He now models himself on Mr Steadies like Jonathan Trott and Jacques Kallis, calm players who seek to act as anchormen in Test teams. Nick told Simon Wilde of *The Sunday Times*, "Kallis is totally deadpan, different from KP who has to dominate. I've tried to steer away from ego. In the long form of the game, ego is evil." Well said!

Gatt didn't have to worry about retiring in the second match against us on a glorious sunny day in early September 2009, with the temperature soaring to 88 °F. When he reached 26 he stretched forward and was bowled by a hasty inducer delivered from the right arm of Andrew Miller for 26. Almost everyone went up, yelling out a loud roar which is now commonplace on cricket grounds all over the world, and the umpire smiled. There was one exception: I had to keep cool in these situations.

As he left, I said to Gatt, "That was a cracker of a delivery."

"Oh no," he said, "I just wanted to give these youngsters a chance!"

Giles Clarke almost found himself being crusted when he batted, just missing a head-high beamer from Lawrence Booth, the editor of the *Wisden Almanac* and a cricket writer on the *Daily Mail*. The recent course of English cricket might have been fouled up if Giles had been mortally struck. Frederick, Prince of Wales and son of George II, a well-known spendthrift and womaniser, was supposed to have died from a blow from a cricket ball in 1751 at the age of 44, but his death was attributed to a burst abscess of the lung. One of the ladies, a Lady of Waiting, might have married him, and she could have ended up as a long past descendant of Lady Diana Spencer, a fact that not many people know. Frederick was a cricket lover and arranged matches to enable him and his friends to place bets on the result.

A Welsh umpire was hit and killed by a cricket ball in 2009, and three years later a boy met a similar end in a school playground in London. Those who nearly met a similar fate were Nari Contractor (who was felled by Charlie Griffith), Raman Lamba of India, Ian Folley of Lancashire and Roger Davis of Glamorgan, fielding at short leg. Lawrence Booth said afterwards, "Before the start Tim Percival, one of the PRs of the sponsors, told me 'don't for goodness bowl a beamer at Giles!' In my second over the ball slipped and it went straight at him. He managed to duck and didn't make a fuss."

The ECB was dismissed for 157 and I found the man I thought might play a match winning innings – Keith Bradshaw, the popular MCC secretary who resigned in 2011. He agreed to nip over from his office across in the pavilion, but had to drop out so I called up a Devon Minor

County player, a friend of Richard Sydenham, and he scored 75 and we won by six wickets. Drop outs in journalists' cricket are frequent, like seeing soldiers drop from exhaustion on punishing training runs. There's more pressure on writers to keep working these days, almost until they drop, and sick notes are very rare.

Two of our best young players, Richard Sydenham and Sam Peters, apologised for missing the third ECB game at the Nursery in August 2010, and I signed up two left handers from the Woodies – Australian all rounder Greg Palmer and Alastair Owen-Browne, a former Tonbridge School first teamer. Greg is a prolific hitter and he smashed 12 sixes in his 91, but it wasn't enough to stop Giles Clarke being on the winning side. Giles didn't bat and was nearly decapitated at short extra cover when one of Greg's howitzers whizzed past his head. Again, it was a near miss. Greg scored 62 per cent of our total of 146-6, and the ECB won with four balls remaining with eight wickets in hand.

The first ECB player to arrive at the Oval in Episode Four of our series – still not yet televised by Sky or even Eurosport – was Peter Such, the former England and Essex offspin bowler. He is the England Lead Spin Coach.

"You shouldn't be playing," I said, "you ought to be at an inquest today in England's shattering defeat against the Windies 3rd XI!" He laughed. He is a cherry soul.

He played 11 Tests between 1993 and 1999, and his 37 wickets cost 33.56 runs apiece. Like Graeme Swann, he started his Test career at 29. "Offspin bowlers don't reach their best until that age," said Suchy, who came from a cricketing outpost at Helensburgh, Dumbartonshire.

Giles had to drop out because of another appointment and an underling said it was nothing to do with the fact that the CWC players were targeting him. Neither Lawrence Booth nor Greg Palmer was included in our XI, but they may have been concerns about Geoff Dean of *The Times*. Formerly a fast, and sometimes erratic bowler who played for Esher CC, he had to be asked to leave the nets once when England were practising before a Test in the West India because he might cause injury.

Normally our players rarely practice, but this time they were eager to sharpen up their skills. They went through a series of relaxed fielding exercises and Sydenham, in particular, wanted a net. Unfortunately there wasn't one. Like some English grounds, there are no nets round the back – the Oval, Trent Bridge, Headingley and now, because of their redevelopments which they can barely afford, Canterbury.

"I've hardly played," said Richard, "and I need that."

At 2.25 Steve Elworthy emerged with his players and the toss ceremony took place in front of the dug out. Andrew called correctly and announced he would bat. He didn't know the strengths and weaknesses of all of our batsmen so I gave him the batting order. Sydenham was number one, partnering our prospective pinch hitter Ben Fulton, a left hander who faces mid wicket and defies gravity by swinging back into line and pummelling the ball hard on the off side. Ben is a solicitor but qualifies by reading the sports section of the *Daily Telegraph* on a daily basis.

Suchy's bowling was immaculate, a lesson to all young offspinners. He didn't turn the ball much, but every delivery was different and he conceded only one run in his first over. Sydenham was smelling the leather, like a Boycott devotee intent on preserving his innings. Our Ben found himself in opposition with the ECB's Ben, Ben Green who bowls medium pace. Our hitter lived up to his reputation, whacking his adversary with 4 fours before he was caught by Rob Johnson for 25 off 12 deliveries. Meanwhile Syders was deflecting the odd ball on either side with deft singles, but wasn't able to punish Suchy's bowling. He couldn't get Robbie Williams away either and was relieved when Suchy's spell ended on 4-0-13-0. Soon Ben was caught by Steve Elworthy for a robust 27. A year or two earlier, Steve had a big toe cut off in an accident caused by a lawnmower. It was sewn back and it is back to normal. Fred Titmus, who had four toes removed, didn't have the same luck. Fred, who died a few months earlier, was never the same.

Sydenham's patient innings of 28 ended when he was bowled, and except for the lusty hitting of Simon Lister who was run out for 21, the tail capsized with four more batsman mustering 0. Helpfully, the ECB men gave away 26 extras in our 133-8. Robbie Williams failed to take a wicket but he did a fine job ruffling Charlotte Edwards, ready for Andrew Miller to bowl her for 17 at first change. "That's two England captains I've got rid of – the other one being Mike Gatting," said a happy Andrew.

The Oval pitch resembled and played like an Indian one – low bounce and little pace – so I advised the skipper to start with the slow left arm Mark Edwards who took an early wicket before losing his length and had to be taken off. We needed to use our mystery bowlers early on and both the loquacious Jarrold Kimber, editor of *Spin*, and the perpetually smiling Ben Fulton, eked out the ECB's middle order by bamboozling their batsmen. Jarrod pitched his leggers accurately – usually a rarity – and took 2-13, and Ben, who bowls both off and legbreaks, had 2-3. There were two fantastic, running catches by Simon "Yosser" Hughes and Geoff "Buffer" Dean, some 80-odd metres on the Archbishop Tennison School side of the ground to finish off the innings of 101 in 18.4 overs.

The victory levelled the series 2-2, and at the end of the eating and drinking in the Long Room, I concluded my speech of thanks saying, "The good news is that the next game will be played at the Newlands in Cape Town, kindly paid for by Giles from the damages he expects to win from his High Court case about the Indian Premier League row." There was a roar of laughter, almost shaking some of the hefty portraits of famous cricketers all around the room. Within days Andrew Miller was honoured (but not by the Queen) by being made editor of *The Cricketer*, one of the most prestigious jobs in world cricket: well deserved, and he is only 33. He'll be looking out for Colin Croft next year!

Six months later, the High Court case was settled without going to a trial, with IMG and the ECB calling a halt to avoid unnecessary further expense. Both sides claimed a winning draw.

16

Shedding Blood in India

A common question asked at quizzes at pubs, clubs and occasionally at the waiting rooms of consultants in private hospitals, but rarely NHS ones, is, "Which English-born cricket captain has the best winning record on tours of India?" The name of Douglas Jardine springs to mind. He was unbeaten on the tour in 1933/4, winning two Tests and drawing another. Tony Greig won three Tests in 1976/7 against Bishan Bedi, not one of the better Indian captains, and lost one, but his successors, Keith Fletcher, David Gower, Graham Gooch, Nasser Hussain and Andrew Strauss had awful records in the subcontinent.

On a 27-hour train trip from Calcutta to Delhi early in 1987 with the Mihir Bose Fleet Street squad, most of the hours were spent with quizzes, and even the Indians joined in. Someone asked the question about who was the most successful England skipper, and both English and Indian contestants struggled to find the correct answer. In 1979/80 Mike Brearley won a Test, but as it was a single match it couldn't count as a series win. Trains often stop in India, often unscheduled, and there are water wallahs ready to step forward and sell bottles of water, or preferably in our case, the hot, sweet tea they provide in plastic cups. We were flagging and each time the train came to a shuddering halt we stepped out on to the side of the track to avail ourselves from some refreshments, and on this occasion, the 55th stop, I said to our group, "We'll be here all day and you won't come up with the answer so here it is – it's me! I was fortunate to captain Bose's side on three occasions and was on the victorious side each time."

No-one had evidence to counter my claim, and Nick Wood, the then political correspondent of *The Times*, bought a round of tea for the teetotallers and pulled out a flask of whisky to share with the hard drinkers who were in the majority.

A young Indian passenger said, "Excuse Sir, am I right in thinking that you played for England?"

I told him he was wrong and I said, "On several occasions I skippered the English Press team in various parts of the world but not the national XI."

He produced a scrap of paper and a pen and said, "Please sir, may I have your autograph?" I wrote, "Be bold! Douglas Jardine." He was very grateful and we shook hands.

Why do the Indians love cricket so much? They didn't invent it: we did, and we took the gentlest of all sports to a number of maharajahs in different parts of India in the eighteenth century and they liked its subtleties and its sense of fair play. They liked having a bet and still do. The sport spread rapidly to every village, town, city and every corner and cranny of the nation. Now the Indians and are running world cricket. At the time of writing, England's South African mercenary Kevin Pietersen was forced to stop playing one-day cricket for his adopted country because he needed to rest, ready to count his rupees after his exertions in the Bollywood-glamour extravaganza of the Indian Premier League.

Back in our reserved compartment, the train was ready to start, and it seemed a perfect time to tell the story. I told the throng, "My first win was completed at the Madras ground, now known as Chennai. We were supposed to play on the main 40,000 capacity Chepauk ground but the England A team were playing there so we had to play on the ground next door. There was a hilarious start to the game. I can't remember who I opened with – Bruce Pavey, the LBC presenter may well have been the man – but I noticed that a young lady wearing a sarong and carrying a wicker basket on her shoulder kept walking behind the bowler's arm, and I said to the captain, 'Can you stop this lady, it's putting me off.'

"He said, 'She is an essential worker carrying the water bottles into the pavilion and she will lose her daily wage if she is removed. Her large family won't be able to buy food. Please, she must be allowed to do her work.' I had to concede and in the next over I was dismissed, bowled. As the bowler released the ball I saw the woman stumble and one of the bottles fell to the ground. I said to my partner at the other end, 'I've been dismissed by a woman who dropped a water bottle!'"

It was an extremely hot, humid day, not surprising because Madras is close to the Equator. We bought a new scorebook and it had some unusual entries. If someone made a mistake in the field, the Indian scorers wrote in "Erring Fieldsman". A batsman who was dropped was described, "Lucky". We noticed that several of their players used "Lucky" as a Christian name.

A bullock cart carrying building materials arrived at the far side of the ground, stopped, and bricks were taken off and put in a pile. Someone said, "I hope the bricks aren't to be used as missiles if we upset them." One of the women transporting water was struck on the back from a wayward six and no-one rushed forward to help her.

Against some quality bowling, our batsmen struggled to take quick singles and they kept calling for more water. Our total, a mere 198, looked an easy target for the local hitters, all experienced regional cricketers. Andrew Sculthorpe, our quick bowler from a Lancashire League club, was the only man to keep them in check, but he couldn't bowl forever and needed a break. Tall and thin, he looked ravaged by the end of the three-week tour. He played in all 12 matches, scored 202 runs with an average of 25.25, and headed the bowling averages, bowling 84.1 overs and taking 31 wickets at 12.19 with the best economy rate of 4.49 runs an over. A herculean effort indeed! When I saw him a few years later it was hard to recognise him.

"You've lost a lot of hair, Scully," I said.

"Spent too much time tearing my hair out in India mate! We held 30 catches and we dropped at least three times as many."

Our slower bowlers, including Richard Heller of the *Mail on Sunday*, were costly, and with the scoring rate rising rapidly a lot of people turned up to see the fun. A Board official explained, "The England A side have just scored 20 runs in an hour and we noted that your opponents scored 130 in the same time, which is why the spectators walked out of the stadium and preferred to see your game."

Phil Neale, the England A manager came over as well. He's a very nice man and he was the longest serving member of the England party. Having a knee replaced hasn't stopped him either. He played for Lincoln City and Worcestershire and was one of the last survivors to play cricket and football in the same era.

The funniest incident came when Heller, looking up into the bright sky with a strained expression on his face on the mid on boundary, started circling in an attempt to spot the ball which had just reached an immense height and was starting to fall in his direction. He held up his arms high to receive the offering, but swore loudly as the ball bounced into the rough behind him for a six.

He wrote later, "In a frenzy of self disgust, I removed my cap and danced on it and then I couldn't find the ball. No one laughed. The scorer made a precise entry under 'Erring Fieldsman'. The crowd turned me into an idol. I could do no wrong for the rest of the match. Applause for every touch of the ball, a yell for my late only wicket. I was looked on as the Hero of Madras. I would like to believe that it was ordained, a demonstration of a great force in Indian life, stronger even than cricket: the working of destiny."

One of our players read it and said to him, "Watch it mate, you need to be certified!"

Some of their batsman, still roaring with laughter, got themselves out and soon I realised that the game might be lost to the Madras Cricket Board XI. One batsman batted sensibly and whenever he faced the bowling, I moved all ten fielders to the boundary to give him an easy run. He fell for it every time, and Scully came on to knock aside the tail. Sweat was pouring down my face, and when the last wicket fell, I felt so emotional that I shed a tear or two as well. You don't win matches like this without having Jardine's determination and single-mindedness! I felt very proud. As the players walked off, I flopped into a wicker seat which must have been left over by Clive of India. A servant handed me a cup of sweetened tea and wiped my perspiring pate with a discoloured towel. What bliss!

Heller won all the quizzes in the train journey and we suggested he should enter the TV programme "Mastermind". A year later he did, and answering questions about President Harry Truman and Gary Sobers, he finished joint runner up.

Mihir Bose's biggest claim to fame was not being BBC Radio 5 sports chief reporter, or exposing sport's corruption in his various newspaper columns including the *Daily Telegraph*, but in attending the same school in Bombay as Sunil Gavaskar. Two years older than Sunny, Bose was seen poking fun at Gavaskar practising his forward defensive shots in the playground, and the school cricket master, Father Fritz, berated him saying, "This boy will play for India." The Father was right, and also right about Bose not becoming a proper cricketer. Immensely keen, Bose never really succeeded in any of the cricketing arts, fielding, batting or bowling. But he could talk a good game and he produced a magnificent work entitled *The History of Indian Cricket*. He arranged three eminently successful tours to India, one in 1986-87 and two others in 1995 and 1999, partly sponsored by the Indian Government. He said, "I hadn't played cricket for almost 20 years since leaving school and my occasional forays for *The Sunday Times* team convinced me that if I were not to spend my Sunday afternoons fielding at third man at both ends I had better organise my own team. One of the perks of captaining your own side is deciding where you bat or bowl and where you field. Very important considerations at our level of cricket."

The first tour was dangerously chaotic and it was hard work being bumped all round India on their overcrowded, under-repaired roads in a rickety coach which kept breaking down. It covered almost 2,500 miles in 19 days and broke down frequently. Each time, the two drivers, who alternated four hours on and four hours off, would clamber under the vehicle armed with spanners and hammers and starting bashing away. It worked every time. Nine years later the smooth talking Mihir found it much easier with government assistance. We flew most of the way.

The 1995 expedition was flung together speedily after a bubonic plague outbreak in five states, which cost the lives of 52 inhabitants the year before. Even today up to 15 per cent of people infected from it has a poor chance of survival, despite taking the necessary antibiotics. The India tourist department feared that many British holidaymakers wouldn't go on their intended tours and they wanted some top English journalists to write favourable articles in their publications. Our heavyweight journos included Roland Watson, the now political correspondent of *The Times*, Mike Evans, the defence correspondent of the same newspaper, Nick Wood, also of *The Times*, Peter Oborne, then of the *Evening Standard* and now with the *Daily Telegraph* and a TV star, Tim Jotischky, then of the *Daily Mail*, now the assistant editor of the *Telegraph*, George Pascoe-Watson, the political editor of the *Sun* and now in PR, and Charlie Thomas and Gavin Scovell of Sky Sports. All jolly men with great stamina: those are the two ingredients needed to tour India. They all took hours and hours queuing up for their visas at India House – good training for touring the subcontinent – and almost as along to catch up on their many inoculations.

The political journalists were invited to John Major's Christmas party at Number 10, and one of them told the PM about the tour. The PM said, "I wish you every success. I hope you are so successful that you don't come back for several years." That was the PM's little joke. Or was it?

Making it easier for Mihir's men in the subcontinent was the presence of Nick Hewer, Sir Alan Sugar's PR advisor on "The Apprentice" and presenter of "Countdown". Nick, a silky PR man with a deft sense of humour, was responsible for Bose's cricket tour booklet, and as a sensible man, his name wasn't mentioned in it just in case there was a comeback. Someone might have caught bubonic plague and it would have made headline news back in the UK. Hewer was 51 at the time and like everyone else in the party, he managed to avoid Delhi Belly. "Keep swigging the whisky," he advised. When Sugar became chairman of Tottenham Hotspur, Nick performed a near miracle. He persuaded some of the leading Fleet Street writers to write favourably about his boss. Sugar was in a constant legal battle with Terry Venables leading up to a costly High Court action, which he won, but it was a hard sell because Venables had a coterie of top football writers who loved him and saw no wrong with the smooth talking Cockney.

Everywhere we went in India we were accompanied by senior officials of the Ministry of External Affairs and dozens of soldiers carrying Lee Enfield rifles. These weapons went out of fashion in the First World War, but we were assured that they could still be fired if necessary. On arrival at airports we were rushed through immigration and our coach was waiting outside to transport us to our five star hotels. At Delhi we were welcomed by young ladies who placed the traditional garlands around our necks at 2 a.m. We wondered whether they were on double time in the middle of the night. Soft drinks with ice were handed round. We had been told that any contact with water or ice should be shunned except at five star hotels, which had their own supply of water. India Airways granted us huge discounts on fares and at the end of the tour, Mihir Bose refunded £150 to every member of the party. We were treated like lords. Lucky people!

I had to share a suite with Mihir on the first night, and at 3 a.m. I was awakened by what appeared to be smoke.

"The place is on fire," I shouted.

Mihir was sitting up in the other opulent king and queen size bed nearby smoking a huge Havana cigar. He laughed. "I'm just catching up on a few administrative matters," he said.

"Well, I'm trying to sleep," I said. Next morning I arranged to move in to another room – very much smaller.

The Rt Hon. Douglas Hurd, the Foreign Secretary, arrived roughly the same time as us in Delhi, although we missed him. He also went to Jaipur, where we stopped off to take another beating before seeing the magnificent Taj Mahal for a second time. This time we turned up at India's greatest monument, possibly the greatest attraction in the whole world, as dawn was breaking and the effect was startling, almost mystic. It certainly had a profound impact on our cricketers and their wives and partners. Eleven million people visited at that period each year, and nearly all of them were Indians. We expected to see Mr Hurd popping up to sit on the seat where Lady Diana, the Princess of Wales, once sat poignantly on her own, but he was elsewhere, vainly seeking an interview with the Prime Minister Narasimha Rao.

One of the outstanding sights of railway travel in India was to see dozens of coffins – large, rectangular boxes filled with cricket gear lying on the chaotic, overloaded platforms taken from our transport and carried by very thin men of all ages. A single coffin would find it difficult to lift for one of Bose's cricketers, but these emaciated under-nourished men had four, five or even six coffins piled up on top of their turbaned heads as they walked, straight-backed, picking their way to their destination. Not a single coffin fell to the ground. Mihir handled the tips and I suspect he might well have not over rewarded them. There's a very strict code of merit in the country with the Untouchables being virtually ignored. The next level of human beings are pretty servile as well, although with mobile phones and ipads things are slowly changing.

In Delhi we were billed to play the staff of the British High Commission, but the city was shrouded by smog so the organisers moved the match ten miles outside to a private ground. In the previous match we were embarrassingly beaten and now we were expecting to win against the Brits and the colonials from the Embassy. No such luck because the most of the Brits were taken off the team sheet and told to stay on to entertain Mr Hurd. Ringers from local clubs were drafted in and once more we were facing a severe thrashing. The temperature was in the high 30s, and there was no smog in this part of the state. We were in the field and after an hour we called for drinks. Some time elapsed before two wallahs came out with jugs of iced water and glasses. Most of our players refused to drink it, fearing that they might pick up the lurgy.

"Can we have something else?" said the polite Mike Evans.

"No sir, this is all we have," said one of the Indians. Some of our hungover players decided to drink the water and gulped down a gallon or two down their parched throats.

It was hard to contain the flow of runs, and inside another hour we called for another break. On came the wallahs with an Australian who worked for the Embassy. He apologised about the lack of drinks other than water, and Mihir said, "I hope lunch will be provided."

The Australian looked sheepishly at our leader. "Unfortunately we haven't made provision for any," he said.

Mihir was furious. "What!" he said. "The British Government can't afford to buy us a lunch – what next!"

In the other games, marquees were set up and a staff of workers served us with vast amounts of curries, sweet cakes and drinks. After play ended, there were more drinks and Mihir began asking me to make the speeches. It was all good fun. I always started by ribbing him and that would set him off, roaring with laughter. Everyone joined in and the hosts didn't mind about the poor quality of our cricket. A good tactic, we thought. They assumed we were county cricketers and I said, "We read the daily newspaper reports of the county cricket, that's all."

Mihir, still fuming, announced he would be going off to ring the manager of our hotel, the Hyatt, and order a similar type of meal, plus copious drinks. The meal and drinks on wheels arrived in the team coach 15 minutes before play was about to restart, and we sat outside chewing away under the cruel sun while the Embassy team finished their own snack and bottles of beer in comfort. Some weeks later, when my stomach had settled down from the incessant curries, I found myself sitting next to Mr

Hurd in a NatWest cricket lunch in London, and I told him about the way Her Majesty's press were treated in Delhi, with no food and drink on a blistering hot day.

"That's extraordinary," he said. "What a way to carry on! I'll see that this is looked into. We can't upset the political writers." We never heard any more.

Before the game at the inappropriately-named Wankhede Stadium against a Bombay Invitation Xl, Mihir accompanied me out to the pitch to assess the state of the pitch. "What do you think?" he asked me.

"The dew is still down and we need to bowl first," I said. "Half an hour or so it will dry out and the pitch will be flat and easy paced. Bowling first is the only chance to take a wicket or two."

"Ah," he said. Twenty minutes later I was in the dressing room where all the great Indian Test players changed over the years when Mihir marched in and said, "Put your pads on."

I was surprised and said, "Am I keeping wicket? I'm no good at it, you know."

"We're batting," he said. I groaned. I duly strapped on my pads, my chest protector, and put on my gloves. I'd never worn a helmet and this might have been an occasion when it was needed. When the first ball was delivered, it swung sharply into the bat and rapped me on the glove. In half an hour we were 12-4, and it was as if our batsmen were being treated like miscreants, stuck in the stocks and being bombarded with missiles. I was the third man out and was happy to return to base unscathed.

As usual in this part of India, the pitch soon dried out and the rest of the innings was much more orderly. Ordinary batsman like ours could survive and Peter Oborne, who dressed like Pandit Nehru, the former Indian Premier, for most of the tour, batted superbly to reach 77. He managed to run out five of his colleagues on the way, and unfortunately for him nine wickets had fallen and the number 11 batsman was Nick Wood, whose highest score on the trip was 9 not out. Oborne thought he had a chance of making a century and called for a run off the last ball of an over. He hit it straight to a deepish mid on and noticing that Wood was still stationary, he screamed, "Run man!" He still kept careering down the pitch like a dervish, although Wood said firmly, "No!"

Realising that his partner was still in his crease, he kept running and shouted angrily, "You xxxx, you've stopped me getting a 100." Without stopping, he ran into the pavilion, went up the stairs and threw his bat across the dressing room. Meanwhile the ball was lobbed back to the bowler's end and the departing Oborne was run out by the full distance, 22 yards. Nick said, "He wasn't going to make me the sixth person to be run out." Later, the one-sided mismatch finished with another humiliation.

1. Playing and missing for the Cricket Writers' Club at Ventnor. What a slope!

2. Cricket Writers' Club XL *v.* Ventnor CC: from right, Brian, John Townsend (WA), Gavin and Peter Roebuck (in white hat).

3. Low flying Spitfire over Goodwood (CWC *v*. Motor Racing XI including Jack Bradham who crashed in practice the next day).

4. Jack Bradham, 2nd from the right, Murray Walker (umpire), the Duke of Richmond and B.S.

5. On the left, the late Gerald Plumbly, Life President of Stoics CC, on their first tour to Sri Lanka in 2008.

6. B.S. (with a displaced chest protector) with former Pakistan captain Aamir Sohail at Dambulla.

7. Chris Rossi, the 71-year-old opener of the Stoics, shows immense stoicism against a game U17 XI in front of the sixteenth-century Dutch-built fort.

8. Woodies non-event tour of the Isle of Wight, 2001. Back: Brian Hitchcock, Qamar Ahmed, Calum Parkes, Robbie Wood, Patrick Owen-Browne, Simon Hare, Gavin Scovell, John Murrin, Larry Robeson, Mark Edwards and Brian Scovell. Front: James Wood, Alan Wood and Chloe Wood.

9. Ian Wooldridge (*Daily Mail*) on left with Trevor Bailey (in blue shirt), with members of the English Press Tour in Barbados in 1975. They were paying tribute to Frank Worrell after his funeral in 1967.

10. The happy English press tourists with organiser Alasdair Ross to the left of the balding David Lacey (*Guardian*). John Jameson, England and Warwickshire opener, is one from the right.

Above: 11. Gary Lineker, chief guest at a Woodies dinner at Lord's.

Left: 12. Geoff Lawson snapping Mark Slater at Wandgas CC.

Right: 13. Chandra Bose, the rebel leader, and Mihir Bose, captain of the Fleet Street Tour party.

Below: 14. A self-satisfied Dominic Lawson with first wife Jane Reading at Hyderabad.

15. B.S., Chris Lander (of the *Daily Mirror*) and Ian Todd (The *Sun*) in India, 1989.

16. Ian Bishop at Marlow Park CC with John Peters (of *The Bill*) 3rd to the right.

17. CWC *v.* Texaco. Qamar Ahmed, 2nd left at rear, Harry Latchman (Middlesex) far right, B. S. Chandrasekhar (India) 2nd from left, front, B.S., Paul Davidson, Sarfraz Navaz and David Frith.

18. CWC (*v.* Giles Clarke ECB XI) at Nursery at Lord's. Rear: Ralph Dellor (BBC), Tim Percival (nPower), Nick Compton (England, Middlesex and Somerset), B.S., Matt Prior (*The Times*), Qamar Ahmed. Front: John Stephenson (Essex and Hampshire), Lawrence Booth (*Daily Mail* and *Wisden*), Dean Wilson (*Daily Mirror*), Hugh Turbovill (*Daily Telegraph*), Mark Pougatch (BBC) and Gavin.

19. St Dunstan's Fancy Dress Party on Christmas Day at Rottnest Island, Western Australia.

20. Maltamaniacs Tour to Alderney, hosted by John Arlott (Master of the Wine).

21. Blocking away at the front at Frant CC. The picture doesn't convey the steep slope.

22. *Daily Mail* tour to Dorset in 2000 (Captain Dave Williams, chief reporter, centre of front row).

Left: 23. Geoff Boycott drives and Gary Sobers grimaces (from Geoff Boycott's Benefit Brochure).

Below: 24. Forty Club playing in Walvis Bay, Namibia, with an oil rig parked on the harbour undergoing repairs.

25. The local custom at Oshokati, Namibia, where players who misfield are struck by a bat.

26. Audrey and I taking tea at Brabourne Stadium in Mumbai, with Nicky Evans on the right and, behind, a reflective Forty Club tour manager Ron Hart with Mike Evans and Nick Wood (both of *The Times*).

27. B.S. and Neil 'Count' Runkel with Nigel Phethean and his grandsons.

28. Mick Hogan, the tearaway fast bowler, bowling at the Thomas Cook ground in Beckenham in 1968, with B.S. watching intently and Tony Salisbury walking in.

29. The Woodies line up in honour of Air Vice Marshal Sir Ken Hayr of the RAF, father of one of the players, James 'Dusty' Hayr, at Leigh CC (*c.* 1700) in 2001. He died in an air crash at Biggin Hill.

30. The skipper goes for a rare slog sweep, watched by a startled keeper, Greg Palmer, at Dulwich College.

31. Action at Tilford CC.

32. Woodpeckers taking on Bat and Ball CC on Broadhalfpenny Down.

That tour ended with joy and happiness for Mihir. In most of the matches he insisted on bowling an over or two and at the Bombay Maidan, a huge flat area like the Savannah in Port of Spain where dozens of cricket matches go on at the same time, he was about to start the final over before lunch. Up to then he had conceded 133 runs on the tour without taking a wicket. The batsman at the far end was Rohan Gavaskar, son of Sunil and he was 49 not out. Mihir bowled a slow full-toss and the left handed Rohan pulled the ball high into the air at deep mid wicket. Standing on the boundary was Sculthorpe, our best fielder. He caught it with ease and Mihir leaped into the air with glee. His 48th birthday had just been celebrated and he was ecstatic that he had been able to dismiss the son of the King of Bombay.

Rohan went on to play 11 ODIs with India, but never took the final step towards becoming a Test player. He was named Rohan after Rohan Kanhai, who did, appearing in 79 Tests and finishing with an average of 47. He still lives in blustery Blackpool and when the England *v*. West Indies Test took place at Edgbaston in 2012, he turned down an invitation to join the other great West Indian cricketers who played for Warwickshire of that era, Deryck Murray and Lance Gibbs, at lunch in the new pavilion. Perhaps he knew something the others didn't know: three days were washed out through rain.

I've known Sunil Gavaskar for many years and after he retired from his illustrious career, I bumped into him at Lord's and wondered whether he fancied a match for the English Cricket Writers' Club for the Roger Knight benefit match at Sanderstead, a club south of Croydon. He thought it would be a good idea and I also invited Tony Cozier to come along as well. I understood the starting time was 2.30, and when I drove them into the ground, lunch was being served, with our team on 194-3. The game started at 11.

I told Roger, "Apologies for that," and said to Sunny, "Pad up, you're next in."

"Oh no," said Sunny, "you deserve to bat first. Also Tony." There was a large crowd and they were waiting to see Gavaskar, not me. I tried to talk him out of it but he refused to change his mind. Tony went in and got himself out and when I came in I tried to do the same. Lashing out wildly, I hit three sixes over the pavilion – unheard of in a long career – before eventually falling to a catch at long on. Sunny came in to a loud reception and he batted out the final 30 minutes for an unbeaten 6. He didn't play a single attacking shot. The rest of the players were astonished.

Then we remembered his performance in the World Cup at Lord's in 1975 in an ODI match when after England scored 334 in their 60 overs, he batted through for three hours for 36 and India came in at 132-

3. He explained, "I couldn't get going!" The same thing happened at Sanderstead!

The Mihir Bose tour in India in 1987 was much different to the previous ones. It was almost backpacker class despite being sponsored by Air Canada. When we arrived in Bombay – I always prefer the original name to Mumbai – we were billeted in the BCCI (Board of Cricket Board India) rooms across the road from the Wankhede Stadium. Incidentally, why do these Indian cities squander trillions of rupees on changing their names? Is it anything to do with these try-to-get-rich companies whose staff are asked to telephone angry people in the UK at all hours? When you ask the caller, "Where are you speaking from?" they say, "Mumbai" to confuse us!

Most of our the players stayed at the top floor and the suites were large and airy, filled with pre-Second World War furniture, including leather suites, but in the next floor the rooms were more Spartan. One of the girl friends soon fell out with her man and moved into the communal washing room, and it was embarrassing to turn up with your smalls and see this lithe, middle-aged German, half naked doing her exercises. Gavin, then 17, stayed with me in my suite along with John Dunkin – who was to be given out in a later game lbw when the ball hit him in the backside – Jamie Oborne of the famed Oborne family, and the Woodpeckers opening quick bowler Richard Morrow, an Australian who resembled Bob Massie in size and bowling style.

Nick Oborne, who went on the first Bose tour, is the best of the Obornes in cricketing terms, and was sorely missed on this expedition. Peter is more of a chancer with the bat, and also with his spread betting. He acted as the tour bookie and took a pasting from several of the more successful members. Ten hours after the time we arrived, we were out in the middle practising, and afterwards we were invited to a reception at the nearby Oberoi Hotel, a five star establishment. It was a balmy evening with little humidity and we decided to walk up the Emerald strip, the posh road alongside the bay. The local authorities were rather reluctant to provide many street lights outside and another problem was trying to avoid treading on to the hundreds of people who were sleeping on the pavements. Half of them appeared to have had an arm cut off, and as they heard foreign voices, they would suddenly jump up and rush up to the hapless tourists shoving out their stumps in our faces and asking for cash.

I was stepping to my right to miss another one when I walked straight into a low sited traffic sign and cut my forehead. The resident doctor at the Oberoi Towers insisted I should go to hospital, but seeing so many injured people around I felt guilty about wasting the nation's medical resources.

"You need stitches," he said, and bundled me into one of those tiny low-roof Ambassador taxis which seem to proliferate in India. As I tried to get in, my head hit the roof, knocking off the wad of gauze and its piece of sticking plaster, causing another outflow of blood. I stuck a hankie on it, but found myself being pestered by one of the armless brigade, jabbering away and holding out his hand for money. I pointed to my head and proffered my hand towards him, intimating that a rupee or two might come useful for my taxi ride. The man scowled and withdrew and another beggar was only thwarted when the driver sped off. At the aptly named Breach Candy Hospital – an English architect built it in 1958 – I seemed to be the only patient. The doctor, Dr Minstry, was a cricket lover and we had a convivial half an hour talking about cricketers and their exploits after he stitched my wound. As I tried to leave, he said, "I shall be in London next year and can I stay with you?" I gave him my address and numbers, but I never heard from him. Next day the local newspapers carried stories about the incident and I loved the report in the *Afternoon Despatch* and *Courier*:

> Bombay's badly-lit roads claimed its first victim among the visiting fourth rate Fleet Street Journalists' team. As the team members were walking leisurely to the Oberoi Towers for a party, Brian Scovell of the *Daily Mail* dashed his head against a road sign opposite the Air India building. Bleeding profusely from his bald pate, he managed to make it to the top floor of the hotel where he was attended by a house doctor and taken to the Breach Candy Hospital. But brave as he is, he turned up for the next day for the match.

Turn up sir? I actually played against the Bombay CC XI at the Brabourne Stadium and helped to put on 42 for the first wicket with Bruce Pavey, a batsman of similar ilk, namely good at blocking but short of strokes. The temperature was in the top 30s with 60 per cent humidity, and it wasn't easy having a plaster on top of your head under a sweat-soaked cap. We blamed our defeat of 186 runs on not having enough time to acclimatise. Two days later we switched to the Wankhede and lost by eight wickets against a Bombay U19 side. Twenty-four hours later on the same pitch we impressed the owner and builder Sheshrao Wankhede and the VIPs by beating the Bombay Bank of Commerce with Gavin, then aged 17, scoring a match-winning 57.

By this time it was like playing in a Test match with no rest day. Three games in as many days, but after being rested for the previous one – probably the reason why we won – I opened and managed to edge my way to 80 out of a total of 181 on the Bombay P. J. Hindu Gymkhana ground, which staged the inaugural Test against Douglas Jardine's England side in 1933. There was a high wall on one side of the ground opposite the sea, and hundreds of people were sitting on it waving to us, saluting every run. Most of them were beggars and when Gavin raced 20 yards and dived to hold a fantastic catch they rose to their feet to cheer and clap. Gavin got up, turned to them and raised his pink Fleet Street Xl cap in acknowledgement. There was no chance of a collection for him: the audience would want payment for themselves. Some of them must have been surprised to learn that our 51-year-old opener managed to bat for two and a half hours in these taxing conditions, and without reaching a century, and the *Daily Telegraph*'s Nigel Dudley, of the same vintage, bowled 13 overs in succession to capture 3-27. After expending all that sweat we still lost to the Bombay journalists by four wickets. Wynford Hicks, our travelling photographer, deserved a mention having scored an unbeaten 20 and taking 3-15, but in the scorebook he appeared as Windord Hicker.

Next day we embarked on a 17-hour journey to Hyderabad, and I remember I didn't pee for all that time. I must have been dehydrated like a dry prune. A 19-year-old student volunteered to act as my baggage wallah when we stayed at the BCCI, and I accepted his offer. But when we moved on to the next place, he was still there, travelling with us in the same coach.

"I can't put you up in our hotel," I said to him.

"No Sir, I'll sleep in the coach with the drivers." So for a menial sum, he stayed with me throughout much of the tour. Later he said, "Is it possible to take your place in the side, Sir?" I had to decline for obvious reasons. But he was a good net bowler.

The Hon. Dominic Lawson, the son of Nigel Lawson, the Chancellor of the Exchequer, and brother of the famed cook Nigella, was in our party, and he was a bona fide journalist who rose to become the editor of the *Sunday Telegraph* and various other publications including *The Spectator*, which he edited for several years with distinction. In 1990 he interviewed Nicholas Ridley, a cantankerous Cabinet member about Europe, and when his article was published in *The Spectator*, it caused a major row and Ridley had to resign. The story hinted that Prime Minister Margaret Thatcher shared Ridley's anti-German views. Several MPs called for Lawson to be sacked, but the owner, Conrad Black, backed him.

The match against Hyderabad and Secunderabad was a 40-overs encounter and Mihir was over ruled: he always wanted a declaration game. Dominic learned his cricket at Westminster School and though he was reasonably quick as an opening bowler, his slingy action counted against accuracy. He had to come off after his first expensive spell, and when drinks were called he came over to see his wife Jane, who was an actress, sitting in front of the recently painted pavilion and asked how things were going with her.

"Fine," she said as she continued to read her book.

As the game restarted, the home side swept past 200 and were heading for 300 when Mihir brought Dominic back to bowl. Suddenly he took two wickets in two balls and celebrated like an over-excited schoolboy. Neither delivery was particularly accurate. Both batsmen got themselves out without much help from the bowler. A hat trick was looming. Would it be his first ever? He couldn't remember one. He wanted the field brought in, but Mihir said no. The next ball whizzed harmlessly past the wicket. Soon afterwards, Dominic repeated his astonishing feat – two more wickets in two deliveries, both from two full tosses with fielders holding catches on the boundary. More intense celebrations, with his colleagues mobbing him. Once more the chance of a hat trick evaporated, but Dominic took another wicket to end the innings and came in looking like a proud peacock. His figures were 5-61 off eight overs. He veered away from the rest of the team as they came off and went up to Jane and said, "Did you get a picture of my wickets?"

She looked up and said, "What wickets?"

"You didn't take any pictures then?" he asked.

"No, I'm afraid not, I've been sleeping," said Jane. The pair married two years earlier and that incident may well have proved to Dominic that his spouse had no interest whatsoever in watching cricket, and not long after they were divorced. He went on to marry the Hon. Rosamond Mary Monckton, daughter of the 2nd Viscount Monckton of Brenchley. Dominic's heroics in taking five wickets were in vain. The home side made 301 to our 88, hardly a close call.

The Hotel Karan in Hyderabad was an interesting place. It had four stars and they charged £12 a double room, and most of us had our hair cut for the equivalent of 35 pence. Mihir took a liking to the hard stuff on the second night, and was in a rocky state when he eventually retired. In the following match against Hyderabad Blues, which contained a much younger side including a 12 year old, we came much closer, losing with their 156 runs to our 103 on a matting pitch, sharpened by occasional rain. Mihir was probably upset by the fact that the train we were booked on to travel to Bangalore had failed to materialise, and we faced a 14-hour coach ride on his birthday. We were rushed straight into action against the U19s and lost by 70 runs, almost a moral victory.

Two teenagers played, one on each side. Gavin took 2-61 with his legspin and 17-year-old Anil Kumble bowled a few accurate legspinners for the home team. Like Gavin, Kumble was tall and slim and I can't remember if he took any wickets. But between 1990 and 2008 he took 619 Test wickets, making him the third highest wicket taker in the history of the game, and 337 ODIs wickets, also a record. I remember he bowled at the wicket almost every ball, which was why he gained another record, for lbw decisions. Just over a quarter of his wickets fell to lbws. These days too many England bowlers deliver the ball wide of the off stump. Forget about flying down the corridor of uncertainty, go for the stumps! With the introduction of the Decision Review System, slow bowlers are now taking lots of wickets and doubtless Kumble would have loved to extend his career had he stayed fully fit.

We needed a break and most of us went off to play golf in the best golf course around. We soon found that the many caddies were cheating. Someone hit a 250-yard drive down the fairway and when he arrived to look for the ball, his caddy said, "The ball has disappeared, master." There was no rough, no bunkers, only flat, very dry ground.

"Must be there," the golfer said.

"The crows have stolen it," said the caddy. This went on almost every hole and the caddies must have had a large stock of balls secreted on their person because no-one saw a crow picking up a golf ball.

In the final match in Bangalore we were bowled out by the U19s for 107, and I tried to put up some resistance, scoring 26 in 24 overs at Jonathan Trott speed. After a while when I was giving plenty of practice to my forward defensive shot, the teenaged wicketkeeper said to me, "Wonderful shot sir. Your straight bat is an example for all our younger players to follow."

I wondered whether he was trying to be sarcastic. But he wasn't, the Indians are like that: they love cricket, proper cricket. I wrote several articles in Indian newspapers saying that one day cricket could eventually kill off declaration cricket, and with the Indian Premier League drawing big crowds, my words were proving to be right. Test matches attendances are dropping alarmingly.

The last leg of the tour was a 350-mile coach trip to Goa, which lasted 14 hours on potholed roads filled with loads of pre-historic vehicles, battered lorries which rarely gave way to our coach, a few modern cars and loads of rickshaws and tuk-tuks, accompanied by lots of cows, dogs and monkeys. How we survived was almost miraculous. On the day of the match the temperature had risen to 42 °C, and we were up against a team that had just won a national competition. We were slaughtered by dehydration, and by seven wickets.

There was two treats left. Our coach took us to a prime beach 20 miles outside, and it was a relief to dive in for a relaxing swim. There were no huts or any protection from the sun, and it is dangerous to sunbathe too long. There were a number of European tourists sunbathing, including some young girls wearing bikinis. We noticed lots of heads popping up behind the sandy dunes behind us, moving up and down, and I asked one of the locals what was going on. He was a student and he said, "They are old men looking through their binoculars spying on the girls. Now and again they ride their bikes to a better vantage."

"This would be an offence in England!" I told him. "We call them Peeping Toms."

After dinner, most of us went out to use binoculars to see the stars in the magnificent, clear sky. Our final day was spent back at Bombay, watching India beating the Pakistanis at the Brabourne in an ODI in front of a frenzied crowd of 33,000. We had VIP treatment and had a chat with Imran Khan, whom I had met on several occasions over the years.

"We needed you to play for us," I said, "we were short of all rounders."

He smiled. "No chance, I don't qualify!" he said.

He was staying with the rest of the Pakistan team and I was hoping to renew my acquaintanceship with the flamboyant Mohsin Khan, who scored that memorable double century at Lord's in 1982. Mohsin coached the Pakistan side which knocked England off the top of the ICC unofficial Test League in the Emirates in 2012, and earlier starred in Bollywood films, and was married and later divorced to Reena Roy, a film star. Imran had left him out and Mohsin told a newspaper, "I have come to the firm conclusion that my exclusion is because of planned, filthy politics."

Our eight defeats and only one victory must have helped the morale of young Indian cricketers, or maybe not. The 22 Fleet Street players and their WAGs paid just £750 for their three-week extravaganza of a tour.

"They put their future Test players against us," said Mihir, "because the last time a team of journalists brought some county players." It must have been another tour, not his.

The 1999 Bose tour brought fresh talent – Michael Cockerell, the political TV interviewer who specialises in getting his subject to tell all, Ian Walker, assistant editor of the *Daily Express*, a keeper who spends most of his time on the ground, Peter Foster of the *Telegraph*, William Sitwell, features editor of IPC Magazines, Alan Simpson, the MP who upset Tony Blair, and David Brook and Oliver Bond of Channel 4. We went to Calcutta, Chandigarh, Delhi, Jaipur, Udaipur and Mumbai, and I missed the last two venues because the *Daily Mail* required my services back at home.

Once again we were partly sponsored by the Ministry of External Affairs, but their financial support failed to cover my accident in the first match against the Calcutta Journalists. A feature of our matches was our spectacular dropped catches. I stuck out a hand at gully and the ball, which had a high seam, split the webbing between my thumb and forefinger and blood poured out at a fast rate.

"You'll have to go to hospital," said Mihir. "We'll call an Ambassador."

"Preferably the British Ambassador!" said a fielder.

I managed to stem the flood of blood by using a clean white handkerchief and came off the field. Tuk-tuks handle more than 90 per cent of taxi business in Calcutta, and I rejected scores of them before I found an Ambassador, one with an engine.

The ride was perilous, but I managed to get out without repeating my experience following the Breach Candy incident. The hospital looked like one from the Crimea War, and when I was shown into a treatment room it was like turning back time by 140-odd years. The attendant – not a trained doctor – asked me to sit on a table which was covered by a grubby looking sheet. There was no sign of medical equipment. The attendant, who spoke little English, said, "Two stitches, sir," and took a scrubby piece of cloth on which he poured a few drops of iodine. There was no sign of antiseptic protection and no injection to deaden the pain, and he pulled out a needle and started threading in a piece of gut. The stitching operation didn't really hurt, but anyone squeamish might have reacted differently. A few minutes later it was all over with the man sticking a plaster over the injury and smiling, saying, "Thank you, sir," as I gave him my change, 60 rupees, less than a pound at the current rate.

Back at the ground, I took my place in the field, and later batting proved a problem. Luckily I was dismissed before I did any further damage.

The next day was spent travelling in an overcrowded train from Calcutta to Delhi, another 25-hour-long endurance test. We were in the middle of the winter and there were more stops caused by fog. Eventually we staggered out of our compartment to go to our coach which transported us to the five star Imperial for another reception. After an early breakfast, we were back in the vehicle to take us to fog-shrouded Chandigarh, a city of 1 million inhabitants, which was created by a team of international architects with the most prominent being the Swiss Le Corbusier in the late-1950s. It is now called Mohali. Close to the Himalayas, there is no other city like it in India, with its roads beautifully laid out in circles. Inderjit Singh Bindra, the President of the Punjab Cricket Association, took some of our senior veterans around town, and we were still punch drunk with all the assorted travel and never ending official receptions. He was rightly very proud of the modern cricket ground, and his face lit up when we said that the dressing rooms were the best we had seen.

I was back in charge as captain and the skipper of the Punjab CA President's XI insisted on putting us in on a wet pitch with poor visibility. The opening bowlers both played for the state and they were almost unplayable. The fog thickened and half an hour into the game the captain wanted to call it off. I suggested we ought to put the floodlights on and he demurred.

"We only have a single fixture in this wonderful ground and it's tough that we have experienced such a short time at the wicket." I said.

"Someone might get hurt," he replied. We had to agree and the match was abandoned. My unbeaten 8, both fours off the edge, had to be counted as one of my oddest and most hazardous innings. The Punjab coach came up to me and said, "Congratulations, sir, for sticking out there in those conditions."

Next day we were back at Delhi for a night before catching another "express" train to Jaipur, where the temperature was hardly above freezing. Fortunately we were wearing thick cable-stitch cricket sweaters and windcheaters. Our opponents were mainly elderly cricketers and we managed to win taking my tally as captain to three winning matches and no defeats. It was a good time to declare on my touring activities as leader in the subcontinent, and I took the flight back to Delhi, and on to Heathrow, with Nick and Katherine Wood, *The Times* political man who became a PR for the Conservative party, and Nick and Catherine Hewer.

People often say, "What was the best tour you ever made?" You can't beat India, especially if you manage to avoid severe stomach disturbances. I was one of the lucky ones ... except for the blood I shed on behalf of Mihir Bose.

17

JFK Sought Relief From Young Ladies, Not Dangerous Games of Cricket

For someone who supposed to have had a sound defensive technique at the crease, I've recorded some majestic ducks in some historic places. This one took place across the River Potomac in Washington, just across from the Arlington National Cemetery. You could just see the Eternal Light which commemorates the burial place of President John Fitzgerald Kennedy, his wife Jacqueline and their two children. It was one of Mihir Bose's last tours, to the USA, where he transported his media-cum-celebrity squad with great efficiency to San Francisco, Santa Barbara, Los Angeles (where they beat the Hollywood Oldies Xl), Philadelphia, Washington and New York in the fall of 1996. I was unable to go on the first half of the tour in California and later travelled with the BBC's Chief Economics correspondent Hugh Pym to Philadelphia on the East coast leg. Hugh is a quickish bowler of six feet three inches, with a Bob Willis build without his speed or menace. He's a very equable man. There was barely time to dump our gear at a Holiday Inn – one of dozens in the area – before we travelled from Philadelphia to Washington in a packed coach full of boozy, smoke-enveloped cricket fanatics. We were very tired when we arrived at our hotel, the Washington Quality Hotel (not quite up to 4 star ratings) after midnight, coughing and spluttering.

There was an early call for our players and when we arrived at the "ground" there were no proper changing facilities. The opponents were the staff of the British Embassy and they apologised, as diplomats have to do. "But the view is stunning," one said. "It's the second biggest cemetery in the US with 624 acres and more than 400,000 graves starting from the time of the American Civil War right up to now, with up to 30 new ones every day."

It was difficult to see the supposed square in the middle of a large patch of grass, and we noticed that some of their players were carrying a very long rolled up coconut mat out to the middle of nowhere. They put it down carefully, unrolled it, and started banging metal tent pegs into the ground to hold the mat firmly down. Two of the players were of subcontinent origin, either Indian or Pakistani, and they turned out to be very useful bowlers. It was a late start and no-one was keen to open the innings, for obvious reasons ... self protection.

My first ball lifted over my head and the second squatted along the ground. None of us brought along a helmet and I glanced across the river to the beautifully treated white gravestones. I remembered what Sarfraz Nawaz said to Merv Hughes when he shouted at the hirsute Australian terror bowler, "We've saved a grave for you!" He was referring to a cemetery not far from the county ground at Northampton when they played against each other. If I was crusted, perhaps even killed, at least I would be in good company if I was buried across the road at Arlington. The third ball I received lifted disconcertingly and thankfully I managed to edge a simple catch to the keeper and departed with some relief. The rest of the match was rather a blur, except that no-one was injured.

The publication of Mimi Alford's book *Once Upon a Secret – My Affair with John F. Kennedy and Its Aftermath* in early 2012 might have cut the number of tourists visiting Arlington. Many years ago Judith Exner, one of Kennedy's many mistresses, which include Marilyn Monroe, first exposed the President's partiality for serial adultery, and almost 50 years later, Ms Alford, a former intern at the White House who retains her slim figure and looks at the age of 69, finally confirmed the damning, lewd evidence. She came from a privileged background in New Jersey and attended Jackie Kennedy's alma mater in Massachusetts, and she wrote to her asking if she could go round the White House. With indecent haste, she was invited to meet the President and was signed up as an assistant in the press office. Four days later, the President took her virginity in Jackie's bedroom, while the First Lady was on a trip. The Cuban Missile Crisis was taking the world to the brink at the time and one of Kennedy's advisors explained, "He needs relief." David Lloyd George, the Prime Minister in the First World War, had similar needs, but he didn't have a coterie of sex workers, unlike JFK.

Most cricket aficionados know that the first Test match played at Lord's took place in 1884, but our tourists probably didn't know that a team from Philadelphia toured England that same year, winning eight matches, drawing five and losing five. One of their players, J. B. Thayer, went down with the *Titanic* in 1912. There were several tours from England to Philadelphia around that time and one included The Great Cricketer,

W. G. Grace. WG always started the same speech at the many lunches and dinners he attended, saying, "I have never seen a finer group of young athletes than yours." A good way to win friends!

We were surprised to learn that cricket emerged in America as the Civil War was ending, as though fair play and sportsmanship needed to be injected into the US psyche. For a while the sport flourished, especially in Philadelphia, but it was soon overtaken by baseball, and these days most of the current players are ex-pats from other countries, including England and most of the countries of the Commonwealth. Most of the matches in Philadelphia took place at Haverford College, which was founded in 1833. The college was one of the first to introduce an Honor Code in 1896 to govern academic affairs, and in the 1970s it was extended to showing respect to each other. In disputes, the students were encouraged to admit mistakes and be honest. The ICC could follow that lead in world cricket. They could ask batsmen to admit whether they had nicked the ball, or that fielders had actually caught the ball fairly, or otherwise. No chance of that happening, of course.

My first game at the college ground was against the Prior CC, which appeared to be full of Indians and Pakistanis. They'd forget to cut the grass in the outfield and it was like walking over Twickenham's rugby ground out of season. One player, a former Pakistan regional player, soon showed us the way to score quickly – he hit almost every ball in the air as far as possible.

Peter Oborne, our distinguished political columnist, had an arm in a sling, and he said, "Dislocated my shoulder out in LA. It's probably broken." He was dressed in his whites and insisted on taking part. The burly Pakistani kept hitting sixes but fell just short of a century, and the man who caught him on the boundary was Peter. As the ball came down from a great height, we wondered how he could catch it while one arm was entrapped in a sling. But he caught it in one hand above his head and held it up in triumph. Unfortunately for him and his Facebook friends, there were no videos or TV cameras to record the event.

We managed to take the remaining wickets in the 85 °F heat, as the home side, mainly employing baseball-style swipes, subsided to 192 in 40 overs. Unless we had a born-again Botham or a Colin Milburn in our ranks, our chances of winning were remote. Every time I tried to drive the ball it would come to an abrupt halt. Wickets tumbled, and though it was an overs match, I thought someone ought to stay there and do a David Steele. Having removed his sling to go to the wicket, Oborne tried unsuccessfully to find the boundaries and soon departed, rather grumpily, back to the pavilion. Eventually we came in as losers on 137-8 with most of our players moaning about my scoring rate. I suppose an unbeaten 28 in 40 overs was rather sluggish, but I was somewhat concerned that no-one on our side clapped. At least we put up a fight.

There were a number of pictures and memorabilia around the two-floor pavilion, which was built in the early 1880s, and one of their officials said, "This building is historic. The first international cricket match, England *v*. the US, took place here, and it's a graded building." After the speeches and the presentations, I noticed that two young children were ripping up boards upstairs and throwing them down a gap to the floor below. They turned out to be related to one of our players. We had to tell them to desist. They thought it was a fun game, throwing the caber down the hole, an old Scottish escapade. Later the boards were put back in their proper place by stewards.

I was relieved to know that I hadn't been dropped for next day's match on the same ground, but Oborne, who was skippering the side, demoted me to six in the order. Determined to hit out, I scored 7 in ten balls, a strike rate of 70. Not bad. If I had scored that rate the day before I might have neared my century. Again, we lost.

The train journey to New York on the next day turned out to be a highly entertaining occasion. Mihir wanted all his squad in a single section of the train, but sitting up the far end was a smartly dressed, elderly man reading the *New York Times*.

Someone said to Mihir, "How do we get to the ground?" and he named the area.

"Excuse me sir," said the man, "that's not strictly true. I can tell you where it is."

He was about to explain when Mihir said, "This is a private discussion. Please do not interrupt."

The man was slightly bemused by this and said, "Okay, never mind."

Some time later, when the meeting broke up and most of the others were looking for refreshments further up the train, I went to speak to the man. I discovered he was a four star US general on his way to a military conference and he had served throughout the Vietnam War. We had a good laugh.

As we took leave of Grand Central Station, the world's largest railway station with 44 platforms, soon to be 48, we had to take our coffins and other gear ourselves, or else pay exorbitant tips to porters. How we longed to see a few Indian porters! The coach took us to a litter-strewn field in Brooklyn with minimal facilities, no hot water, no kettle, and no cucumber sandwiches or chocolate cake. Our opponents were a Pakistan Select Xl, and once again we were rolled over very comprehensively.

Our final match was at Staten Island where we travelled on the famous ferry for a modest 50 cents. It is one of the world's greatest bargains. A year later the charges were dropped and the 5-mile-each-way trip is courtesy of the City of New York.

We faced representatives of another country, Trinidad, and their players were even better than the Pakistanis. The pitch consisted of green astroturf on concrete. Heads dropped ... not another fearsome surface with life and limb threatened.

The Trinnies began with an extremely fast bowler charging down the hill, and I was hardly started when I collapsed on the astroturf with a torn thigh muscle, going for a third run. Having blocked, or missed, a number of deliveries, I was overcome with joy when a thigh-high full toss arrived at great pace just outside the off stump, and I managed to divert the ball up the hill with the outside edge of the bat. On a normal ground it would have raced over the boundary, but the grass was only marginally shorter than the Haverford grass. The nearest fielder retrieved the ball and threw more than 70 yards towards the far wicket. I had to strain for extra speed to beat his throw, and I heard this snapping noise as I fell headlong. The ball was about to reach the hands of the waiting fielder as I stumbled back on one leg and succeeded in diving with an outstretched bat, just avoiding being run out. I got up and brushed myself down and realised it was too painful too continue.

The home side included a doctor and he inspected the injury and said, "That's a six-week job. As you can see, it's left a big hole. These athletes do this all the time. Once you tear the muscle, there's not much you can do about it except rest." He was right: I still have an indentation on that part of my leg. That ended my career in American cricket, 4 not out.

"But we won most of our matches in California," said Mihir. "We didn't have enough time to acclimatize to these odd pitches in the East." Perhaps we should have brought along the General. He would have sorted things out.

After the tour, when we were back in Britain travelling in trains appreciably faster than ones in India, I took a Woodies "team" to the former Midland Bank ground in Beckenham on 11 September 1994 to play against a Bose XI. In the millions of cricket games played at all levels all around the world, this must have been one of the oddest. Four of us turned up, Alan Wood, Larry Robeson, Gavin and me, but six others were travelling in a minivan and hadn't arrived. These were early days for mobile phones and we had no contact with them. Bose insisted on tossing up, and I won the toss and said, "As we have only four players, we'll have to bat first." He agreed. I said, "Can we wait until they arrive?"

"We could be waiting all day," he said. "Let's start."

So we did. If two wickets fell, the game would soon be over depending on how many runs we scored, but he refused to budge. I went in with

Alan, and Gavin and Larry went out to the middle to umpire in their pads. Larry did the scoring as well. They may well have been the first umpires to stand in pads, thigh pads and boxes, leaning against their cricket bats.

The Bose Xl had nine men and I wasn't in a position to lend them substitutes. Richard Morrow, a former Woodie from Australia – a fine bowler of swing – had absconded to the Bose team, and we had to be careful about taking chances against his bowling. In the fourth over I was caught by wicketkeeper Bruce Pavey off the bowling of Mark Edwards (another Woodie, now our treasurer), and Gavin took my place at the wicket to partner Alan Wood, while I went to square leg to umpire still wearing my pads and gloves. I had my fingers firmly crossed that no more wickets would fall. Two more and the innings would be over.

But a miracle happened. Nigel Dudley, the hero of Madras, Mumbai and Goa, bowled stoutly, and so did Peter Oborne, and another player named Castle came on later and bowled reasonably straight. None of them troubled our stars. Boundaries piled up and they added 182 for the second wicket when Alan was out for 56. The absent six showed up half an hour late and they took turns to umpire and undertake the scoring, but none of them wanted to field for the opposition, who still only had nine men. Gavin retired on 116 to give someone else a go, and I declared on 199-3. The Bose Xl were dismissed, rather unmercifully, for 65, handing us a triumphant victory of 134 runs. Oborne used to conduct the betting on the Indian tours, with setting the odds, collecting the money and paying out to the winners. We should have asked him a price on a Woodies win with just over a third of a team. Long odds one suspects. We could have cleaned up.

18

Why Don Bradman Never Played
a Game at Rottnest Island

Having been born and bred in the Isle of Wight, the Caulkheads, the name for the indigenous population, are proud to say, "I come from THE Island." Caulk is an old sailing term meaning "stop up seams in ships with oakum and melted pitch". Queen Victoria, who spent much of her life there, always referred to the Isle of Wight as the Island, which gave the regal stamp. I started playing and watching cricket at Ventnor, which has finally produced an England cricketer in Danny Briggs, the 21-year-old Hampshire slow left-arm bowler, and of all the many islands I have visited and played cricket in, up to now 35 in number, the most novel was Rottnest Island, 11 miles off Fremantle in Western Australia.

The Rottnest Island Authority bans cars, doesn't allow private ownership, and there was no supply of fresh water when St Dunstan's School, Catford, paid a three-day stop there in 1988 to take part in the last official event in the Australian Bicentennial Celebrations. The small island is only 7.3 square miles, with a population of a mere 300, against the 148 square miles of the Isle of Wight, which has a population of 140,000. Currently around 250,000 visitors go there every year, and there are 2,850 units of accommodation. There are 63 sheltered beaches, and it is famous for its snorkelling, diving, surfing and swimming. One thing that they don't mention in their publicity is the flies. There are no estimates of the number of flies, but having been outside in the glaring heat – the temperature rose to 38 °C most of the short time I was there – I think Rottnest may have more flies per square foot than any part of the world. Insect repellent was an absolute necessity, and even if your face was coated with it, you were still bombarded by them. The locals wore the traditional

Western Australian broad-brimmed hat, which has up to 20 bottle corks attached by string. The idea is that when you are under attack, shake your head vigorously and the corks take retaliatory action, smacking the flies to all parts. Or that's what's supposed to happen. But the best way to avoid the flies is to swim under the water.

The Australian Test grounds don't have the same problem as Rottnest, but in the Bodyline series in 1932-33, a barracker shouted from the mainstand in Adelaide, "Don't swat those flies Jardine! They're the only friends you've got in Australia!" Rottnest is also known as the home of the quokka, a small kangaroo-like marsupial. They are a rare breed, and most of them frequent Rottnest. For some reason, the flies do not molest quokkas, only humans, particularly Pongos, the description Paul Hogan uses to call us poms.

The Rottnest Cricket Club has unusual (modified) rules – 30 overs per side, each player can bowl a maximum of three overs, leg before wicket no longer applies, each batsman has the first ball free (this must be a legitimate delivery), the batsmen have to retire at the end of the over in which he makes 30, and any ball over the shoulder is a no ball. Kevin Pietersen would have supported the idea about abolishing the leg before law. He said once, "I'm getting out lbw because of the Decision Review System and a few years ago the umpires wouldn't given me out. I've had to change my technique." He was still getting out lbw to spinners.

Ian Murray, the club's archivist, said, "Our hallowed ground, one of the very few naturally level areas of the island, was first used in the Bradman days, and it was unfortunate that it was the western extremity of the airstrip and it soon became apparent that flying and cricket was somewhat incompatible. Planes would be forced to circle the field to avoid landing at a delicate stage of a game. Pilots with an appreciation of the game would wait between overs before landing, but non-cricketing pilots chose to land without consideration, scattering players in all directions and requiring the removal of the stumps to enable them to land with a minimum discomfort to paying passengers. Fortunately no cricketers were lost in this dangerous practice, but eventually the club moved to another area leaving the airport to its proper use."

In their publicity, RICC describe the ground as, "not the best playing surface". Very true as we discovered. The outfield was sand based and grass and plants were scarce, but the artificial pitch – with hardly any bounce but true – ensures that no-one is likely to be carted off to hospital. As there is no hospital, the problem doesn't arise. The nearby corrugated roofed building used for overnight stops had bunk beds but very few toilets.

Coming from well-heeled families in the Borough of Bromley, the St Dunstan's boys found that the conditions woefully short of facilities, but they were well stocked with beer for a New Year's party. They were billeted to the Kingstown Barracks, used in both world wars, and they had to carry their own gear for a considerable distance. For more than a century, several hundred Aboriginal criminals were housed in other buildings, and many of them died, mainly through influenza.

Colin Matten, the very able master in charge, asked the boys to submit write-ups each day for an end of tour booklet. One of them read:

We were all looking forward to the Rottnest trip. We had heard that it was a holiday haven and we weren't disappointed. The journey itself, on a high speed twin-hulled craft, was an experience in itself. It coasted up the Swan River where we were able to get some splendid views of the beautiful Perth skyline. Once beyond Fremantle Docks, it picked up speed and sped across the sea and 20 minutes later we were there. It was a glorious day. In fact we were not to see a single cloud during our week's stay in Western Australia. Our first stop after disembarking was to visit the Bike Hire Shop. Bicycles are the only means of travel and the Cricket Club arranged for us to have one each. That was 32 bikes!

We then cycled to the Old Barracks, which has now been converted into an environment study centre. Ours was considered to be an educational tour and we qualified to set up home there for three days. It was very Spartan but very reasonable. The boys didn't complain. In fact, what comforts they were supplied with most tended to ignore, for example, sheets and pillow slips. Apparently only Matt Dowse had ever made his own bed at home. Having found that tucking sheets into mattresses was an impossible task and most gave up! In the evening we were the guests of the Cricket Club at the Rottnest Lodge Hotel. On this, the last night of the year, we were all determined to enjoy ourselves. We barbequed, imbibed and joked the night away. We won our first contest against RICC which was a Boat Race. Certainly we all got drenched! There was a very good band playing live in the forecourt, and the squad were to be seen dancing with the Sheilas as the bewitching hour approached. The clock struck midnight, 1989 was greeted in, here we were, 12,000 miles away from home under a starlit sky with the temperature in the 80s, and perspiration pouring off, bonhomie ... and all that!

A "Boat Race" is a drinking game with the contestants having to consume his drink without stopping. The Rottnest players, mostly tubby and jolly and with a big thirst, were well beaten by Matten's teenagers. By the end of a memorable night the boys collapsed in their bunks and few were able to be fit to play cricket. The report went on:

1st January 1989 – Thankfully, being a fun match, we were not obliged to play our strongest XI. The team included Brian Scovell (Gavin's Dad who won the Man of the Match Award scoring 31 in 23 overs), Eric Davies (Henry's Dad who did not get the bowling prize), Chris Tooley (we needed his batting and did not get it), Graham Alderman (less said the better), Tour Manager (Colin Matten – brilliant performance, top score, unbeaten on 36). A few regulars did play and the resulting rabble was skippered by James Allen, in his first match of the tour because of a broken wrist.

In the evening we didn't do very well! We lost by six wickets – 134 in 30 overs to 136-4. It would be difficult to describe the game more fully. Only photographs do it justice, but there was just one feature that perhaps communicates the spirit of the game. As the bowler ran up to bowl he would often stop and start to applaud in the direction of the boundary. This seemed to be a general direction for the rest of the fielders to take up the applause and then the umpires would join in followed by the spectators and eventually the batsmen were encouraged to clap their hands too. All this was in appreciation of a pretty girl who just happened to pass by on the way to the beach. She would be applauded until she scampered, red faced, over the sand dunes! This, apparently, was all in accordance with local rules and was termed 'players' comfort.

The evening brought another Boat Race and SDC kept their 100 per cent record. After the match we all gathered in front of the pavilion for the presentations. As if by appointment, RICC's President arrived in a dirty pair of shorts, a pair of old trainers, a stained T-shirt with the Club tie slung around his bronzed neck, sitting astride a beat-up old tractor which had conveyed him across the island. He was heartily cheered. Obviously a popular figure. Following the President came the West Australian Minister for Sport – no less! He had no legs, but came hurtling around the corner on his wheelchair until it got bogged down in the sandy topsoil which was now turned into choking dust! James Allen made a nice little speech of thanks and presented various mementoes to the opposing skipper and the Minister of Sport. The Tour Manager said his piece and presented the President of RICC with our tour tie which was promptly tied on to the tractor. All this was huge fun and the group was duly photographed to produce probably the most memorable snap of the tour.

John Inverarity, the former Test player, former coach of Warwickshire and Kent and now Chairman of Selectors of Cricket Australia, attended the final event at a reception at the Prindiville Stand at the WACA ground.

Along with Test stars Rodney Marsh and Ian Brayshaw, he passed on some good tips to the boys. "Invers" was Headmaster of Hale School in Perth between 1989 and 2003, and is a great guy. I first met him when he toured England in 1968, and he played his sixth and final Test at the Oval in 1972. He is a Mike Brearley-type leader and has transformed the Australian side by introducing younger, fitter players.

After leading Western Australia to four Sheffield Shield triumphs in five years, Invers went on to win the Shield again for South Australia in 1981-82. He made history that season when he was bowled for a duck by Greg Chappell and started to leave the crease when umpire Col Egar called him back. Egar explained that the ball deviated after hitting a sparrow which died on the spot. Egar was the scourge of the chuckers in Australia, no-balling eight bowlers for throwing. With the wholehearted support of Sir Don Bradman, he ended the career of Ian Meckiff, and soon after the game's rulers barred bowlers with suspect actions.

When the SDC party first arrived in Perth there were problems about billeting boys with hosts, and some of them had to stay at the Christchurch School pavilion. John Dall had some indifferent stays earlier in the tour, and was upset with the prospect of staying in a cricket pavilion, so Colin Matten arranged for him and another boy, Lee Tyler, to stay with Rodney Marsh, and they did. Two of Marsh's sons played for Christchurch Grammar School, and with SDC winning by eight wickets, neither of them were on the winning side. Nick Middleton, Jon Andrews, Chris Tooley and Henry Davies reluctantly accepted the idea of lodging in the pavilion when it was explained to them that it backed on to a nudists' beach. Their mood changed when they learned that there was also a six-lane motorway and an SAS firing range within hearing distance.

In any Australia *v.* England cricketing encounter sledging of some description occurs, but on this tour there was very little sign of it. Most of the ten schools St Dunstan's played against in Sydney, Canberra, Melbourne, Adelaide and Perth were fee-paying ones, and discipline was reasonably strict. Some of the SDC boys were fined for breaking the curfews Colin Matten and his coach Peter Clare-Hunt imposed, but none of them disgraced themselves. Former England and Surrey batsman Micky Stewart wrote an article in the tour brochure and advised the boys not to retaliate if they are sledged.

"They will come up to you and say things like 'where have you come from, intensive care?'" he said. "Don't respond."

Matten taught Religious Studies at SDC and he was the ideal man to speak about behaviour. He presided over the school's best cricketing period in 1987 when they won 11 successive matches. In the 1960s, he spent two years in Australia and played for two leading clubs in Melbourne. Peter

Clare-Hunt taught French and the main sports, and is a national cricket coach. He is a very respected man in his field.

There was one unusual happening against Prince Alfred College in Adelaide on Christmas Eve. After losing the first four matches and then winning the next one by just one run, SDC were determined to keep winning on the hottest day so far. They heard that the home side's opening batsman Greg Blewett, who went on to play in 46 Tests and 32 ODIs between 1995 and 2000, had just scored three centuries in succession, including a double hundred against Millfield, and they were desperately keen to get him out early. In the pre-match publicity, the boys were asked a number of questions for the tour brochure, including one about their nicknames, and Nick Middleton said he was "The Whinger", and David Gale, "Hurricane". They were the SDC's opening bowlers in this match and both had aggressive fields. When Blewett was on 7, Middleton bowled an outswinger and the fielders behind the wicket went up with a roar of howzats as the keeper threw the ball up in the air. The umpire signalled out. Blewett looked distinctly unhappy and hesitated before leaving the crease.

Apparently some boys clicked their fingers when the ball passed his bat and that made the noise which influenced the umpire to give him out. Cheats never prosper to use an old cliché, and in this case they didn't. Prince Alfred were reduced to 80-5 on a Test-class pitch, and Middleton and Gale both went off suffering from sunstroke and exhaustion. Threadgold, their number 7, had just created a school first team record of six successive ducks, but then scored 66, taking his side to 208-6 at the close of the innings. Dowse, nicknamed "Hammer" and Dall, who was known as "The Sulk", were both run out and with no-one scoring a half century – Gavin Scovell and skipper Julian "Fred" Platford just missed a jug on 45 and 42. Blewett's offspin bowling removed five batsmen and SDC collapsed to 162, losing by 44 runs. So justice was done.

Blewett scored a century on his Test debut against England on his home ground at the Adelaide Oval and followed with two more in his subsequent Ashes series, but was just short of being a top-class Test player. He kept failing to Mushtaq Ahmed and Anil Kumble, and was replaced by Matthew Hayden. When he first became an international cricketer he took 14 Test wickets and the same number of wickets in ODIs, bowling quicker at around 125 kph. He went on to play for four counties – Yorkshire in 1999, Nottnghamshire 2001, Kent 2003 and Surrey 2004, and was a popular addition to county cricket. He is now a cricket commentator.

Celebrating Christmas Down Under was certainly different. One of the boys wrote:

The whole squad seemed to have difficulty in accepting that the season of Yuletide had finally arrived, with the thermometer well into the 80s. We were helped by the driving rain on Christmas morning, a sight we were used to at home. We had a large (English) breakfast and Father Christmas (alias Dodo, alias Colin Matten) turned up and gave us our presents, followed by an extremely civilised Bucks Fizz party. The afternoon was spent on Brighton Beach playing cricket, football and rugby, and swimming in the Southern Ocean. We had a turkey dinner with the trimmings at the hotel and the fancy dress competition followed with some very good costumes. Everyone entered into the spirit of the occasion. Homesickness was prevalent and longing for colder climes, but Christmas was, like the rest of the tour, a new and overall thoroughly enjoyable experience.

SDC won the final three matches giving a 4-6 record, not bad against good opposition. Gavin, who was two years older than most of the others, was presented the Outstanding Player of the Tour by topping both batting and bowling averages. He scored 323 runs, average 35.9, and took 31 wickets at 10.2 in eight appearances with his legspin and googlies. The late John Iberson, one of the school's most loved teachers, was his hero. John bowled slow left-arm Chinamen and googlies and took a vast number of wickets for Beckenham and other clubs in Kent.

It took three years to do the groundwork to take 18 players and a party of supporters to Australia, and with the help of 150 Friends of the Tour, mainly parents, including a committee of up to 20, it went off superbly well. The appeal raised £20,000 – worth more than double these days – and I was in charge of producing the brochure. Roger Lacey of the *Mail on Sunday*, brother of *The Guardian*'s David Lacey, designed it and it brought in more than £4,000.

The biggest gamble was taken by the late Alice Newman, mother of opening batsman Peter Newman who was a National Fives champion. Her idea was to hire a Concorde, the supersonic airliner, to attract people who wanted to take a quick spin out to the Bay of Biscay and back. She was the London-based PA of Sulaiman Abdul Aziz Al Rajhi, the chairman of Al Rajhi Bank, one of the largest companies in Saudi Arabia and the largest Islamic bank in the world. In 2011 Forbes estimated his wealth as $7.7 billion, making him the 120th richest man in the world. He is now in his nineties and has 23 children. Alice's husband Bill said:

She booked a huge amount of work on his behalf with British Airways, all first-class seats, and she said to me it would be a good idea to organise a trip. She said Brian Trubshaw, the first pilot to fly a Concorde, had the idea to raise money for a good cause in his village Cherington, near Tetbury, Gloucestershire, and he organised a short flight and it was very successful and we could do the same. The members of St Dunstan's fund committee gasped when she told them that it would cost up to £28,000. They thought it was a big risk but eventually they agreed to go ahead. We were advised to charge £330 a head and arranged a reception afterwards. There were 100 seats available and the first few tickets sold quickly to parents at St Dunstan's, but we were stumped on 40. It was very nerve wracking time, but I stuck an ad in a newspaper and people began ringing me and we managed to sell out. BA wanted to give Alice a free ticket but we compromised because I wanted to go as well and there was only one ticket left. Alice sat in the cockpit on the ascent and we changed over and I sat there on the way back. We were probably the only married couple who sat in a Concorde cockpit in the air! BA laid on a wonderful lunch on the flight and with our reception as well, the customers left very happy. I still have a bottle of champagne at home.

It was a fantastic flight, very smooth, just like a BAC 111, except the Concorde was flying up to 1,350 mph rising to 60,000 feet and you could see the curvature of the world. The trip took about two hours, well worth the money. It was an experience of a lifetime.

In the committee's financial report it showed the venture costing £23,836.39, leaving a profit of £4,101. Alice received a huge number of congratulatory messages. She was a very demure, nice lady, with a wonderful smile. Only 20 Concordes were built and the British and French Governments lost huge sums before realising that the super slim aircraft was unprofitable, and the last flight took place on 26 November 2003. The first flew on 2 March 1969, from Filton airdrome in Bristol to RAF Fairford. BAC (now BAE Systems) made theirs in England and Sud-Aviation Aerospatiale (now EADS) in France. Concordes made an awful noise and today's noise laws wouldn't tolerate it. One crashed at Gonesse, France, in 2000 and all 100 passengers and three crew died, and that sealed their fate. Brian Trubshaw died eight months after the crash at the age of 77. He was the cricket captain of the first team at Westminster School, and in 1942 he signed up for the RAF while visiting Lord's cricket ground.

Profits for the SDC fund also came from selling Christmas trees, calendars and ties, and from social events. One event was a black tie dinner at the school. Some people thought it might lose money. However, it was financially successful except that a number of people went down with food poisoning afterwards! Fortunately the story didn't leak, otherwise it would have been a PR disaster.

I managed to commission an article written by Sir Don Bradman for the 24-page A4-size brochure, which he typed out himself on a battered old typewriter when he was almost 80. He had some worthy advice for the players. He told them to keep a diary and retain all newspaper cuttings about themselves in case they become famous. I've managed to do that which is why I have been able to write this book and also my memoir *Thank You Hermann Goering – The Life of a Sports Writer*. Other articles came from Micky Stewart, Chris Cowdrey, David Gower, Douglas Jardine, E. W. Swanton, who had St Dunstan's connections, Gary Lineker, who once played a cricket match at the school, Frank Tyson, John Woodcock, Ken Barrington, Arthur Morris and John Edrich, and short pieces from Denis Compton, Len Hutton, Tim Robinson, Tom Graveney, Bill Bowes, Gary Sobers, Mike Brearley, Bob Taylor, Keith Miller, Bob Willis, Malcolm Marshall, Brian Luckhurst, Peter Richardson and John Arlott.

Sir Don started his piece saying:

I learned with very great interest that St Dunstan's celebrated its Centenary in 1988, and among the functions being organised was a cricket tour of Australian schools by their senior team. It caused me to reflect on my own youth, the relative paucity of facilities at a tiny country school and to wonder whether the St Dunstan's boys fully appreciate the marvellous opportunity that is coming their way.

As I approach the octogenarian stage, I often wonder which are the best years of your life. In the sporting world I am sure it is the period when there is the maximum blend of youth and experience. By the age of 50 there may be experience to burn but no longer can the eyes pick up the spin on the ball, the muscles don't respond to the brain with that split second timing, and moreover those muscles have a horrible tendency to tear rather than to stretch. It is useless knowing what to do if you cannot get there on time. So perhaps, according to which sport one speaks of, the marriage of youth and experience generally reaches its zenith between 20 and 35, though I am well aware of those boys and girls of genius who reach world standard in their teens.

The purpose of the foregoing is mainly to impress on the boys the need to understand and build for the future. In retrospect, I am sure my life would have been greatly enriched had I been more aware of the need to embrace learning and knowledge as distinct from pure enjoyment. No boy should fail to keep a diary and meticulously record places, events and people in full detail. It should be written up every night, or perhaps, using the advantage of modern technology, recorded on tape. Just five minutes at the end of each day could in later years prove to be an invaluable asset. To keep newspaper articles or cuttings, always dated as to time and place, is another rewarding matter because nobody in his youth ever knows what sort of career might unfold in the future.

It was my good fortune to find myself, as a very young man, on friendly terms with community leaders. Cricket had made those contacts possible. Sports can so easily prove a catalyst for lifelong friendships. I would exhort the boys to seriously appreciate how desperately the world is always searching for leaders to take the place of those currently holding the torch. There will be room at the top for people of courage, wisdom and vision.

Wise words from the Greatest Batsman of all Time. Where are the leaders today? Incidentally, he never played at Rottnest – too many flies!

19

Forget the Isle of Wight, On to Serendipity

The Woodies have only made one tour, in 2001 to the Isle of Wight, and it was such a wipeout that we never tried another one. It was doomed from the start. My wife Audrey, who loved going on most of them, died on Christmas Day, four months previously, from cancer of the liver at the age of 58, and the day before we set off to Queen Victoria's favourite summer resort in the Isle of Wight, my best friend Bryon Butler, the former BBC football correspondent and author, died from the same disease at the age of 67. His first love was cricket, not football, and he was still playing occasionally as an offspinner for Merrow CC in his sixties, despite having regular doses of chemotherapy over several years. Bryon wrote more than 20 sporting books and one was the autobiography of Alec Stock, the much loved football manager. Alec's funeral took place on the same day, at Poole crematorium. Both were born in Somerset, and Alec, who was severely injured as a tank commander in the Second World War, had a favourite way of describing the state of football – "It's all about a little thing called pride." I spoke to him not long before he died and he said, "Pride seems to have disappeared. It's all about grabbing the last shilling."

I was born in St Lawrence, a village next to Ventnor, where a number of famous authors and poets lived or stayed, including Charles Dickens, John Keats, Lord Alfred Tennyson, Alfred Noyes, Algeron Swinburne and Karl Marx at the south tip of the IOW. Almost every time I make another visit I discover another famous author. The latest was Ivan Turgenev, the Russian writer who wrote *Fathers and Sons* and other masterpieces. Walking along Ventnor's promenade recently, I spotted his Blue Plaque hidden off the road on a wooden shack, commemorating his stay in 1860.

We had little trouble to arrange a two-match tour in April, one at the newish ground at Brading and the other at Ventnor where I first started playing cricket at the age of 11. St Lawrence is unique. It has a large acreage stretching along the coast and there have been significant landslips over the centuries, the most recent being in 1978 and 1994, when harder strata slips down towards the sea over Gault clay, locally known as "blue slipper". This gave rise to the name Undercliff, and it is one of the most beautiful, unspoilt parts in Britain, almost semi-tropical. A few years ago the main road collapsed: it needed £20 million to put it right and it is still in a bad state. One of the road signs says "Beware of Badgers!"

A German philanthropist named William Spindler fell in love with the place in the late-1880s and built an odd collection of large houses which were called "Spindler's Follies" before his premature death stopped him turning St Lawrence into a town. Today there are hardly any rows of houses or blocks of flats and the electoral roll comes to just 624 inhabitants, with few children.

Ventnor's cricket ground at Steephill was renowned for having one of the steepest slopes at the road end, and a countless number of visiting cricketers found themselves tumbling over as they tried to run down the hill, finishing flat on their faces having failed to hold a catch. Upper Ventnor, where my family moved to at the start of the Second World War, has similar slippage problems with 30-odd houses being demolished, including the next one we lived in, because of vents in the ground. The town, famous for its hills, winding narrow roads and hundreds of steps, was named Ventnor because of the intermittent openings in the ground. The Harry Potter films should have been filmed there. A telephone box opposite a third house we rented in a short space of time suddenly disappeared down a massive hole, and the next morning we wondered whether someone had been using it at the time.

Ventnor CC started around 1840 and Jack Hobbs played there once in 1931. An umpire named Walder gave him out lbw for 65 and the local newspaper reported that The Master had nicked the ball. The reporter wrote, "Mr Walder was subjected to a barrage of vicious barracking from some of the 1,600 spectators while Hobbs took the decision laughingly and like the true sportsman he was, he didn't refer to it." Twenty years later Wally Hammond played for Shanklin against Ventnor and a Mr Howell, an umpire from Ventnor, gave Hammond out lbw in similar controversial circumstances for 12. We are told that Wally wasn't as nice about it as Jack's "dismissal".

The club boasted having four Lords of the realm in their ranks – Lord Tennyson, captain of Hampshire and England, Lord Jellicoe, the Vice President who led the British Grand Fleet at the Battle of Jutland in

1918 and who in 1936 had a secret meeting, less than a mile away at St Lawrence, with Hermann Goering regarding a peace treaty, and the Lords Ebbisham and Maddon. I gather the appeasement talks broke down. As Jellicoe died not long after, hardly any details emerged.

Hugh de Selincourt, the writer and journalist, often stayed at St Lawrence and once wrote, "What matters is that games – win or lose – should be good games, well worthy of remembrance." His book *The Cricket Match* was published in 1925 and was described in the same complimentary manner as A. G. Macdonell's *England, their England*. Some years ago Ventnor qualified to play in the Hampshire League but was banned because of the excessive slope of their ground. Another philanthropist, a British one named Brian Gardener, spent £1.5 million on a new, sumptuous, flat ground at Newclose, just outside Newport, and Ventnor now play there regularly. The former ground is still used for the junior sides – the youngsters don't complain about tumbling down the hill.

The ill-fated Woodies mini tour wasn't worthy of remembrance. The weather forecasts were dire – rain, wind and an occasional glimpse of the sun – and we were warned that the Brading ground was flooded and only a sudden heatwave would enable the match to take place. No such heatwave occurred, and it was cancelled the night before. Nevertheless our multinational force turned up on time – a Kiwi named Brian Hitchcock who is a cricket TV producer, South African Calum Parkes, Pakistan all rounder and cricket journalist Qamar Ahmed, Australian swing bowler Simon "Sav" Hare from Perth, and eight Englishmen including our vice captain Alan Wood, a deputy head of a comprehensive school in Croydon and his three delightful children. After experiencing choppy waters on the Portsmouth to Fishbourne car ferry on the Friday we had our nerves soothed by welcoming drinks at a hotel in Shanklin, where the owner, Brian Porter, a cricketer himself, was well versed in keeping the bar open well past the usual closing time. Most of our players were wearing their Alaskan training outfits and we were relieved to have them with us.

With nothing to do except boring ourselves with stories of past matches, and drinking shandies, coffee and an odd whisky, we set about arranging a team dinner in the Old Village, one of the prettiest parts of Shanklin. Brian gave us some names of restaurants which would be open and some of us walked the half mile from the hotel to the restaurants and hotels, mainly thatched, and selected an Italian middle-range pizzeria called Pavarotti's.

We were making good progress about agreement on a group discount, when I told the manager, "We are a wandering cricket team from South London." His face stiffened.

"We had a rugby team the other day and their behaviour was shocking," he said.

"Cricketers are a different breed," I said. "Most of our party are top bankers and journalists." He didn't show much enthusiasm.

"Bankers throw their weight about and journalists make things up," he said. He accepted the booking with reluctance – for 16 – and we turned up in jackets, blazers, slacks and jeans but no ties. After we downed a few pints and glasses of cheap wine, POB said to a member of staff, "Any chance of our first course? We've been waiting for almost an hour."

Suddenly we were on a war footing. The manager rushed out to say, "If you expect good food, you'll have to wait for it. You're not at Knightsbridge or Kensington." When the food eventually arrived, some of our members were keen to leave immediately but managed to sit through the first two courses before departing. Not surprisingly, the business failed and the property was last used by a charity.

On the way back, as 11 p.m. struck, the town appeared to be subject to a war-time blackout. Only our hotel was lit up. A few hardy of our cricketers stayed up for a final round before trudging up the stairs to their rooms. Next morning Brian confirmed that the second fixture was off as well, and some of our athletes wanted to fix up net practice. There was no progress on that either and most of them caught an early ferry back to Portsmouth. Not a ball had been bowled, not even in a hotel corridor.

To play cricket for many years you need to be stoical. There is always someone who has had a bad day. A batsman can travel half the day to a match and be bowled out first ball. Worse than anything else is seeing nervous bowler suffering the "yips" – losing his line and length. So many handicaps are placed in front of you it is not surprising that the incidence of suicides among cricketers is higher than any other sport, and double the rate for normal males.

Andrew Ernest Stoddart, who captained England at both cricket and rugby, shot himself in the head in a flat in St John's Wood in 1915 after losing a fortune on the gaming tables at the age of 52. A stockbroker, gambler and the archetypal Victorian sportsman, he played a key part in starting a wandering club called The Stoics Cricket Club in 1877. The name comes from the school of philosophy founded on the teachings of Zeno of Citium (333-264 BC) and stoicism teaches self-control, fortitude and being indifferent to pleasure and pain, allowing oneself to become a clear thinker. Chris Heron, a member who has also played for the Woodies, says, "The ethos of Zeno is still to be found in club members, some of whom have played Test cricket, including Trevor Gripper of Zimbabwe, Adam Gilchrist and Raman Subba Row. However, members of lesser note still distinguish themselves by their competitive spirit."

On 4 August 1886 Hampstead played The Stoics at the Hampstead ground, and Stoddart was playing for Hampstead at the time. He had been playing poker through the night, but batted for six hours and 15 minutes to score 485, the highest individual score at the time. It included 1 eight, 3 fives, 64 fours and no sixes. Hampstead batted all day for 813 and there was no time left for Stoics to bat. Their number 4, S. D. Fairless (appropriately named in these circumstances) was one of several who thought that was extremely unfair, and at a committee meeting shortly afterwards, the Stoics proposed a new Law of Cricket about bringing in declarations. It was sent to MCC, who wrote and administered the Laws, and it was adopted.

The Stoics moved quickly and decisively about helping to ban single innings matches, but took 122 years before they organised an overseas tour to Sri Lanka, originally known as Serendipity and then Ceylon, before gaining independence to become Sri Lanka. Gavin, who has directed the TV coverage of many Test matches in Sri Lanka, was the initiator with co-manager Chris Heron, and it took place in February 2008. Thirty people, including wives and partners, came and the playing members of The Stoics were joined by several Woodpeckers, who have a reputation for both stoicism and a sense of fun. Realising that the Stoics Life President Gerald Plumbly, who was in his nineties and had a fall down the stairs in his house in Soho, wouldn't be fit to travel, they arranged a ten-foot-high picture of him which was unveiled at every match and function during the tour. As it was unrolled on to a frame and displayed, they would announce, "And this is our Life President ... Gerald Plumbly and he apologises that he has a pressing engagement at Buckingham Palace and can't make it today." That drew instantaneous applause and uproarious laughter. Once it was blown over and someone said, "He's tipsy – again!" It was not quite as tall as the picture of Kim Jong Ill, which was paraded on a 1976 Lincoln Continental town car in the funeral of the North Korean dictator in January 2012.

Soft spoken and full of charm, Gerald acted as a veterinary surgeon treating the Queen's horses for more than 20 years, but was better known as a revered bohemian who loved cricket with an intense passion. He was only a mediocre player – he never scored a century and dropped too many catches for comfort – but was the backbone of the club, serving in almost every post. John Pretlove, the former Kent player, said, "In his latter years he would be sitting in the scorebox on a freezing cold day – sometimes on his own – and he didn't need any help putting up the score. And his scorebook was immaculate. He was an amazing man. He enjoyed life to the full and was rarely in bed before 2 a.m."

Gerald Percival Plumbly was born in Hither Green on 30 October 1914, and his father had a blacksmith's business near Fitzroy Square. His love of horses came from that. At one of his many celebratory dinners he was asked if any of the Queen's corgis bit him and he said, "No, I didn't have any contact with any, thankfully! I worked with horses, particularly the heavy ones. I love them. They are more intelligent than most people." One of his claims was that he was the last vet to deliver a foal in central London.

His early education was gained at Malvern House School, and at the age of 11 he entered Form 2C at St Dunstan's College, originally founded by King Henry Vl in 1446, before moving to Catford in 1888. In the school magazine in 1934, he was described as "One of our Idols" and the author wrote, "He is the hardest person in the school to draw on one side as one always has to fete him from a circle of admirers. But he will converse generally and that shows him to be possessed of an interest in cultural forms like literature and music, and animals especially and he has a wit that might give a long reign. His career is to be that of a veterinary surgeon but remember how long he once kept an experimental snail until it was almost a pet, one cannot help wondering if he will be able to stiffen his sympathies with an admixture of ruthlessness."

One of Plumbly's contemporaries at St Dunstan's was the legendary Battle of Britain pilot Robert Stanford-Tuck, DSO, DFC with two bars, who had 27 kills, 14 probables, was shot down four times and was mortified later when he shot down a German bomber near Cardiff in 1942 and a stray bomb from the aircraft killed a soldier at an army training camp. The soldier was married to his sister. Stanford-Tuck died in 1987.

Plumbly qualified as a vet at London University and opened his surgery at his father's property. In 1943 he married Josephine Mary Rayner and she qualified as a vet and also acted as his secretary. He soon built up a wide circle of friends, including theatrical people and Val Parnell, the band leader, was a good friend. Actresses from the West End shows were clients of his and he was frequently called out late at night when their pets were ill. He also treated the animals at circuses and pantomimes. One day a manager of a Soho strip club rang to say one of his girls had a problem with a boa constrictor.

"The snake has dug his teeth into her lip and it won't let go," he said.

By this time Plumbly lived in Wimpole Mews and drove his Rolls Royce round to the club. The girl was in a bad state and he said to the manager, "Pull the curtains. We don't want the audience to see this." After the curtains were drawn, he pulled out his lighter and put the flame under the snake and it soon released its hold. Plumbly gave the signal to the manager who drew the curtains to tumultuous applause from a packed house. Said one of his friends, "I think he was a bit careful about naming the part of the girl's anatomy. He didn't want to make a fuss. That was one of his much used phrases – 'don't fuss!'"

The Old Dunstonian who wrote of him needing to be more ruthless was right. Peter Grender (OD, left 1955) said after his funeral, "Some of my favourite stories are when we opened the batting together and his instincts as a vet took over. On the first time we were at the Old Haberdashers coping with a terrible pitch when a dog fight started on the boundary. Gerry said, 'I can't let this go on. Bring your bat with you.' Whereupon we strode up to the scene and broke up the fight to Gerry's great satisfaction. On another occasion we were playing in Knowle Park. It was the rutting season. One of the girls who had come with us was wearing a bright red plastic type of coat. Whilst we were batting, there was a terrible yell and we turned to see a deer had got his mouth locked around the girl's arm. Off we went again and Gerry did the necessary to free the girl's arm. Batting was never dull with him!"

Another OD (John Malone, 1953) said, "I adored him. He used to turn up in a convertible Rolls and always told me you should enjoy your cricket and rugby but put women and drink first! Now there was an eccentric!"

Plumbly fitted in his appointments to suit his cricket engagements and often played three or four matches a week. He was a member of the MCC and also played occasionally for The Romany. He was a habitué at The Cricketers Club near Baker Street, drinking with the likes of Denis Compton, Keith Miller, Bill Edrich, Reg Hayter, the journalist and agent of Ian Botham, and dozens of famous Test players visiting from aboard. When he learned that someone had dropped out of the Stoics side, he was the first to volunteer. He said, "When there were withdrawals from the side, we have to show fortitude and make the best of things."

Some of his finest achievements on the field took place at The Saffrons ground at Eastbourne where he hit his only six of his 80-year-long career, over the roof of Eastbourne College. A team mate said, "He was fanatically keen. He would put his name down to play but often he was delayed by work. One day he turned up at the county ground there and we were in a pretty bad state with one wicket left. Raman Subba Row, the former England left hand batsman who was later the reforming chairman of the Test and County Cricket Board for some years, was still in and Gerald came in at 11 to join him, and they batted out time to save the game. He was rather pleased about that. He felt it was worthwhile to make the 142-mile round trip from London."

His exploits at the wheel of his old Rolls Royce were legendary. "He drank a lot at clubs, pubs and cricket clubs but he never lost his licence and was never prosecuted for traffic offences," said a friend. "One time he lost control and the car ended on a ledge. It was like a scene from 'The Italian Job' and I said to him, 'you ought to have another driving test,' and he said, 'in those days you didn't need one and I don't think it would be a good idea now.'"

A cricketing colleague said, "Often we were hanging on for grim death, fearing the worst. He was oblivious to it. He was still driving in his nineties and by that time his eyes were going. One day he was driving along the A14 in the outside lane at 20 mph and it caused an accident when another car tried to get past him and the road was blocked for some time." The only brush he had with the police came in mid life when he was stopped and a police officer asked him to get out of his car. He stepped out and started swaying and the officer thought he was drunk and told him to empty his pockets. He refused but was taken to a police station and examined by a doctor who diagnosed that he was suffering from Legionnaire's disease. He was put into intensive care at St Mary's Hospital and only his strong constitution enabled him to survive. It was discovered that the germ came from water at a squash club and he sued the club and won damages. Bill Frindall, who sometimes met him at cricketing events, died of the same disease much later."

When he was 92 he had a fall and needed a tetanus injection. He asked the doctor, "How long will it last?"

"Ten years," he was told.

"I'll make note to come back and get the next one in 2016," he said. He didn't make it, sadly.

His other sporting interest was squash. He founded a club called The Swans and ran it for many years. He died at midday on 26 January 2010 at the age of 95 and is survived by his daughter Geraldine and his grandchildren Charlie and Natasha. His wife died in 1996. His private funeral took place at Golders Green Crematorium, where A. E. Stoddart was cremated.

Before setting off for Sri Lanka, our party attended a cocktail gathering at the High Commissioner's house near Tyburn, the last place in London where miscreants were hanged. The fighting in the north of the island provoked demonstrations in the area with Tamils showing their anger about the way the government was handling the civil war. When we arrived the road was sealed off by police and we were rather apprehensive about the outcome. But the person in charge, Ksenuka Senewiratne, a jolly lady with a great sense of humour, said, "I can assure you that you won't be killed on your tour. We've never lost a tourist yet and that will continue."

She was right, but there were two scares during the tour. On the single-lane road from our hotel, the Cinnamon in Dambulla, we saw a yellow bus blocking most of it with lots of children playing and police officers trying to keep them back. All the windows were blown out and the front of the vehicle was mangled by a bomb which went off two weeks earlier with a number of casualties. A police superintendent was standing there and I asked him, "Why is it still there?"

"We're conducting forensic tests," he said.

One of our tourists piped up. "You won't take good fingerprints, with all these children milling around." Everyone laughed.

More than 40,000 people died in the civil war and it lasted almost a generation before it ended within two years. The United Nations are still investigating complaints about alleged war atrocities in the north.

The day before we set off for our flight to the Maldives for the final leg of the tour there was another bomb attack on a bus near the five star Colonial Heritage hotel named the Mount Lavinia Hotel, the last hotel we stayed at. This time someone gave the alarm and all the passengers got out and ran off before the bomb went off. Brigadier Udaya Manayakkra said, "Casualties would have been far greater but an alert passenger spotted the booby-trapped package and shouted at people to leave. The terrorists' beastly intention to commit carnage against civilians was foiled by the vigilance of the civilians themselves. The bus was totally destroyed. Eighteen people were treated in hospital." If we had been there 24 hours before, we could have been caught up with the attempted massacre.

I have stayed at the Mount Lavinia on five occasions and love it. It was built in the early 1800s as a home for the Governor General Thomas Maitland, a bachelor, who fell in love with a mestizo dancer named Lavinia of Portuguese-Sinhalese descent. He had a tunnel built to smuggle the girl into the house to protect his reputation. His governorship lasted only six years, 1805-11, before he was transferred to Malta, leaving his grief-stricken dancer behind. Nothing seems to have changed since then, except the tunnel was blocked up. The name remains and also, its high reputation. The last time we dined on the open air terrace next to the swimming pool looking over the Indian Ocean a gigantic electric storm started up and it was almost as exciting as watching the Sydney Bridge New Year fireworks display.

I have been fortunate to have visited 23 countries on various cricket tours, including: ICC Full Members of the ICC – Australia (2), India (2), New Zealand (2), South Africa (5), Sri Lanka (5), West Indies (1) and Zimbabwe (1); Associate Members – Gibraltar, Guernsey, Hong Kong, Italy, Kenya, Malaysia, Namibia, Holland, Singapore, Thailand, UAE and USA; and Affiliated Members – Cyprus, Maldives, Malta and Spain. I haven't been on the winning side too often. This is because the home clubs want to win and don't want to be disgraced. Our clubs are forced to take a lot of older, wealthier cricketers, and they usually stress they prefer to take on similar strength sides – the old fogeys. Except for New Zealand – where they do put out wholly Golden Oldie sides – none of the countries play the game in the right spirit, as we see it. They always slip in younger, quality players to ensure victory, especially the Aussies and the South

Africans who pile food and booze into their visitors to weaken their will to win.

Neither Trevor Gripper, Raman Subba Row (who was staying with a former Sri Lankan Test star during our tour) nor Adam Gilchrist were available to play for The Stoics Crusaders tour, but we were successful in signing former Pakistan captain Aamir Sohail and the New Zealand swing bowler Danny Morrison, both 42 and recently retired from first-class cricket. They have worked as TV commentators under the directorship of Gavin at various Test series and were eager to take part without any payment. Quite a coup! Yes, we actually won a game and both played key roles. Two other games ended in honourable draws after rain and our elderly side were thrashed twice by two schoolboy XIs (when our Test stars were injured). Christopher Martin-Jenkins once said of Sohail who played in 47 Tests, but should have made many more, "He was temperamental, tempestuous and aggressive by nature." Fair comment, but he also loved the game and he was one of the first Pakistani players to draw attention to the match fixing which started to afflict world cricket in the early 1990s. His revelations probably curtailed his reign as captain because one or two leading administrators were just as corrupt as some of their dodgy players.

I wrote a number of articles about him in my role as the *Daily Mail's* cricket news reporter, and he was keen to sell his story about match fixing and spot betting to a national newspaper in England. I remember meeting him on that piece of grass in the roundabout at Marble Arch Corner. With so much traffic, he felt his words couldn't be picked up by anyone else to avoid detection. He wanted £50,000, and if he had named the guilty people, with all the relevant evidence, that figure wouldn't have been excessive. Hacking of mobile phones was at its infancy, otherwise a private agency might well have cracked the story. Bryan Cooney, the then sports editor, knew little about cricket and he was prepared to offer £10,000. I had another meeting with Sohail at another venue, less noisy, and he was reluctant to name names. Exasperated, Cooney offered £500 for a feature article without any real revelations and I went ahead with it. It was published and the last time I asked about it, no payment had been made. Eventually, several well-known Pakistan cricketers were found guilty but none were imprisoned. Another 15 years went by before three Pakistan cricketers were convicted in Southwark Crown Court.

Before setting off for the game at Dambulla, two of our players, Chris Aeschlimann, a six-foot-five-inch legbreak bowler and slogger of Swiss extraction, and his Sanderstead CC colleague Tom Sherlock, a teacher and wicketkeeper, joined me on a walk round the hotel grounds next to a lake. Simon Barnes of *The Times* would have loved to be present. He's written more words on birds than almost anyone and this place is one of the best in Sri Lanka to spot birds. We saw a tall mahogany tree with steps and climbed to the top to get a better view. Suddenly I noticed someone had scratched an A and three XXXs on the trunk of the tree. I realised it was like the last St Valentine's card Audrey sent to me before she died. It was so reassuring!

The hold up by the blown-up bus delayed us for only a short while and we arrived at The Rangiri International Dambulla Stadium well ahead of time. It was built on a World Heritage site in 2001 in just 155 days and it is an imposing structure almost in the jungle. The sun was cruel, the temperature was 37 °C and we brought several crates of water and needed every drop. The police superintendent we had spoken to at the stricken bus turned out to be in charge of the security at the ground and he assured us there would be no trouble. Chris Tooley, a former St Dunstan's Old Boy, ex-captain of Oxford University and a former opener at Bromley CC and now chairman, was captaining the side and he asked me about my fitness.

"My knee has swelled up slightly but in this heat it will clear up," I said.

"You're opening with Aamir," he said.

"Don't be silly," I said. "There are plenty younger and fitter players who love to partner him."

I had just been elected as Life President at the Woodies and he said, "You can fill Gerald's anchor role."

When we inspected the pitch it had the appearance of a road – rocklike. No sign of a crack anywhere. The home skipper won the toss and decided to bat on this pluperfect pitch.

Danny Morrison is an ebullient, very likeable Kiwi with a smile and a joke and he wanted to bowl at the other end from the four-storey pavilion.

"I've got bit of a hammy," he said. "But I should be able to bowl my quota, the usual one over! No, we'll see how it goes." Born in Auckland, his mentor was Richard Hadlee, the greatest strike bowler ever produced from New Zealand and he learned a lot from him. Much shorter than Hadlee, he made up for his lack of inches by his enthusiasm and willingness to keep going when things get tough. He never stinted himself. These days he is a TV commentator for TVNZ, Sky Sports and Fox Sports and is a presenter of several radio programmes, and one of his charitable interests is a meningitis appeal. He is popular not only in New Zealand but around the cricketing world. He took 160 wickets in his 48 Tests and held the word record of 24 ducks, a record which has now been overtaken by Chris Martin, another New Zealander, who has much less hair. In 1997 he brought out an autobiography entitled *Mad as I Wanna Be*, and it was well received except for one critic, Richard Whiting, who said, "It's mental."

The Dambulla side was filled with regional cricketers of a good standard, but they had no Test players. Danny was soon working on the ball, bringing up the shine on one side and right from the outset he was pitching it up and swinging it both ways. He bowled one of their openers with a slower ball and followed up with an inducker which trapped the other opener. Most Sri Lankan batsman like finding the boundary from the first ball, but now they had to show caution. The rest of the batsmen found themselves being pressurised: this man can still bowl! Aamer Sohail came on with his accurate slow left-arm orthodox bowling to tighten the grip and wickets started tumbling.

"You all right?" Tooley asked Danny.

"You bet," said our strike bowler.

To their astonishment, the Dambulla Combined Xl found themselves dismissed for 117 on a pitch which should have produced three times as many runs. Danny was helped back to the pavilion by his colleagues for a rub down. His figures were 4-25.

After a buffet curry lunch which saw the home players ignoring knives and forks and using their hands, the usual custom, our Anglo-Pakistani pair of Sohail and Scovell took over the central stage. Aamir was recognised to be one of the hardest hitters of all the Pakistan batting stars and he started in his usual manner, smashing the ball back through mid on and mid wicket with tremendous power. One extra cover drive sizzled away to the boundary and brought back memories of the West Indian shout when Brian Lara was at his pomp – "No Man Move". The fielders on that side were left standing, gasping.

Batting with a great player takes all responsibility from your partner and I relished letting the ball go or stopping the straight ones with a ramrod straight bat. You don't have to take any risks. It was batting bliss! Once Aamir hit the ball straight back to me and I managed to jump aside to see it fly to the sightscreen at the pavilion end. Soon we were on the way to 50 and I succeeded in collecting a few runs, mainly behind square on the off side. Aamir was unstoppable. Another rocket shot aimed to my stomach could have knocked me down, but again, I was just able to squeeze out of range.

"Can you please adjust your target areas?" I asked him. He apologised.

The home skipper tried all his bowlers and none of them worried him. Nor me either because there was no swing to help them. A Waqar Younis, and certainly a Danny Morrison, would have achieved it. With our total at 95, Aamir fired another ferocious shot towards my unbending right leg, and the ball hit my pad and ricocheted on to the off stump – run out for 15, eked out in 18 overs. I was quite relieved. I could have finished up in hospital: one of these dangerous shots of his may well have done serious damage. And in that heat it was time to have a rest and let someone else take over. Aamir finished unbeaten on 75 and we won by eight wickets. Albert Stoddart and Gerald Plumbly would have been proud of us.

We had small, gold coloured (not real gold) trophies to present to successful players, and to my astonishment Chris Tooley named me as The Best Batsman. If the ICC Anti Corruption Unit was in action at the time they would have investigated the betting patterns if there were any. Aamir was the only contender and I might have been 1,000-1, or more. I mumbled a few, embarrassing words and what I really should have done was to credit Audrey. She was my greatest supporter and though she hardly watched cricket – she was too busy doing sketches when she toured with me, ready for her next prize etching to be submitted to the Royal Academy's Summer Exhibition – she always offered encouragement and support. Before I faced my first delivery at Dambulla I looked for the tallest tree and said, "Please God that I don't let her down!" In my 80-odd minutes at the crease I never concentrated harder. It was a very exciting and emotional time.

Trillions of words are written about cricketers being depressed or committing suicide, but very little is written about the loyal, loving wife. While I was writing this chapter I saw on Sky Michael Clarke pointing his bat towards his beautiful 29-year-old new girlfriend Kyly Boldy in the members' stand at the Sydney ground when he reached 100, 200 and 300 against an outclassed Indian side. Up to then he hadn't spoken about her in public but on the following Sunday she starred with William Dafoe in a new Jim Beam ad campaign. With the fantastic improvement of television coverage – many of them pioneered by my son Gavin – these moments tell a human interest story to the viewer. When Clarke reached 100, Kyly had a tear in her eye. But by 200 she was showing all her pride and joy in her man, spurring Clarke on to an unbeaten 329 to set a host of new records. A supremely happy marriage or a close relationship makes a cricketer a better one, and two outstanding examples are Andrew Strauss and Alastair Cook.

Aamir missed the next game with a sore muscle in the rib and Danny was laid up as well. A Galle U17 team easily beat The Crusaders by 99 runs at the rebuilt Test ground which was destroyed by the tsunami four years earlier. The next day an even younger side beat them by ten wickets after bowling them out for 62. When the boys took the field they were astounded to see two elderly grandfathers opening the batting – Chris Rossi, aged 69 and me, aged 72. They smiled and were very polite, calling us "Sir". The first bowler was a left-arm slow bowler who pitched every ball on the spot and the second one bowled offspin, just as accurately. Chris and I were able to block a few deliveries but the prospect of scoring a run, in a 35-over match, was a distant memory. Chris was soon bowled for a duck and I lasted five overs for a single – bowled shouldering arms to the left armer who cheekily fired in a fast arm ball. In the dressing room we were filmed by our video man and we sang the refrain of "Dads' Army" which was later released on Amazon.

Our final match was supposed to be at the Sinhalese CC, the MCC of Colombo. There was no sign of opponents and an official said, "There is no game here today. Try the ground of Moors CC where the pitch is very good." Our coach driver located the new ground and again, there was no opposing team in sight. We were told that a school's side, St Antonians Old Boys, was being hauled out of their classrooms and transported to the scene. They were good young cricketers and scored 151-7. We managed to con them by saying it had to be a declaration game because The Stoics invented the declaration. We held on to claim a draw on 118-8. After a late night and a jolly fine session we were up at 6 a.m. to fly off for three nights at a luxury five star hotel in Paradise Island in the Maldives. It was wonderfully relaxing way to end a hilarious tour. We had a number of injuries – that was our excuse – and Her Excellency the High Commissioner was right. We made it back safely. No-one was blown up.

20

In and Out of Deepest Africa

Breaking new ground, 23 intrepid Forty Club former athletes, well past their sell by date, and 16 ladies had a memorable three weeks in the autumn of 2009 in one of the loveliest desert countries of the world. Namibia – the name come from the Namib Desert – is much bigger than Great Britain, and the 2.3 million population is thinly spread over 824,000 square km. It has the fifth lowest population density in the world – 2.7 people per square km – and half the population lives below the poverty line. It was taken over by the Germans in 1889 and after the First World War, South Africa had a mandate to rule it before granting independence in 1990. Though some of the German streets have been changed to the names of despots like Robert Mugabe and Fidel Castro, names like Kaiser Wilheim and Bismarck still remain. We needed a few Bismarcks to stand up against the young Namibians whose national side is seeking to qualify for the next stage of the ICC Associates' competition after unluckily losing to Afghanistan some years ago.

The members of the national training squad, average age 23, thought they would be playing against sides in their early forties. Ours wasn't Dad's Army: it was Granddad's Army. Alan Spencer, our former Worcestershire player who played for the county between 1957 and 1961, was still using the metal box which Fiery Fred Trueman dented 52 years ago. Alan said, "It hurt when it hit me in amidships but if I had been wearing one of those pink plastic jobs of the time I would have been in real trouble. I'm now 65 and I think it will see me out."

After a quick count we discovered that most of the players took between 8-10 tablets each day and there were suspicions that some of them were on viagra. No-one owned up to that. Some were taking steroids to increase their normal running pace from its usual 5 mph. I was the last to undergo a thorough examination by a member of the German security department at Frankfurt Airport on the way out from London. As he placed his detection rod next to my heart, he said, "What's that?"

"My heart," I said. "I had two metal stents in an artery some years ago after a heart attack." I showed my bottle of Simvastatin cholesterol tablets.

The rod was passing my left knee and he said, "What's that?"

"An artificial knee made of titanium." Now he was going up the other side. It reached my right hip.

"And what about that?"

"More titanium, and I have to tell you that the 2,500 members of the Forty Club have caused an acute shortage of titanium through the world."

He laughed. "Ah," he said, "some years ago you would be confined to wheel chairs. Now you are lucky to play sport." I told him some of our players played in an Over 70s League and I expect some will take part in wheelchair cricket in the 2016 Olympics, if the sport is added to the events.

The Namibians made every possible concession to old age. Their batsmen retired on 50, nearly all their players bowled and sometimes they failed to remove the bails when a run out was imminent. It was sportsmanship of the highest standard. Our air-conditioned coach travelled 2,500 miles on mainly gravel "roads" and despite the bumps and scares, we survived. And we weren't hampered by the 6,000 feet altitude, the 35 °C temperatures in the north, and the howling wind that often whips up in the capital Windhoek (means "Wind round the corner"). At one match I was flattened when a metal frame of a tent which housed the scorers crashed into my head, but I was soon on my feet.

The Rudolf family is the driving force in Namibian cricket. Johan Jacques, the father of Jacques, the SA Test player who played for Surrey and Yorkshire, was the national coach and his other son Gerhard is hoping to be the KP of his adopted country. "You need to live in the country for four years and I did that," said Gerhard. The way he battered our bowling in the opening match against a United Invitation Xl showed that he has all the assets to make the grade. He made a rapid 45 in his side's 310 and Mike Plumridge mustered a gallant 41 in our 146, 164 runs short. A Development Xl, all teenagers, continued the punishment next day on the same ground. Skipper Wilber Stabbert restricted his team to 30 overs before declaring on 200-6 and in our 50 overs we straggled to 118 in 40.3 overs against nine, very kind bowlers. Wilber's players relished meeting our veterans, some of whom were 70-plus. "I wish I'd met you a few years earlier," he said. "I would have learned so much." That was very encouraging!

We had three lob bowlers in Norman Gray, Mike Wicks and Japp Vogelaar who, on a good day, can lob the ball 30 or so feet into the air and still land on a length. I told them they should have faced Tony Macdonald-Barker, our highest lobber. "He sometimes causes panic with low flying helicopters and aircraft pilots when he performs," I said. Unfortunately be couldn't come this time.

A swarm of bees held up play in one game. The home players flung themselves to the ground and remained there for several minutes. Rather apprehensive, our batsmen and umpires remained on their feet. One said, "Having had two knee replacements, it's hard to get up once you lie down."

A few minutes later the home team captain said, "We were expecting to see a swarm but they've passed by. It is okay now. It happens a lot out here." A fact few people know: bees fly up to 15 mph, no more.

Our party was quartered between the eleventh and fourteenth floors of a 4 star hotel in the centre of the city overlooking the Supreme Court which was built by the Chinese. "It's falling down already," said a sceptical local. Namibia is looked on as one of the most stable and progressive nations in Africa but the 83,000 whites are worried about being outnumbered by the new invaders, the Chinese. Like most African countries, Namibia is tainted by corruption in varying degrees and it is part of life. But they are cracking down on it after the 76-year-old President pulled off a Ronnie Reagan, winning a second term.

Halfway through the tour, the players had an exceptionally early wake up call to discover than the lifts weren't working. Alan Spencer, our senior pro who had a part-time job with a lift company, said, "I've known people dying in high rise towers because rescuers can't get to them." Hardly reassuring news. Well, we all got down safely although Greta Groves, one of the partners, was stuck in one for several minutes before the lift started moving again.

Outside on the road more problems piled up. Our coach driver couldn't open the door of his coach and a mechanic had to squeeze through a side window to break in to make the repair. Our opponents, a Namibian U17 side, agreed on a time game and sportingly declared on 207-2. Gerhard Lotter, aged 16, struck an immense six into the nearby railway line and climbed over a six-feet-high fence to retrieve the ball, still wearing his pads. One of our veterans said, "I can't imagine any of us doing that. It's hard enough to bend down to strap the pads on."

Again, it was a generous declaration but their nine bowlers pinned down our batters and in a cool, windy late afternoon we sneaked a draw on 166-8. Up early again, we spent three hours driving to Otjiwarongo, 150 km north of Windhoek. Suspecting that some of our players were of pensionable age, the local undertaker turned up. He was married to Estelle Hauccu, a Dutch lady who was the match scorer. The U17s showed no mercy as our popgun bowlers were hit to vast distances, with four of them retiring on 50. Robert Smith nearly had some teeth removed when a ball on the boundary jumped up straight at his face. He ducked just in time. Alan Spencer impressed the boys with his courageous 46 and Robbie Barker, one of our most consistent batters, made 33 to take us to 139-8, losing by 169 runs. Andy Meads, one of the few who took his coffin – I hasten to say that was his rectangular cricket box containing his gear – up and down all the stairs to the top floor at the hotel, said, "The boys were wonderful. So polite and friendly. They were a credit to their school." Some of the schools in England which we visit would have learned from their example.

Tour leader and casual, very casual, bowler Ron Hart opened the bowling with his pie throwers to everyone's surprise, and perhaps disorientated by being slammed for several sixes, he later walked into a window in his hotel. Fortunately there was no damage. The undertaker departed after the end of play drinks with no business but he did leave his card.

Next we were at Oshakati, near the Angolan border where the North Koreans are trying to buy up most of the uranium, and we played on a lake – another XL first. In the rainy season there is a five-feet-deep lake, well stocked with fish. When the temperature shoots up in the spring, the fish disappear underground in the remaining nine months and the huge sandy ground, with 90-yard boundaries, has a surface of rolled sand and the players laid down a green mat in the middle. The ball either shot along the ground or jumped up at head high on this horrendous "pitch" but our unexpected two-wicket victory came from stoicism, improved bowling (Peter Owen 4-45 and Japp Vogelaaar 3-41, neither English through and through), the batting of Denham Earl, with 55, Robert Smith 33, and 45 welcome extras.

The locals staged a peculiar Afrikaans ritual after the match which featured the smacking of bottoms by another player wielding a heavy bat – punishment for misfielding. As all of them were guilty, the ceremony took some time. They had to bend over and be whacked by a rather muscular rugby-style man with cauliflower ears and he relished it. Peter Roebuck and Max Mosley would probably have relished it as well. Our total of dropped catches and misfields were higher than theirs and some of our athletes were ready to make their excuses and go to the coach. If they had been thumped we wouldn't have been able to sit down on the 350-km trip back to our hotel. After handing out glasses of obnoxious liquid, which we had to drink, accompanied by an interminable number of toasts, we were finally allowed to leave.

After our lucky escape, there was a welcome four-day mid-term break to tour the alluring waterholes, the dunes, the desert and the mountains before taking another beating from the side from Walvis Bay, Namibia's port, close to its main seaside town Swakopmund. It turned out to be one of the most uplifting stories of our tours we have undertaken around the world, and it concerned 24-year-old Helmut Mack who was Man of the Match and son of Otto Mack, the hardworking organiser of the event. When he was born, both of his arms were less than half of the normal size, like one of the thalidomide children of a previous generation who received large sums in compensation from drugs companies.

"It wasn't like that," he said. "It was just an unexplained event but I got on with it. I started playing cricket at an early age and began bowling in different styles, including legbreaks and googlies." He has a finger and a thumb on one hand and astonished some of our batsmen while taking 4-10. His batting was even more extraordinary. He was unable to use batting gloves and didn't use a box or an arm guard. He crouched over his bat and that accentuated his congenital problem with his back which has worsened since being in a car crash. Some years earlier, he was also attacked by two pit bull terriers, savaging his left leg.

Normally a number 11, he scored a career best 31, nearly all to leg, and hit three fours, the first boundaries he has scored for five years. "I have straightened my life out," he said, "I've cut down on drinking and smoking." Apparently, he was a naughty young man but has reformed. We saluted his courage: it was an inspiration to anyone with disabilities.

At one stage Walvis were 57-7 but Cape Town-born Esau Heyns struck a thrustful 78* and their 163 was too much on a slow artificial pitch and we were dismissed for 112. Esau works on the oil rig from Angola which is being repaired and dominates the ground. Robbie Barker, with 58, helped to make more of a game of it, with XL losing by four wickets with 16 balls remaining. Helmut summed up our visit to this interesting place, saying, "Your players taught us a lot, especially your very slow, flighted bowling. We were very grateful to them."

In the north, we experienced the fascinating close ups of lions, rhinos, giraffes, springboks, zebras and many more animals and now it was time to take to the water in the cooler south. We were woken at dawn to be taken on a perishingly cold, four-hour trip in boats around the vast harbour to see thousands of sea lions, dolphins, otters, seals and other sea life. Several seals jumped on to our boats to be fed and they were well behaved. When we waved them away, they dived back into the water.

The final match took place at the Lord's of Namibia, the ground of the senior club Wanderers CC and we went down to another heavy defeat against the Knightwatchmen led by 65-year-old Namibian CO Laurie Pieters, who has done more than anyone to bring Namibia's cricket up to international standard. We lost by 99 runs although we reached our highest total of 185-5. Andy Meads, who was good enough to be a professional but preferred to go into teaching, made a Colin Cowdrey-like 52 and Alan Spencer, 32. When I came in, Johan Jacques who played a lot of first-class cricket in South Africa, was bowling legspin. It gave me a chance to use my favourite shot, the sweep. Twice I swept him for boundaries, but he soon switched to his faster version of years ago. The next ball was a fizzing bouncer which I managed to avoid and I edged the next one to give a catch to the keeper. Time to go, I thought. These South Africans don't like being shown up. They are even harder than Aussies. The Knightwatchmen side was packed with rugged over 40s, experienced practitioners, and some of them were former internationals. They were far too good for us.

In our nine matches – seven defeats, a win and a draw when we wheeled out a declaration result – the locals amassed 120 sixes to our 2. "But ours was more stylish," said Robert Smith. Peter Owens, who bowled 82 overs in his eight matches without blowing up, deservedly won the Man of the Tour award, and in the final dinner Greta Groves, our Dancing Queen, led the dancing in the dining room of the swish Windhoek Golf and Country Resort, surprising the other residents and staff with her elasticity. We thought she ought to have been invited to take part in "Strictly Come Dancing", the BBC TV series, and not Ann Widdecombe. Ron Hart and three of his colleagues then took over from the karaoke singer to keep the momentum.

Culturally, the highlight was to see the staff of the hotels and lodges emerge from the kitchens to entertain with us with songs and dancing after the meals were finished. Nearly all of them were very talented, singing in their own style and dancing wearing broad smiles. We always took a whip round and the money probably exceeded their wages. On the final day we coached a hundred or so black orphans, some of whom had AIDS, and we launched an appeal to members to support four homes for them around Windhoek. It raised £400. MCC and the Eton Ramblers have toured Namibia and we were the third club to do it. But we knew that ours was the most enjoyable, and the most meaningful.

Namibian cricket has to be complimented for their efforts to raise standards and extend to us such wonderful hospitality. Some of our tourists thought it was the best of tour ever. Forget the cricket, just remember Africa in the raw.

21

Sorry I Got That Wrong

This is an admission of guilt: I was wrong about Twenty20 cricket. The explosion of sixes in the West Indies has finally converted me after seeing England rise up and win a quickie cricket tournament at last.

It happened almost on the exact date of the 50th anniversary when I first reported on international cricket for Associated Newspapers for the *Daily Sketch*. The match was MCC against the South Africans at Lord's and the average scoring rate over the three days was 1.5 runs an over. When England won the ICC World Twenty20 Trophy the scoring rate in the final was 8 runs an over. It wasn't just the speed of the way Paul Collingwood's players scored their runs, but their blistering strokeplay, their extraordinary fielding and their varied bowling showed millions of viewers around the world that the game is now hugely entertaining and viable. It will save the counties, there is no doubt about that.

In 1960 the cricket writers used phrases like "occupying the crease" and "building a winning position before going on to the offensive". Some of England's captains were like General Montgomery – refusing to take chances which is why Australians nearly always won the Ashes. Geoff Boycott typified the way England took the attritional route. Desperately poorly paid, batsmen selfishly played for their averages, helping them to get an untaxed benefit at the end of their careers.

With crowds dwindling, Colin Cowdrey and Ted Dexter suggested a 60 overs a side competition in 1963 to encourage spin bowlers and improve the run rate. It didn't really work. It was boring. John Player sponsored a rival 40 over tournament and that that raised the pulse a few degrees although the audience remained sceptical. Then Kerry Packer came along with his World Series in Australia in 1977-79 when he signed up the best players. It was hard, unrelenting cricket and the introduction of helmets probably saved serious injury, or death. Once Packer snatched the TV rights of Australian cricket he demobbed the stars of WSC and the attendances at Tests, except in Ashes series, continued to fall.

Seven years ago the English Cricket Board took up an idea first adopted after the Second World War when people had to work six days a week. It was called time limit cricket with each side batting 20 overs. As a teenager I played it on a concrete pitch covered by coir matting in Newport in the Isle of Wight, and it was brutal stuff but we enjoyed it. When 20/20 was included on the English cricketing calendar experts like Brian Close, England's most successful captain, and Sir Alec Bedser were horrified. Speaking at a Forty Club forum Close said, "I switch it off when it comes on. The batsmen are hitting across the line and the bowlers can't bowl on the spot. It's not proper cricket and it's going to ruin the game."

I agreed with him, especially watching the overcharged, Bollywood version of the IPL in India with its incessant breaks filled with adverts. But in the West Indies, I realised the leading countries were updating methods to take the game into a better and more enjoyable experience. A prime aim was to hit as many sixes as possible. The total worked out 11 per match. Sir Don Bradman, the Emperor of batting, hit just six sixes in his Test career and you couldn't imagine a reborn Bradman belting a succession of sixes nowadays. Most of the matches had close finishes, the sportsmanship displayed was encouraging and the TV coverage reached a new standard.

The Caribbean organisers redeemed themselves for the failures of the 2007 ICC 50 overs competition when everything went wrong, and the Barbados Government used the chance to launch a campaign to curb the incidence of HIV. Their 166-square-mile island with 300,000 inhabitants and almost as many cars has one of the worst records for HIV.

Two key matters need vigilance. First security. ICC are spending enormous sums on it and unlike the IPL, they ensured there were no incidents with the 500-strong Barbados Defence Force putting a protective curtain around the Afghanistan side, and armed, plain clothed agents were attached to every team. A similar plan came into effect when the Pakistan side arrived a month later. Outside the seventeenth-century St Ann's Fort in Bridgetown a huge placard urged the BDF troops to show "Responsibility – My Platoon deserves it, My partner deserves it, My life depends on it – Use your condom always, at everytime."

David Morgan, a former ICC chairman, has warned cricket to be watchful about illegal betting. It is very difficult to prove that players gave information to bookies but some experts in the IPL felt that some had been tempted. The betting is on things like dot balls at beginning and end of overs or wides and no balls, not so much on the result of matches. We need more arrests and convictions, otherwise spot betting will continue.

Two thirds of England's runs in the semi-final and final were scored by two players, Kevin Pietersen and Craig Kieswetter, both South Africans, and as John Woodcock, the former *Wisden* editor and *The Times* cricket correspondent, said of Tony Greig, "He is not English through and through." Nor are KP and Kieswetter. The dynamic KP and former Millfield schoolboy Kieswetter, who played some exceptional shots while he rode his luck, are qualified to play for their adopted countries under the rules, but I share the feelings of many cricket lovers who say signing players who were born and brought up in South Africa is not cricket – it's mercenaryism. KP's "loyalty" to his adopted country was stripped bare in 2012 when he opted out of one form of one day cricket and was barred from taking part in another when the ECB put their feet down.

Most important, there has to be a right balance now between Test cricket, the highest form of the game, the classical music of cricket, and 20/20, which is the equivalent of pop music. They can co-exist but if the short form gets too big Test cricket will suffer.

22

Maniacs Prowling Down Under

Mihir Bose was a hardmaster on his cricket tours, but Bill Frindall, cricket's "Bearded Wonder", made him look like a softie. When Bill was working as the world's greatest scorer in the Test Match Special boxes all over England, commentators like Brian Johnston, who gave him his nickname, Fred Trueman, Ian Botham, Chris Martin-Jenkins, Jonathan Agnew and others would try and put him down. They would say things like "not now Bill" and the producer Peter Baxter would tell him only to speak when he was asked. But when he took his many cricket tour squads abroad, he made sure he was the unchallenged leader and he soon was given another nickname – "The Führer".

Most of it was friendly banter but he often lost his temper with managers of hotels, porters, waiters and fielders who spilled dollies (easy catches that weren't). When we arrived at a hotel in Alexandra, the driest spot in New Zealand on the Maltamaniacs tour to NZ and Australia in 1984, he said to the lady clerk, "This is not up to the standard we were promised. Show me your superior rooms."

The woman said, "They're all the same." Frindall cursed and stormed off to our waiting coach where the rest of the players, wives and friends were waiting.

"Return to your seats!" he said. "We're going to look at another hotel."

The clerk called up the manager who dashed out to intercept the coach when the driver was about to drive off. He shouted out, "Mr Frindall, we actually have a suite."

"Let me see it," said Bill. The two men walked off to inspect it. After a few minutes, Bill returned and said, "Everyone out. We've sorted it out. I'm having the suite."

It was the time the *News of the World* broke the story that Ian Botham had taken drugs and shared a room with a former Miss Barbados on the England tour to the West Indies. Tom Clarke, the sports editor of the *Daily Mail* at the time, tracked me down to the Alexandra hotel and asked me to interview leading cricketing figures in New Zealand about the story, and I filed a short piece with Graham Dowling, the chairman of the NZ Cricket Board saying precious little. Bill had a very loud, deep chuckle, and he laughed uproariously when he heard the bed had collapsed. As a bit of a Lothario himself, he saw the joke. In one profile of him in the tour booklet he gave his hobbies as wine, women and stamp collecting and someone said, "I never saw him talking about stamps." His clubs – the cricketing ones – were MCC, Lord's Taverner's, SPARKS, the English Press Cricket Association, the *Sunday Telegraph*, the Pioneers, the Maltamaniacs, the Oxford Clergy, the Banstead Mental Hospital and the Gamecocks. He also had something in common with John Arlott – they both made a single appearance for the Hampshire 2nd XI.

Frindall started taking tours to Malta – a windswept, bare speck of rock, 122 square miles and 50 miles south of Sicily with no grass cricketing pitches – in 1976 and the locals thought some of the players had manic qualities, particularly the captain, and Alan "Leapy" Lee, the former cricket correspondent of *The Times* and current racing correspondent who came up with the name Maltamaniacs. There was no subscription and members were asked to contribute a fiver, or more, to the Guide Dogs for the Blind Association. Bill had a very fine reputation for helping charities.

Alan had a tumultuous debut on that tour when he split the webbing of his hand when he dropped a catch in the first over, he was denied a bat when the rain caused an abandonment as he walked to the wicket, and after a few drinks later in the night, he sprained an ankle while running to embrace a young lady named Helen Gould on the marble floor of a hotel. The Revd Hugh Pickles, the mystery non-spin bowler of the Oxford Clergy, was one of Frindall's players on a number of tours, and he was in charge of taking confessions which kept him busy.

Frindall once reminded me how we met. "It was a benefit match for Ken Higgs, the Lancashire and England bowler (now no longer with us) at Didsbury on the rest of the Old Trafford Test of 1968," he said. "You opened the batting with Trevor Bailey and it was some time before the public were informed that it was 'The Boil' who was crashing the ball to all parts and 'Souters' (he nicknamed me after my mother's maiden name for passport purposes) was demonstrating the most famous forward defensive stroke in Britain."

The Great Scorer loved stats and that was how he earned most of his money. When he died on 29 January 2009 aged 69, he left behind a record of scoring in 246 Tests in England for BBC's Test Match Special and a further 133 Tests abroad in an unbroken period of 43 years. For someone who sat down throughout the day he was amazingly fit and was still playing occasional cricket matches when he contracted Legionnaires' Disease through a default in the air conditioning of a hotel in Dubai where he was on a tour with the Lord's Taverners. He would have been fit enough to carry on for some years but it was doubtful whether he could beat the record of Bill Ferguson, the Australian scorer who did a similar job for 52 years.

Frindall met when him he was 14 in 1953 during the Australia tour and he vowed he would make a living out of scoring. The generous Ferguson (1880-1957), who didn't have a beard, showed his linear scoring which was invented by John Atkinson Pendlington (1861-1914) who did have one. "Bearders" called it the Frindall System and resisted all efforts to change to more modern methods. He served in the RAF for ten years and in his final years in the service, he became an accountant and that proved to be useful in his scoring career. He grew his fearsome-looking beard in the RAF and kept it for the rest of his life. His scoring sheets were meticulously accurate and his writing was clear and easy to understand. If Brian Johnston or anyone else spilled tea or coffee he would let out an angry roar. He brought his own flask of tea or coffee and also sandwiches whereas the rest of the team were served with proper meals by the sponsors.

He was good at mimicking the accents of the TMS team and probably his best was impersonation was of Fred Trueman. He thought himself as a fast bowler of the F. S. Trueman ilk but he wasn't in the Trueman speed frame. He was fairly rapid and one of his favourite tricks was to bowl a split ball. The first time I saw it was at Hayes Cricket Club playing for the Maltamaniacs. He rushed up, arms pumping and the startled batsman saw one half of the ball cutting in and hitting the off bail and the other half went straight through to the keeper who held up the remainder of the ball. The batsman started to walk off to the pavilion before Bill shouted, "Not out, come back! It was my joke ball."

One of Frindall's most descriptive stories about Fiery Fred Trueman was about the great bowler's refusal to tour India. He said, "He was asked about why he wouldn't go to the subcontinent and Fred said, 'Well, the best way I can describe it is to say that if you could produce a fart out there, you'd immediately be awarded a gold medal!'"

His favourite among his Maltamaniacs was Richard "Jaws" Davies, a county-class batsman who was born in Selly Oak, went to school for

four years in Auckland, played in 13 countries and appeared for English
Schools, Warwickshire's first team (once) and Berkshire (a few times) and a
lot of other clubs. He coached Worksop School and Lancing before retiring
too soon, to Malta. The Stephen Spielberg film "Jaws" came out in 1975
and "Jaws" Richard earned the nickname when playing for Maltamaniacs
at the swish ground at Benenden three years later. He tried to hook against
the local hairdresser and had his jaw fractured. The tour to Malta was
imminent and he went with his jaw wired up and was confined to drinking
only soup and gin and tonics. He played in a 50-overs match against Malta
Combined Civilians and scored 212 not out in 42 overs (135 minutes, 129
balls, only 3 sixes and 24 fours). It turned out to be the highest of his 70
or so centuries and the first to go into Frindall's records as "batsman's
jaw encased by metal". Frindall said afterwards, "We declared at 373-3
off 48.3 overs and won by 240 runs. Several of the opposition announced
their immediate retirement and the subsequent British withdrawal from
Malta may not have been a coincidence." A few months later, on 1 April
1979 the British forces left the island.

"Jaws" was the batting star of the 1984 Maltamaniacs tour to NZ and
Australia and the bowling star was 51-year-old David Morgan, of whom
Frindall said, "is always last to bed and the first at breakfast". David ran a
successful financial consultancy in Carshalton and as he was self employed,
he had the time to go off on a 29-day tour. Trevor Bailey was in the sixth
form at Dulwich College when David started there, and like "The Boil"
he became a medium-paced outswing bowler who took plenty of wickets.
Called up on National Service, he served in the 17th Gurkha Regiment
in the Emergency in Malaya in 1952-53, and after a season coaching on
concrete pitches in Denmark he returned home with a defective knee. He
was advised to take up spin to preserve his knee and became the highest
wicket taker in the Surrey Championship which began in 1968, taking
almost 3,000 wickets at 12.7 per match. On his 50th birthday he took
9-75 against Guildford's first team. He was one of those rare bowlers who
improved with age. He always wore a rather huge support on his knee but
often bowled 20 overs in succession. He was termed an offbreak bowler
but he hardly turned the ball. His line, on off stump, was immaculate, and
his most prolific wicket taking ball was the floater that drifted away from
the right hander by an inch or two.

Besides being a heavy drinker, he smoked profusely. Smoking was still
permissible on aeroplanes in 1984 and after stopping at Bombay, Perth
and Melbourne before arriving in Auckland, my clothes stank of smoke.
Why the airlines allowed it to happen is one of those questions that should
have been asked from the first days of flying. Our pleasant hostelry, the
Kenley Motor Motel, was close to the Eden Park Test ground where

England played New Zealand two days earlier. The Führer wanted to use the nets the following day and permission was granted by the Auckland Cricket Association, and the match, against the Auckland Cricket Society, took place on the picturesque Outer Oval. Playing for the Society were two NZ Test stars, the left-hand batsman Bert Sutcliffe, the former NZ captain who was one of the most cultured, most successful and popular players in the world, and all rounder John Sparling. I was asked to open the innings with Jon Harris, a top-class amateur batsman, and that was a relief. It took the pressure off me and we put on 66 with me chipping in with a dour 26.

Bert, who was 60 at the time, showed our men how to play beautifully crafted cut shots, and when he was on 66, he suddenly pulled up with a muscle strain. He continued with a runner before he was dismissed. In 1953 he was damagingly hit in the head by a bouncer from South African fast bowler Neil Adcock – one of the game's awkward brigade – and had to go off with treatment. Like Denis Compton in a similar position when Compo was hit by a short-pitched delivery from Ray Lindwall at Old Trafford in 1948, he insisted on going back out there. No-one wore helmets and they never flinched: they took the blows and always came back for more. In 1965 a bouncer from Fred Trueman struck Bert in the ear and again, he returned to the crease to carry on his innings. But the injury was too serious and was forced to miss the rest of the tour. He was a very nice man, and a great ambassador for New Zealand cricket. He died in 2001.

In 1963 I played for Brian Statham's side in their testimonial match at Dewsbury and Denis was in full flow when Brian asked me to bowl. There was a crowd of 3,000 or more and most of them wanted to see Compton score a century. I said to Brian, who was a very upright, ordinary man with no ego, "I'm not really a bowler these days. I used to bowl Chinamen, like Denis."

"Denis will like that," said Brian. In my first over, one of my slow deliveries slipped out of my hand and Denis came down the pitch, played too early and the ball went high into the air. I looked round to see who might want to catch it and realising that I was the best positioned person, I stood under it, hesitatingly ... and managed to hold on to the ball. There was a feeling of disappointment around the ground. Compo was out for 75 and robbed of a hundred. As he walked towards me, he put his arm round me. "Well bowled young man." He was a true sportsman.

My moderate success at Eden Park was followed by a flop at Wellington's Basin Reserve, the windiest Test match ground in the world. Originally a swamp, or in NZ a "basin", the effect of the earthquake in 1956 was to lift the area and drain it and it turned into a playing field, or "reserve". We played Midland St Pats CC and we beat them. Early on I dropped an easy catch at first slip off the Führer's bowling and he was furious. "Go to square leg," he shouted. I didn't complain. Not being able to bend my right leg – caused by septic arthritis following a German air raid at the end of the Second World War – it was difficult to catch low balls on the right, close to my body. I never complained about it, nor about the Führer's insistence on humiliating me by putting me on the legside.

At tea, when he announced the batting order, he said to me, "You're six." He obviously thought I would be too slow to keep up the run rate. A few wickets fell but "Jaws" was making up the loss with his bold strokeplay and the leader made a further change. "You're now 11," he said. I decided to take over as umpire because of the local umpires had to leave. Fortunately for him, the Führer didn't get in otherwise I might have fingered him!

Having been to New Zealand on two occasions, I believe it is still the most civilised and nicest country of the 206 countries in the world, and I have been lucky to go to 88 of them. There's no hustle, no sign of stress and you can travel from one end at the top of the North Island down to the bottom of the South Island without meeting gridlocked traffic. We used the same coach and the same driver and it was a pleasure to sit back and take in the stunning views of the many mountains, forests, lakes and rivers. You have to admit it's a bit boring and as Tony Taylor, the Maltamaniacs manager, said, "If your mind is wandering you can always count the sheep. They outnumber the population of 4 million by ten times!" Captain James Cook brought the first sheep in 1773 and at one stage the figure rose to 80 million in 1982 before it fell to the current 40 million. Most of them are exported alive on huge vessels to countries in the Middle East.

The Führer introduced an element of stress when the coach arrived in Christchurch. As we approached the town centre, he announced, "We can only spend an hour here because we have to check in and attend a party early in the evening and then go on to the official dinner at the Town Hall." Anthony Fincham, a solicitor who played one first-class match for Oxford University and took five wickets and was never picked again, piped up and said, "Come on Bill, we'd like to spend a bit more time here." He was quickly put in his place. The locals were extremely sociable and most of the squad returned on unsteady legs. Not surprisingly, we were well beaten by the Old Collegians CC next day at their tree-surrounded ground.

Queenstown is the tourist mecca of the South Island and it lived up to its promise. But the Queenstown Recreation Ground should be renamed:

it nestles in a beautiful setting and it might have affected the concentration of our men being mentioned in the same breath as a recreation ground because we lost again.

The flight from Auckland to Sydney took up 14 hours because the aircraft landed in Melbourne on the way, and the Führer's mood darkened when we learned that the private accommodation which was promised had fallen through. He had to book us in with rooms in a Travelodge: certainly not up to our usual standard of hostelry. In most of the stopovers, he stayed privately. It was an early departure on the next day to take on the Primary Club of Australia at the beautiful Lemon Tree CC ground in Dooralong. The Führer told us, "I had the honour of helping the Primary Club of Australia inflict a narrow defeat upon the Cricketers' Club of London when they included such hired assassins as Doug Walters, Brian Taber and Trevor Chappell." None of the trio were available to face us and we went down to an embarrassing defeat of eight wickets. I managed to shoulder arms and be bowled to record a duck, thus qualifying for the Primary Club tie.

Two days were spent walking around Sydney and seeing "Conquest of Carmen Mirandes" at the Opera House, one of the world's unusual, and most arresting buildings. I'd met Lindsay Hassett and Bill O'Reilly in previous Australian tours to England and the others of our group were enthralled to hear my accounts of their pungent views about the state of the game. Lindsay, short of stature and long in memory, brought back visions of the Bradman era and how the peppery O'Reilly hated Douglas Jardine and his upper class mates in the Bodyline series. He never forgave them. O'Reilly wrote his own column and he too spared no-one.

More accommodation problems arose on arrival in Perth and the Führer lost his temper, yet again. I stayed with friends. Kent's Derek Aslett played for the Lord's Taverners at Hale School and after bowling for an hour, Frindall went off when Aslett came to the crease.

"He's lost a contact lens and needs another one," one of our fielders said. After 90 minutes when Aslett was out for 81, Frindall returned to resume bowling. "Took some time to find that contact lens," said the fielder.

In the next match Craig Serjeant, who played 12 Test matches for Australia in 1977, came in and Frindall did his disappearing act. Serjeant rattled up 35 before he was dismissed and on came Frindall again. "We've had some problems with the scoreboard and I had to sort it out," he explained. A pharmacist, Serjeant seemed a very well mannered, intelligent young man. In Perth they are better behaved than those in the East.

On the flight back to Heathrow, we were in the smokers' section again and learning that Willy Newlands, the *Daily Mail*'s travel writer, was in first class, I spent some time talking to him about what was happening at Northcliffe House, the GHQ of Associated Newspapers. Willy wasn't a cricketer but he said, "That Frindall ought to be in the travel business. Taking a tour of that size and length takes some doing."

"You need someone like that to take charge," I said, "otherwise it descends into mass confusion!"

Like everyone who loves cricket, I was shocked to hear about Bill's sudden death. One minute he was in full flow, roaring with laughter and jokes, a few days later he was gone. He won't be forgotten.

The Complicated Mr Roebuck

Many people who met Peter Roebuck liked and respected him but few actually knew him. When I first talked to him in his younger days playing professionally for Somerset, I thought he was an interesting, highly intelligent but slightly odd man, and I never thought he would finish up preying on young males. When he arrived at the County Ground on April Fool's Day 1974, he found himself looking up to cricketing gods like Ian Botham and Viv Richards. Thirteen years later, he was responsible for their abrupt departure. A bachelor, he had little or no interest in women but took an inordinate interest in young men. Later, he became a champion of the best values of cricket and a highly talented writer about the game, and he made many enemies including Botham and Richards. Not men to take on in an argument.

When he established himself in the Somerset side he was being considered by the selectors as a possible successor to Mike Brearley as England captain. He took over as county captain in place of Botham in 1986, and surrounded in controversy, he resigned after three years to become a full-time writer. The closest he became to leading England was when he skippered a B side against Holland, when the Dutch avenged the Battle of the Medway.

Some of his writings were almost in the same class of those of R. C. Robertson-Glasgow, a former Somerset fast bowler who committed suicide at the age of 65 in 1965 after taking an overdose. Twenty-seven years later, Roebuck's secret life was exposed when a judge in Taunton gave him a suspended jail sentence after pleading guilty to three charges of common assault. The police were supposed to have done a deal with him

– pleading guilty to a lesser charge. Henk Lindeque, one of his victims, said, "The problem was not so much that he caned us but wanted to look at the marks. That's when I decided to get out of his house." Roebuck's father, a mathematics teacher, described his son as, "an unconventional loner with an independent outlook on life, an irreverent sense of humour and sometimes a withering tongue," and that was an apt summing up.

I was fortunate to have met "Crusoe", Robertson-Glasgow's nickname, early in my career, and he was a very humorous and jolly man when he was up but totally depressed when he was down. I loved that line he wrote in one of his books, "there was a total absence of teetotalism". That was, and still is, a rarity in English cricket. Another of his books was entitled *I was Himmler's Aunt*, published in 1940, and it showed he had a penchant for the work of P. G. Wodehouse. With Harold Gimblett, the Somerset opening batsman who also took an overdose, and the latest Somerset star Marcus Trescothick confessing that he was a depressive, it makes you wonder about the air in the cider county.

In 2001 when Roebuck was spending the summer in England and working in Australia for the rest of the year, I asked him if he wanted to play for the Cricket Writers' Club team to take on the Australian Crusaders at Longparish. John Woodcock still lives in Longparish and was a good friend of both of us, and Roebuck was keen.

"I can probably bring along a couple of young colonials," he said. "One is South African and the other two are Australians who are staying with me in Devon." Next day he said they were willing to play and I rang one of them.

"Peter will give us a lift and we're looking forward to it," one of them said. Some weeks earlier, Roebuck was charged with assaulting three young men and was waiting to appear at his court case. I wondered whether they were the same trio because the judge gave an order that the ones who were spanked weren't allowed to live in his house or approach it within 300 metres. I never did discover the answer.

We were short of players at Longparish so we didn't want to go too deeply into the affair. All three played and all did well. Our total of 208 was on the low side and the match was decided by a shameful episode when Roebuck cast himself as a cruel housemaster. The Crusaders lost early wickets and a stylish left-hand batsman from New South Wales started pounding our depleted bowling. When he was 40, he mishit a drive and it went high towards a 17-year-old local boy whom I had called up as a stand in when someone dropped out. The boy looked nervous with his hands shaking and not surprisingly, he dropped the ball. Roebuck shouted at him, "Get out to the boundary. You've let the team down." The boy had tears in his eyes.

"Steady on Peter," I said, "that's not the way to talk to a youngster who is helping us out."

He looked at me and said, "These boys need discipline." The fielders who heard his comment were rather shocked.

I said to the boy, "Don't worry. He's a bit over competitive. It's only a friendly match."

The batsmen reached his century and the Crusaders won by five wickets. Ian Redpath, the former Australian Test opener played for the Crusaders and John Woodcock and his brother Hugh invited me to dinner so I missed the hard drinking that followed in the pavilion. Christine, Ian's wife, is a vivacious lady and she told me her mother, who came from Geelong, is living at a Catholic retirement home in Bromley named St Raphael's. I said, "My mother in law lived there for some years. What a coincidence!"

When Roebuck appeared in court, the prosecuting lawyer said he met three 19-year-old cricketers and offered to coach them in England. They stayed with him and he was said to have warned them that he would use corporal punishment if they didn't obey his house rules. He admitted caning them on their buttocks on several occasions. He said in court, "Obviously I misjudged the mood and that was my mistake and my responsibility and I accept that."

Roebuck was christened "Rupert" when Keith Fletcher, the absent-minded captain of Essex, forgot his proper Christian name. After that incident at Longparish, I began to realise he was a spanker. Teachers in public schools, in particular, are sometimes spankers and though Roebuck went to Millfield School, it was very unlikely he was spanked there because his parents were teachers at this unconventional sporting school and would soon know. Having reared six children, they weren't in a position to pay school fees and Jack Meyer, a former Somerset skipper who was the Headmaster, did them a favour by hiring them as teachers and giving scholarships to four of their children. Roebuck's father was a cricket enthusiast and his mother kept wicket for Oxford University Ladies. The family lived in a third floor flat in Bath and the young Roebuck moulded his cricket by hitting a plastic ball against an adjoining flat and giving a commentary on his performances. When Graeme Wright, the Editor of *Wisden*, nominated Roebuck as one of the Five Cricketers of the Year in 1987, he wrote, "Unfortunately, the adjoining flat was used by a group holding séances and having misinterpreted the tappings and the voice, they were very cross when the real source was discovered."

In his book *It Never Rains*, Roebuck wrote about the way Meyer awarded him a scholarship. "I found an orange flying through the air towards me and I wondered whether he would have got me in if I had dropped it." Fortunately he did catch it. He went on to study law at

Emmanuel College at Cambridge and graduated in first-class honours. He thought law was a bore and became a professional cricketer at Somerset. With his glasses and scholarly look, he was often ribbed by his team mates and was looked on as outsider. But his strength of mind and his leadership qualities gradually won them over and in 1987 he helped organise the putsch which led to the sacking of Richards and Joel Garner. Botham, who never spoke to him again except to insult him, left the county in protest.

Roebuck told Eric Hill, a former Somerset player who was the most respected and longest-serving journalist working on Somerset cricket, "Bowlers like Marshall, Hadlee and Sylvester Clarke seemed to bowl better at me than at others."

I discovered that was true in August 2000 when Ventnor Cricket Club invited the Cricket Writers' Club to take part in their 125th anniversary game, sponsored by Blue Heaven Productions. I never learned who Blue Heaven were but Roebuck finished black and blue when he batted against the South African fast bowler Walter Masimula, the club's professional. The home side batted first in front of a reasonable crowd and Roebuck announced, "I've broken a toe but I am fit to bowl." So I put him on to open and he bowled accurately without bothering too many of the batsmen. When I suggested he ought to have a rest, he said, "I've just got into a rhythm." I gave him a couple more overs to placate him.

Will Swanton, one of the Australian cricket writers, played for us and when he came on to bowl I told the announcer, "He's the illegitimate son of Jim Swanton" just as a joke. The announcer read it out and everyone was impressed, especially as two other Aussie journalists were playing as well.

"I never heard that Jim had a son," one said.

"He didn't," I said, "he married late in life."

At tea, I asked Roebuck if he was happy at coming in at 7. As an opening batsman who scored 17,558 first-class runs, with 33 hundreds and an average of 37.27, he was obviously not best pleased, to use a Swantonism, and he said, "That's too low. When are you coming in?"

"Six," I said. "You opened the bowling and bowled 11 overs and we have to give everyone a game. I was born just round the corner and the locals have come to jeer me!" Both of us were padded up and when the fourth wicket fell, I began walking down the steep slope towards the pitch. Suddenly I found myself being overtaken by Roebuck.

"I don't want a runner Peter," I said.

"I'm not running for you, I am going in ahead of you," he said. "We need some runs." With that, he speeded up and I realised it would cause an incident had I continued walking. The spectators might well see some jostling and pushing. A rare example of two batsmen fighting for the right to bat first. Roebuck walked on and the spectators must have been surprised to see me returning up the slope to retake my seat in front of the pavilion.

By this time the light was fading and when another wicket fell, I joined Roebuck out in the middle. Masimula, who played against England in 1999 in an ODI match, was the first black South African from the townships to play at provincial level. He bowled fast, fast enough to earn the nickname "The Black Express" in South Africa. When he saw Roebuck coming in, he wanted to bowl again and marked his full run out and bowled several fearsome bouncers at Roebuck. One was heading towards the batsman's face until the ball hit his left glove and flew into the air and ran up the hill towards the English Channel. The ball finally came to a halt close to the edge of the cliff. Another short delivery whacked him on the hip.

As I took guard, Walter halved his run and bowled to me at half pace. I scored a single and he lengthened his run again and charged in to bowl short to Roebuck's ribcage. It was obvious that he wasn't an admirer of "Rupert". He got him out eventually but we held on to draw. Eighteen months later, Walter died in his sleep at the age of 26 in a house in Guildford. The reason for such an early death was given as a heart attack. He signed as a coach at King Edward's School at Witley, Surrey, and was to play for Brook, another village club the Woodpeckers have played at for the past 40 years. Mark Garaway, who was born and bred in Ventnor and was a coach at Hampshire and in the England set up, said of him, "He was as fit as any cricketer I have played with. He put hundreds of man hours into coaching the youngsters. He was a super guy and enormously liked by everyone." And another player said, "He loved the ladies!"

After he retired as a professional cricketer, Roebuck emigrated firstly to Sydney and then to Pietermaritzburg in South Africa, and owned properties there and also in Devon, and in each of his properties he invited young men to stay with them. In the case of young Zimbabweans, he gave them educational scholarships as well as other services. He looked on them as his extended family.

He often spoke about a premature death for himself. After he committed suicide jumping out of a sixth floor window of the Southern Sun Hotel close to Newlands, the world's best looking Test match ground, at the age of 55 on 12 November 2011, many who knew him confirmed that fact. One was Troy Crosland, an Australian cricketer who stayed with him at Roebuck's home in East Sydney and later, at Bondi Beach.

I met him on a Forty Club tour to Italy in 2007 and after a rare win, we were invited by Simone Cipolli, President of Gambassi Valdarno CC, to attend a dinner in Bucine. Our tour leader Ron Hart said, "Wear your best gear." The ladies dutifully wore their expensive finery and when we turned up we were surprised to see a marquee on a car park filled with tables and benches like school dinners, and the other 50 seats were filled by men and women in jeans and sweat shirts. Most of them looked like pop fans or political agitators. As Ron began his speech, they continued to jabber away in Italian. The newly elected Mayor, wearing a chief's apron and a sweat shirt emblazoned with an anti-war slogan, yelled for quiet and introduced a small, young, dark haired lady who turned out to be Malala Joya, an Afghan MP. She called on our Brits and their Dutch colleagues to support the campaign to end the fighting in Afghanistan and withdraw all foreign troops. Duco Ohm, a former international Test umpire who is six feet eight inches tall, came up to the little lady, towering over her, and told her to be quiet.

"This is a private cricket event, not a political meeting," he said. Bedlam ensued. Soon, our troops withdrew to our hotel.

Troy was at the wonderful party with us the following night he said of Roebuck, "I was 18 when I first met him and he talked about me going to play some cricket in England in 1990. I sincerely liked the guy. He never spanked me but he did some odd things, like turning a light on and off when I was asleep and saying, 'I am testing you'. He talked a lot about death and once said, 'I will choose when to go,' but I never thought he was on the edge of suicide. One other thing he said was, 'Isn't it amazing that the waves keep rolling in and always will, once we are gone!'"

The Sunday Times revealed that he ended his life on the day when police burst into his bedroom in the Southern Sands Hotel and confronted him with allegations from a 26-year-old Zimbabwean student who claimed he had been sexually assaulted. They started taking DNA evidence. "He asked to be allowed to take a minute or two to compose himself," said Dan McDougall, the writer of their article. "In that split second, it seems he chose to rush out from the bathroom and threw himself out of the window. He died when his head hit a metal awning below. In his final words, posted on his blog before he died, were 'I am not perfect but I think the good outweighs the bad.'" Cricketing folk think that was an appropriate epitaph for this muddled but brilliant man. Others believe otherwise: that he was a paedophile. It was all very sad.

No-one has ever committed suicide in the history of the Woodpeckers but one or two players became depressed after being dropped. As no-one was charged an annual subscription, I didn't need to go into the reasons. I followed the example of Sir Alf Ramsey: he would always thank the player for coming along and if he didn't want the player back, he just ignored him and didn't break the news about his omission in person.

Unlike professional football, cricket is not about life and death. Our type of refined cricket is about enjoyment and afterwards, having a good chat over a few drinks. I am very proud indeed that I was able to play this wonderful game, the best, for a long, long time. Thank you Lord for being giving the chance!